# The Mystery of the Gospel

# The Mystery of the Gospel

## Hidden Truths Have Been Revealed

Chuck Dieringer

One in Christ Press

Copyright © 2020 Chuck Dieringer

All rights reserved.

Printed by One in Christ Press in the USA.

First printing, 2020.

ISBN 978-1-7346962-0-2

Unless otherwise indicated, all Scripture quotations are from The ESV® Bible (The Holy Bible, English Standard Version®), copyright © 2001 by Crossway, a publishing ministry of Good News Publishers. Used by permission. All rights reserved.

One in Christ Press
info@oneinchrist.net
www.oneinchrist.net

# TABLE OF CONTENTS

**PREFACE** .................................................................................................................. ix
**PART I: The Mystery of the Gospel** ................................................................ 1
   Chapter 1: What is the Mystery of the Gospel? ................................................. 3
      General uses of *mysterion* ............................................................................. 3
      The *mysterion* in Ephesians .......................................................................... 4
      The *mysterion* in 1 Corinthians ..................................................................... 7
      The *mysterion* in Colossians ......................................................................... 8
      An example of the *mysterion* ........................................................................ 9
   Chapter 2: The Ultimate Purpose of the Old Testament is Jesus .................... 13
      History ............................................................................................................. 13
      The Law ........................................................................................................... 14
      The Prophets .................................................................................................. 16
      Old Testament Scriptures ............................................................................... 16
   Chapter 3: Christ Fulfilled the Scriptures and the Prophets ............................ 21
      Jesus fulfilled the prophets ............................................................................ 21
      Moses wrote of Jesus .................................................................................... 22
      The road to Emmaus ..................................................................................... 24
      Everything written about the Son of Man ...................................................... 26
      An appointed day ........................................................................................... 29
   Chapter 4: The Old Testament Covenants Foreshadow Christ ....................... 33
      Abrahamic Covenant ..................................................................................... 33
      Davidic Covenant ........................................................................................... 39
      Mosaic Covenant ........................................................................................... 42
**PART II: New Testament Evidences of the *Mysterion*** ............................. 47
   Chapter 5: New Testament Evidence of the *Mysterion* ................................. 49
      Joel 2 in Acts 2 ............................................................................................... 49
      Amos 9 in Acts 15 .......................................................................................... 51
      Jeremiah 31 in Hebrews 8 ............................................................................. 52
      Psalm 8 in Hebrews 2 .................................................................................... 54
   Chapter 6: More New Testament Evidence of the *Mysterion* ....................... 59
      Matthew 2 ........................................................................................................ 59
      Hebrews 2 ....................................................................................................... 62
      Romans 9 ........................................................................................................ 64
      John 19 ............................................................................................................ 67
   Chapter 7: Evidence of the *Mysterion* in Paul's Writings .............................. 71
      1 Corinthians .................................................................................................. 71
      2 Corinthians .................................................................................................. 72
      Galatians ......................................................................................................... 76
      Ephesians ....................................................................................................... 78
   Chapter 8: Evidence of the *Mysterion* by Various New Testament Authors ................. 83
      Matthew ........................................................................................................... 83
      Acts .................................................................................................................. 86
      Hebrews .......................................................................................................... 92
**PART III: Discovering the *Mysterion* in the Old Testament** .................... 97
   Chapter 9: An Example (Joshua 7) .................................................................... 99
   Chapter 10: Discovering the *Mysterion* in Genesis ...................................... 105
      The light of creation ...................................................................................... 105
      Be fruitful and multiply ................................................................................. 108
      Cain, Abel, & Seth ........................................................................................ 110
      The flood ....................................................................................................... 112
      Circumcision ................................................................................................. 113
      Abraham & Isaac .......................................................................................... 115
      The life of Joseph ......................................................................................... 117
   Chapter 11: Discovering the *Mysterion* in the Wilderness ......................... 123
      The exodus ................................................................................................... 123
      Passover ....................................................................................................... 125
      Manna ............................................................................................................ 126
      Water from the rock ..................................................................................... 127

| | |
|---|---|
| A holy nation | 128 |
| The tabernacle & its furnishings | 130 |
| The Levitical system | 133 |
| The feasts of the Lord | 134 |
| The year of jubilee | 136 |
| The bronze serpent | 138 |

**Chapter 12: Discovering the *Mysterion* in the Narratives ... 141**

| | |
|---|---|
| The conquest | 141 |
| The judges | 141 |
| The book of Ruth | 142 |
| Barrenness | 143 |
| The anointing | 145 |
| Saul & David | 147 |
| David & Solomon | 149 |
| Solomon's temple | 152 |
| Elijah's ascension | 155 |
| Restoration from captivity | 157 |

**Chapter 13: Discovering the *Mysterion* in the Poetic Writings ... 159**

| | |
|---|---|
| Job | 159 |
| Proverbs | 161 |
| Ecclesiastes & Song of Solomon | 163 |
| The Psalms | 165 |
| Psalm 22 | 166 |
| Psalm 30 | 170 |
| Psalm 69 | 171 |
| Psalm 89 | 176 |
| Psalm 109 | 179 |
| Psalm 118 | 180 |
| Psalm 119 | 183 |
| Psalm 24 | 185 |

**Chapter 14: Discovering the *Mysterion* in the Prophets ... 189**

| | |
|---|---|
| Isaiah 1 & 2 | 189 |
| Isaiah 6 | 190 |
| Isaiah 11 & 12 | 191 |
| Isaiah 40 | 192 |
| Cyrus | 193 |
| Isaiah 52 | 194 |
| Isaiah 59 | 195 |
| Isaiah 62 | 198 |
| Jeremiah 18 | 199 |
| Jeremiah 30 & 31 | 201 |
| Ezekiel 11 | 203 |
| Ezekiel 15 | 204 |
| Ezekiel 16 | 205 |
| Ezekiel 34-37 | 206 |
| Ezekiel 40-48 | 208 |
| Daniel | 211 |
| Hosea | 214 |
| Jonah | 215 |
| Haggai | 217 |
| Zechariah 3 | 220 |

**Conclusion: What Does This All Mean? ... 225**
**Appendix: Chiastic Structure ... 229**

# PREFACE

The purpose of this book is to reveal Jesus. More specifically, it is to reveal Jesus in the Old Testament text; to show that the primary point and purpose of the Old Testament is Jesus.

Some people may observe the title *The Mystery of the Gospel: Hidden Truths Have Been Revealed* and perceive that the book is about disclosing some newly-found obscure secret message in the Bible. It may be perceived that it is about something that only the most scrupulous, gifted eye could detect. However, this writing discloses nothing beyond what the Bible reveals. These hidden truths are obtainable for all believers to know; in fact, the New Testament writers purposed to reveal these truths to their readers.

In a way, this book truly *is* about revealing a secret message in the Bible. The irony is that the secret message isn't a secret to Christians at all. The secret message is Jesus.

Christians might be led to believe that only the New Testament is about Jesus. They may be surprised to find that the primary point and purpose of the Old Testament also is Jesus.

Through types, shadows, and pictures, Jesus is the hidden message throughout the Old Testament Scriptures. Jesus is the hidden truth in the Creation account. Jesus is the hidden truth in the lives of the Patriarchs and the events that pertain to the nation of Israel. Jesus is in the Law. Jesus is in the Prophets. We can scope the Old Testament and see Jesus saturated throughout. The secret message of the Old Testament is that it is about Jesus. Jesus is the lens with which Christians are to read the Old Testament.

The problem is that there are many teachings, doctrines, and systems of theology that have been established based on the Old Testament *without* Jesus being the lens. Israel-centered theology permeates the modern English-speaking Church. Let us learn not to read the Old Testament through an Israel-centered lens, but through a Christ-centered lens.

It's also possible to read the Old Testament and view the Law as God's highest expression to mankind. God's highest expression to mankind is Christ. A Christ-centered lens would put the Law in its proper perspective. This book attempts to redirect our thinking by revealing Jesus as the primary point and purpose of both the Law and the Prophets (i.e., the entire Old Testament).

Part I (the first four chapters) presents the New Testament teaching of how to properly view the Old Testament. How did Jesus, the apostles, and the New Testament writers view the Old Testament?

The next four chapters (Part II) examine several New Testament quotations of Old Testament passages. We'll identify the surface-level context of each Old Testament passage and observe the interpretation of said passages by the Spirit-inspired New Testament authors.

Part III then surveys the Old Testament, disclosing Jesus as the hidden truth throughout. Perhaps you may find Part III to be the most life-giving portion of the book. Hopefully, you'll have Jesus revealed to you from the text in a powerfully impactful way.

Therefore, sit back, put on your Christ-centered Bible Vision goggles, and enjoy the mystery of the gospel!

Jesus, reveal Yourself to us!

# PART I:
# The Mystery of the Gospel

# Chapter 1:
# What Is the Mystery of the Gospel?

The mystery of the gospel of Jesus Christ.

Perhaps you've come across the mention of the mystery of the gospel while reading the Scriptures. Maybe you wondered what it meant by the gospel being a mystery. It's possible you gave it a quick thought and then never thought about it again. Or maybe you glossed over it and don't recall having seen it.

Many different theories can be hypothesized as to what it is about the gospel that makes it a mystery: Is it considered a mystery because it is unfathomable for us to think that God would take human form? Is the gospel a mystery in that we can't comprehend why God would redeem sinners, or to do so by offering up His Son to suffer His wrath as a substitution? Those are questions that can certainly boggle our thinking, but they're not what is meant by the gospel being a mystery.

The English versions of the Bible use the word mystery as a translation of the Greek word *mysterion* (moo-STAY-ree-on). For the English word mystery, we may think of something beyond our ability to know, something we are unable to grasp or comprehend, something that baffles the mind, often with no resolution.

The Greek word *mysterion*, however, serves a bit different purpose than does our English word mystery. The *mysterion* represents a truth that is hidden, that which is perceived to be one thing but beneath the surface there is a deeper truth. When that deeper truth is revealed, the *mysterion* is revealed.

## GENERAL USES OF *MYSTERION*

Before we address how *mysterion* relates specifically to the gospel, let's first observe a couple examples of how *mysterion* is used in the Scriptures in general ways to help give us a better understanding of its meaning.

When Jesus appeared to John on Patmos, John wrote that he "saw seven golden lampstands, and in the midst of the lampstands one like a son of man (Rev. 1:12)." John continued in verse 16: "In his right hand he held seven stars..."

We know this much: there are seven lampstands and there are seven stars. We would have no idea but to merely speculate at what might be the truth of their meaning. Fortunately, Jesus explains it to us:

> "As for the mystery (*mysterion*) of the seven stars which you saw in My right hand, and the seven golden lampstands: the seven stars are the angels of the seven churches, and the seven lampstands are the seven churches." (Rev. 1:20)

Okay, great! There's something about the Revelation that is spelled out for us clearly! Praise the Lord!

Initially, the truth of the identity of the lampstands and the stars is hidden from our understanding. The hidden truth is revealed to us in verse 20. That's how the *mysterion* functions; a hidden truth that is later revealed.

Another example is in Matthew chapter 13. Jesus had just spoken the parable of the sower. In verse 10, "the disciples came and said to him, 'Why do you speak to them in parables?' And he answered them, 'To you it has been given to know the secrets (or "mysteries"; *mysterion*) of the kingdom of heaven, but to them it has not been given.'"

Jesus' use of parables was in the form of the *mysterion*. On the surface of a parable is a set of circumstances and characters. The true purpose and teaching of the parable is found deeper, beneath the surface. On the surface, it looks like one thing, but a parable is not meant to be taken literally. The primary point of a parable is found hidden deeper beneath the surface-level circumstances of the parable. The *mysterion* is the hidden truth.

With the English word 'mystery' we may think of, for example, magician David Copperfield and wonder "how did he do that?" For the Greek word *mysterion*, however, we may think of something more like the entertainment duo of Penn and Teller. If you're not familiar with Penn and Teller, during their stage show they perform magic tricks. Then, as part of their act, they show the audience precisely how they did it. The illusion industry hates that they do this because they're giving away all the secrets. That's how the *mysterion* functions, as a hidden truth that is later revealed.

What is it, then, about the gospel of Jesus Christ that makes it a *mysterion*?

## THE *MYSTERION* IN EPHESIANS

The Apostle Paul most mentions the *mysterion* throughout his letter to the Ephesians. In chapter 1, verses 3 through 14, Paul provides a beautiful description of God's big picture purpose in redeeming His people and restoring the world.

## Ch. 1: What is the Mystery of the Gospel?

In the middle of that passage, Paul briefly mentions that God has made known to us the mystery (*mysterion*) of His will which He set forth in Christ (1:9).

Fast forward to chapter 3. Let's walk our way through the first 10 verses:

> For this reason I, Paul, a prisoner of Christ Jesus on behalf of you Gentiles-- assuming that you have heard of the stewardship of God's grace that was given to me for you, how the mystery (*mysterion*) was made known to me by revelation, as I have written briefly. (Ephesians 3:1-3)

Paul proclaims himself to be a steward of God's grace for the benefit of his Gentile readership. The truth of God's grace upon Gentiles was hidden in mystery, but the *mysterion* was revealed to Paul. When he states "as I have written briefly," he is referring to having briefly mentioned the *mysterion* previously in the letter (1:9).

> When you read this, you can perceive my insight into the mystery (*mysterion*) of Christ, which was not made known to the sons of men in other generations as it has now been revealed to his holy apostles and prophets by the Spirit. (Ephesians 3:4-5)

Paul wrote that his readership, as well as you and I, can have the same insight to understand the *mysterion* just as he did. It was not made known in prior generations but it was made known beginning at Pentecost when the Holy Spirit of God indwelt believers.

> This mystery (*mysterion*) is that the Gentiles are fellow heirs, members of the same body, and partakers of the promise in Christ Jesus through the gospel. (Ephesians 3:6)

Until the apostles and prophets made it known post-Pentecost, it was understood for generation upon generation that all of God's promises and deliverance were reserved for Israel. The hidden truth all along was that God was to be about the business of saving Gentiles. Not only saving Gentiles, but also making them heirs of God's kingdom! The thought of Gentiles being heirs to God's kingdom would have been an insult to any Israelite for centuries of generations prior.

> Of this gospel I was made a minister according to the gift of God's grace, which was given me by the working of his power. To me, though I am the very least of all the saints, this grace was given, to preach to the Gentiles the unsearchable riches of Christ, and to bring to light for everyone what is the plan of the mystery (*mysterion*) hidden for ages in God who created all things, so that through the church the manifold wisdom of God might now be made known to the rulers and authorities in the heavenly places. (Ephesians 3:7-10)

The truth of Christ was not known in prior generations, but "has now been revealed." What has been revealed is that Gentiles are heirs to the promises that appeared to be given to the nation of Israel. How can Gentiles be partakers of the promises? Only through the gospel of Jesus Christ.

The truth that was hidden for ages is that believing Gentiles are fellow heirs and members of the same body. Israel had thought that it exclusively was heir to the promises of God and that Gentiles had no part in God's purposes on earth.

Paul had previously reminded the Gentile readership that pre-Christ they:

> ...were at that time separated from Christ, alienated from the commonwealth of Israel and strangers to the covenants of promise, having no hope and without God in the world. But now in Christ Jesus you who once were far off have been brought near by the blood of Christ. ... For through him we both have access in one Spirit to the Father. So then you are no longer strangers and aliens, but you are fellow citizens with the saints and members of the household of God. (Ephesians 2:12-13, 18-19)

The mystery that was revealed through Christ is that Gentiles are now fellow-heirs of the promises of God that for hundreds of years appeared to be exclusive to Israel. The truth that was hidden for ages is that it was not to Israel that God would reveal His manifold wisdom; it would be Christians!

Therefore, what appeared on the surface to be promises made to Israel, the deeper truth is that those promises were ultimately made to Christ and, thus, also to all those who are *in* Christ, which is comprised of believers from *all* nations.

This shocking turn of events was God's plan all along. Here is Paul's clincher:

## Ch. 1: What is the Mystery of the Gospel?

> This was according to the eternal purpose that he has realized in Christ Jesus our Lord (Ephesians 3:11)

It was God's eternal purpose to bring members of all nations into His kingdom. This was no last-minute change of plans. It was no surprise to God. This was His plan all along!

Moving ahead to the conclusion of the letter, Paul asks for prayer:

> ...that words may be given to me in opening my mouth boldly to proclaim the mystery (*mysterion*) of the gospel, for which I am an ambassador in chains, that I may declare it boldly, as I ought to speak. (Ephesians 6:19-20)

We all know that Paul was in prison for preaching the gospel. Had we realized that he was in prison for preaching the *mysterion*? Paul was in prison because he revealed that the hidden truth of the Scriptures (Old Testament) was about the gospel of Jesus Christ, and the Jews hated him for it! The Jews wanted the Old Testament to be about God's promises to Israel; but Paul proclaimed that the Old Testament was about Gentiles becoming members of God's family through Jesus. That's why Paul was imprisoned!

### THE *MYSTERION* IN 1 CORINTHIANS

Paul also wrote the Corinthians about the *mysterion*:

> Yet among the mature we do impart wisdom, although it is not a wisdom of this age or of the rulers of this age, who are doomed to pass away. But we impart a secret (*mysterion*) and hidden wisdom of God, which God decreed before the ages for our glory. (1Co 2:6-7)

In God's infinite wisdom, He hid the truth of His plan for many years. God's plan is one that would result in "our glory." He decreed such before creation and unveiled it in His Son Jesus. Until He unveiled His plan through Jesus, His plan remained veiled. From Creation until John the Baptizer, God's plan remained veiled. He hinted at it. He provided types, shadows, and pictures of it, but the fullness of His plan remained hidden until it was unveiled through Jesus.

> None of the rulers of this age understood this, for if they had, they would not have crucified the Lord of glory. (1Co 2:8)

Neither the Jewish leadership nor the Roman authorities understood God's hidden plan. Had they understood it, they would not have killed Jesus.

> But, as it is written, "What no eye has seen, nor ear heard, nor the heart of man imagined, what God has prepared for those who love him"-- these things God has revealed to us through the Spirit. (1Co 2:9-10a)

What God had prepared for those who love Him is beyond what the heart of man could even imagine. It is beyond anything that we can gather from our senses, such as sight and hearing. God first revealed it in the 1st Century to those upon whom the Spirit fell. The Spirit is still falling on humans today as God continues to reveal to believers the glory that He has prepared for us.

**THE *MYSTERION* IN COLOSSIANS**
Paul also wrote of the *mysterion* in his letter to the Colossians:

> Now I rejoice in my sufferings for your sake, and in my flesh I am filling up what is lacking in Christ's afflictions for the sake of his body, that is, the church, of which I became a minister according to the stewardship from God that was given to me for you, to make the word of God fully known, the mystery (*mysterion*) hidden for ages and generations but now revealed to his saints. To them God chose to make known how great among the Gentiles are the riches of the glory of this mystery (*mysterion*), which is Christ in you, the hope of glory. (Col 1:24-27)

Paul here states that his stewardship to God was to make the word of God (i.e., the message of the gospel) fully known. The gospel message was hidden for ages and generations. Paul is making fully known the message of God that was hidden for ages, for it has been revealed to believers in Christ.

To the Gentile believers God chose to make known how great are the riches of the glory of the mystery. What is the mystery? Something that nobody would

## Ch. 1: What is the Mystery of the Gospel?

have expected! It is that the Jewish Messiah indwells Gentiles! "Christ in you" ("you" referred to believers, mostly Gentile, in Colosse).

God's plan of the *mysterion* was hidden for ages. When? Which ages? The truth of God's glorious plan remained hidden for the period of time throughout the Old Testament, beginning at Creation. Not clearly understood in ages past, the truth has now been made known through Christ. If it was hidden throughout the Old Testament period of time, it's also going to be found throughout the Old Testament writings.

**AN EXAMPLE OF THE *MYSTERION***

Paul provided an example of the *mysterion* in Ephesians chapter 5. Beginning in verse 25, Paul is addressing husbands: "Husbands love your wives." Then Paul quickly shifts the focus to Christ: "as Christ loved the church and gave himself up for her..."

The focus goes back to husbands in verse 28: "In the same way husbands are to love their wives as their own bodies. He who loves his wife loves himself. For no one ever hated his own flesh, but nourishes and cherishes it..." (as the focus goes back to Christ again) "...just as Christ does the church, because we are members of his body. Therefore, a man shall leave his father and mother and hold fast to his wife, and the two shall become one flesh. This mystery (*mysterion*) is profound, and I am saying that it refers to Christ and the church." Finally, in verse 33 the focus goes back to husbands. (See next page for a visual aid to observe which portions of the passage are addressing husbands and which portions are addressing Christ.)

In verse 31, Paul quoted Genesis 2:24: "Therefore a man shall leave his father and mother and hold fast to his wife, and the two shall become one flesh."

We might be confused to think that in verse 31 Paul's quotation of Genesis 2:24 is addressing husbands. But actually, Christ is the focus from the latter portion of verse 29 all the way through verse 32 which includes his quotation of Genesis 2:24. When Paul quotes Genesis 2:24, he is using it, not in the context of husbands, but in regards to Christ and the church. He tells us such in verse 32: "I am saying that it refers to Christ and the church."

What does Paul mean that "a man shall leave his father and mother and hold fast to his wife, and the two shall become one flesh" is about Christ and the church?

> *Italicized text is addressing husbands;* <u>underlined text is addressing Christ.</u>  (Eph 5:25-33a)
>
> *Husbands, love your wives,* <u>as Christ loved the church and gave himself up for her, that he might sanctify her, having cleansed her by the washing of water with the word, so that he might present the church to himself in splendor, without spot or wrinkle or any such thing, that she might be holy and without blemish.</u> *In the same way husbands should love their wives as their own bodies. He who loves his wife loves himself. For no one ever hated his own flesh, but nourishes and cherishes it,* <u>just as Christ does the church, because we are members of his body. "Therefore a man shall leave his father and mother and hold fast to his wife, and the two shall become one flesh." This mystery is profound, and I am saying that it refers to Christ and the church.</u> *However, let each one of you love his wife as himself...*

If reading Genesis chapter 2, when we come across verse 24 we would have no reason to think that this had anything to do with the gospel of Christ. Nothing in Genesis 2 shouts to us explicitly "the gospel of Christ!" But Paul says Genesis 2:24 is "a great mystery (*mysterion*)" (KJV). He is saying that when he reads Genesis 2:24, he sees a deeper, hidden truth.

Paul read Genesis 2:24 and saw the gospel of Christ. When Paul read Genesis 2:24 he saw Christ, who left his heavenly abode with the Father, came to earth to secure for Himself a bride, and the two, Christ and His bride, shall be united together as one. Thus, Jesus left his Father to hold fast to <u>His</u> wife, and we are joined with Him as one.

It is true that, generally speaking, a man shall leave his father and mother and hold fast to his wife, and the two shall become one flesh. It will never be <u>not</u> true that a man shall leave his father and mother and hold fast to his wife, and the two shall become one flesh. However, Paul is saying that the hidden truth of Genesis 2:24 is the gospel. It is about Christ and the church, as is the grand scope of the entire Old Testament.

The New Testament reveals to us how to properly view the Old Testament. We are to view the Old Testament in this manner, that of the *mysterion*. The New Testament teaches us that the primary point and purpose of the Old Testament is that it is about Christ. It is about what Christ accomplished and for whom He accomplished it. The hidden truth buried throughout the entire Old Testament is that it is about Christ and His bride. The New Testament reveals what the Old Testament was about all along.

# Chapter 2:
# The Ultimate Purpose of the Old Testament is Jesus

The hidden truth of the Old Testament is that it is ultimately about Jesus. It is about the message of the good news of God's kingdom ushered in by Jesus via the New Covenant realities we can experience today. Layered beneath the surface of the history of events throughout the Old Testament era, all of redemptive history leading up to Jesus was doing exactly that: leading up to Jesus. It was all building up to and culminated in Jesus who came to fulfill all of God's promises. The history of Israel, the law Israel was given, the prophets who spoke to Israel, and Israel's Old Testament Scriptures all find their purpose in Jesus.

**HISTORY**

The history of the nation of Israel served as a foreshadowing of the realities that were to be found in the kingdom of God that was ushered in by Jesus.

> For I do not want you to be unaware, brothers, that our fathers were all under the cloud, and all passed through the sea, and all were baptized into Moses in the cloud and in the sea, and all ate the same spiritual food, and all drank the same spiritual drink. For they drank from the spiritual Rock that followed them, and the Rock was Christ. Nevertheless, with most of them God was not pleased, for they were overthrown in the wilderness. **Now these things took place as examples for us**, that we might not desire evil as they did. Do not be idolaters as some of them were; as it is written, "The people sat down to eat and drink and rose up to play." We must not indulge in sexual immorality as some of them did, and twenty-three thousand fell in a single day. We must not put Christ to the test, as some of them did and were destroyed by serpents, nor grumble, as some of them did and were destroyed by the Destroyer. **Now these things happened to them as an example, but they were written down for our instruction**, on whom the end of the ages has come. (1Co 10:1-11 ESV)

The Greek word *typos* is here twice translated "example." It is *typos* from which we derive the word "type", as in a foreshadowing or a pattern.

The events that happened to national Israel were:

1. "Examples." What Israel experienced we can learn from.
2. "For us." The things that happened to Israel weren't even for Israel's learning. It was for us! It was for Paul and the members of the New Covenant to whom he was writing. It is still "for us" who are in the New Covenant 20 centuries later. What Israel experienced was not for Israel's instruction, rather "they were written down for *our* instruction."

From Israel's experiences in the wilderness, they could not enter into God's rest because of unbelief. For those of us who are in the New Covenant with belief, we have entered God's rest (Heb. 4:3) and we get to learn from Israel's mistakes.

## THE LAW

The ultimate purpose of the Law was to point forward to Christ. The Law's regulations, its festivals, the Sabbath, etc., were but a shadow of the reality it prefigured.

> These are a shadow of the things to come, but the substance belongs to Christ. (Col 2:17)

> ...the law has but a shadow of the good things to come instead of the true form of these realities... (Heb 10:1a)

The Law was merely a shadow; a shadow of good things to come (i.e., better things than even the Law itself). The Law was the shadow, Christ is the substance. The Law was the shadow, Jesus is the true form of its realities.

The substance of the Law is not the Law itself. The true form of the realities of the Law is not the Law itself. The Law is neither the reality nor is it the substance. Jesus is. The Law points forward to Jesus.

The Law was temporary. It was temporary by God's design.

> Now before faith came, we were held captive under the law, imprisoned until the coming faith would be revealed. So then, the law was our guardian until Christ came, in order that we might be justified by faith. But now that faith has come, we are no longer under a guardian, (Gal 3:23-25)

## Ch. 2: The Ultimate Purpose of the Old Testament is Jesus

The Law served as a child-conductor (or "guardian"). When the child matured, the child-conductor was no longer utilized. When God's redemptive plan "matured" to its fullness, in the revealing of the kingdom of God through Jesus, the Law was no longer necessary.

The Law served as a guardian "until Christ came." Once Christ came and ushered in God's kingdom, the Law's purpose was fulfilled: "now that faith has come, we are no longer under a guardian."

God intended for the Law to serve a temporary purpose. It was surpassed by a much greater purpose:

> Not that we are sufficient in ourselves to claim anything as coming from us, but our sufficiency is from God, who has made us sufficient to be ministers of a new covenant, not of the letter but of the Spirit. For the letter kills, but the Spirit gives life. Now if the ministry of death, carved in letters on stone, came with such glory that the Israelites could not gaze at Moses' face because of its glory, which was being brought to an end, will not the ministry of the Spirit have even more glory? For if there was glory in the ministry of condemnation, the ministry of righteousness must far exceed it in glory. Indeed, in this case, what once had glory has come to have no glory at all, because of the glory that surpasses it. For if what was being brought to an end came with glory, much more will what is permanent have glory. (2 Corinthians 3:5-11)

The New Covenant is not of the letter (i.e., the Law) but is of the Spirit. The Law kills but the Spirit gives life. What does Paul describe as being "the ministry of death"? Letters carved in stone. What letters were carved in stone? The Ten Commandments. Paul refers to the Ten Commandments as being a "ministry of death"! The Law was ushered in with great glory. The New Covenant ("the ministry of the Spirit") far exceeds it with much more glory! The Law was a "ministry of condemnation." The New Covenant is "the ministry of righteousness." The Law once had glory. When the New Covenant was ushered in, the Law came to have no glory at all. The Law "was being brought to an end" (verses 7 &11).

The hidden truth about the Law is that it was to be temporary by God's design, fulfilled in Jesus.

## THE PROPHETS

The hidden truth about the Old Testament prophets is that their ultimate purpose was to point forward to the coming kingdom of God and the salvation that is offered through the grace of Jesus.

> Concerning this salvation, the prophets who prophesied about the grace that was to be yours searched and inquired carefully, inquiring what person or time the Spirit of Christ in them was indicating when he predicted the sufferings of Christ and the subsequent glories. It was revealed to them that they were serving not themselves but you, in the things that have now been announced to you through those who preached the good news to you by the Holy Spirit sent from heaven, things into which angels long to look. (1 Peter 1:10-12)

Peter wrote that the Old Testament prophets predicted the sufferings and subsequent glories of Christ (i.e., the Crucifixion, Resurrection, and Ascension). He stated that the prophets actually *knew* that they were writing of the coming Anointed One. They searched out diligently to try to find out when and who their prophesies were concerning.

Peter added that the prophets were not serving themselves. Nor were they serving their contemporaries. They were serving the New Covenant people of God! They were serving those who would respond to the preaching of the good news! The prophets were writing for the benefit of those who would later receive the gospel of Jesus!

> Paul, a servant of Christ Jesus, called to be an apostle, set apart for the gospel of God, which he promised beforehand through his prophets in the holy Scriptures, (Romans 1:1-2)

God promised His gospel through His prophets during the Old Testament era. In upcoming chapters, we'll examine with increased attention and detail how the Old Testament prophets promised the gospel.

## OLD TESTAMENT SCRIPTURES

The entirety of the Old Testament writings foreshadowed Jesus, His gospel message, and His people with whom He is in union. The ultimate purpose of the

## Ch. 2: The Ultimate Purpose of the Old Testament is Jesus

39 writings as a single collective entity is to reveal Jesus. Shrouding the realities of the New Covenant in mystery, the Old Testament preaches the gospel of Jesus in picture form.

> But as for you, continue in what you have learned and have firmly believed, knowing from whom you learned it and how from childhood you have been acquainted with the sacred writings, which are able to make you wise for salvation through faith in Christ Jesus. (2 Timothy 3:14-15)

"Salvation through faith in Christ." That's the gospel! Paul tells Timothy the Old Testament Scriptures are able to make him wise to know the gospel of Jesus Christ.

Of all the things Paul could have said the Old Testament would make someone wise to know, he says the Scriptures are able to make one wise to know that salvation is by faith, "which is in Christ" (NASB).

What are things Paul did *not* say the Old Testament would make Timothy wise to know? What would some believers like to suggest that he possibly could or should have said?

Paul did *not* say that the Old Testament is able to make you wise to know:
- God's gracious dealings with Israel
- a future millennial kingdom
- the Law of God
- the 2nd coming of Christ.

These are all things that many Christians believe that the Old Testament would most make one wise to know. But of all the things Paul could have written but didn't, what he did write is that the Old Testament Scriptures are able to make you wise to know the gospel; that salvation is through Christ.

> For whatever was written in former days was written for our instruction, that through endurance and through the encouragement of the Scriptures we might have hope. (Romans 15:4)

What was written in the Old Testament was written for the instruction of members in the New Covenant. Those same Scriptures provide *our* encouragement and hope. The Old Testament Scriptures were intended to provide New Covenant Gentiles with instruction, encouragement, and hope.

Paul proceeds, just a few verses later, to provide a small sampling of Old Testament passages relating to the Gentiles being recipients of the promises of God:

> For I tell you that Christ became a servant to the circumcised to show God's truthfulness, in order to confirm the promises given to the patriarchs, and in order that the Gentiles might glorify God for his mercy. As it is written, "Therefore I will praise you among the Gentiles, and sing to your name." And again it is said, "Rejoice, O Gentiles, with his people." And again, "Praise the Lord, all you Gentiles, and let all the peoples extol him." And again Isaiah says, "The root of Jesse will come, even he who arises to rule the Gentiles; in him will the Gentiles hope." May the God of hope fill you with all joy and peace in believing, so that by the power of the Holy Spirit you may abound in hope. (Romans 15:8-13)

Here Paul provides Old Testament quotes from passages found:
- in the historical narratives (2 Samuel 22:50)
- in the books of the Law (Deut. 32:43)
- among the books of poetry (Psalm 117:1)
- and from the prophets (Isaiah 52:15)

All 4 categories of Old Testament writings are used to provide evidence that the Old Testament was teaching that Gentiles would be heirs of the promises made to Israel; more specifically, the promises made to the patriarchs: Abraham, Isaac, and Jacob.

And by what means do Gentiles have access to these promises? Through the gospel of Christ, which was promised in the Old Testament.

# Chapter 3:
# Christ Fulfilled the Scriptures and the Prophets

The previous chapter briefly established that the ultimate purpose of the Old Testament's history, Law, prophets, and Scriptures is the gospel of Jesus. The truth of Jesus and the good news of His kingdom is hidden beneath the surface of the Old Testament. This chapter examines that truth more fully with additional passages that indicate that Christ fulfilled the prophets, the prophetic aspect of the Law, even the entirety of the Scriptures.

## JESUS FULFILLED THE PROPHETS

> "Do not think that I have come to abolish the Law or the Prophets; I have not come to abolish them but to fulfill them. (Matthew 5:17)

This verse is often addressed regarding the Law because the Law is the context of Jesus' teaching throughout the rest of Matthew chapter 5. On six different topics Jesus begins each teaching by stating: "you have heard that it was said...but I say unto you..."

How did Jesus fulfill the Law? He fulfilled the Law by perfectly keeping it, thus bringing it to its fullness. The Greek word *pleroo*, translated "fulfill", means "make complete", "bring to fullness".

Imagine an empty barrel. In his description of *pleroo*, Thayer includes the notion that it means to "fill to the brim", "so that nothing shall be [lacking]."[1] The barrel is filled as much as can be; one more drop and it starts dripping over the edge. The Law provides the framework, the shell, the barrel. Jesus fills the barrel to the brim. The Law supplied the barrel, Jesus filled it up. Jesus "makes full" the Law; He "brings to completion" the Law.

It is interesting to note that He doesn't merely say "Do not think that I have come to abolish the Law." Because of the context of the rest of Matthew 5, this is typically handled in reference to the Law. However, He also addressed the Prophets to likewise say He did not come to abolish the Prophets; but to fulfill them.

---

[1] Thayer's Greek Lexicon, s.v. "πληρόω"

How did Jesus fulfill the Prophets? Jesus fulfilled the Prophets the same way in which He fulfilled the Law. The Prophets supplied the barrel, Jesus filled it to the brim. There is no available space remaining in the barrel, it has been completely filled.

The common, modern perspective is that Jesus has yet to fulfill the Prophets, that the prophetic nature of the Prophets awaits its fulfillment at Jesus' Second Coming. Contrary to such suggestions, Jesus said He already came to fill to the brim the prophetic nature of the Prophets.

Is there any part of the Law that is left unfulfilled? Does the Law remain in any way such that some of it has been left unfulfilled and currently continues on, awaiting its fulfillment at His Second Coming? No, Christ is "the end of the law" for everyone who believes (Romans 10:4). Jesus has fulfilled the Law.

In the same way, Jesus has fulfilled the Prophets. In Jesus, the Prophets were "brought to completion." They were "filled to the brim" by Christ. Just as the Law does not continue forward as unfulfilled, so too do the Prophets not continue forward unfulfilled. Jesus has fulfilled them. The Prophets have been brought to completion. They have been filled to the brim.

**MOSES WROTE OF JESUS**
Prior to Jesus revealing to Nathanael that He saw him under the fig tree (John 1:48), Philip was called by Jesus. Philip rushed to Nathanael to give him the news:

> Philip found Nathanael and said to him, "We have found him of whom Moses in the Law and also the prophets wrote, Jesus of Nazareth, the son of Joseph." (John 1:45)

Moses wrote of Jesus when he wrote the books of the Law. The prophets also wrote of Jesus. Philip knew when he met Jesus that he had found the One of whom Moses and the prophets wrote.

> You search the Scriptures because you think that in them you have eternal life; and it is they that bear witness about me, ... Do not think that I will accuse you to the Father. There is one who accuses you: Moses, on whom you have set your hope. For if you believed Moses, you would believe me; for he wrote of me. (John 5:39, 45-46)

## Ch. 3: Christ Fulfilled the Scriptures and the Prophets

When the New Testament mentions the Scriptures, it is speaking of the writings which we refer to as the Old Testament. Jesus proclaimed that the Old Testament writings wrote of Him. He also reinforces what was previously expressed by Philip, that when Moses wrote the books of the Law, he was writing about Jesus. If they truly believed Moses, they would have believed Jesus because what Moses wrote was about Jesus.

> So whatever you wish that others would do to you, do also to them, for this is the Law and the Prophets. (Matthew 7:12)

The Golden Rule: do unto others as you would have them do unto you.

It makes perfect sense that the so-called Golden Rule would be a summary of the Law because we know that elsewhere we are told "love is the fulfilling of the Law".[2] Therefore, if we do unto others as we would have them do unto us, that wraps up how we may put the Law into action.

Why, then, does Jesus state that "do unto others as you would have them do unto you" is also a summary of the Prophets? This is regarding the writings of the prophets as a whole, the collection of utterances that the prophets spoke/wrote.

How do the Prophets (as a whole, as a singular entity) express "do unto others as you would have them do unto you"? That sounds like a bizarre thing to suggest!

The Prophets, as a collective whole, were prophesying of the gospel of Jesus Christ. The prophets were foreshadowing the same thing the Law was foreshadowing...Christ! They were foreshadowing the life of Christ, and the life of those who are in Christ! How else can the Prophets be summarized by "do unto others as you would have them do unto you" unless the primary point of the Prophets be the very gospel of Jesus Christ?

> "Teacher, which is the great commandment in the Law?" And he said to him, "You shall love the Lord your God with all your heart and with all your soul and with all your mind. This is the great and first commandment. And a second is like it: You shall love your neighbor as yourself. On these two commandments depend all the Law and the Prophets." (Matthew 22:36-40)

---

[2] Romans 13:8-10, see also Galatians 5:14 and James 2:8

The two greatest commandments in the Law: love God & love others. Just like both 5:17 and 7:12 previously in Matthew's gospel account, it is no shock to us that the Law is dependent upon (hangs on, is suspended on) love. Without love, the Law loses its stability or support. The Law <u>needs</u> love, relies on love, for the functioning of the Law to be effective.

Once again, it's easy for us to overlook that right along with the Law is included the Prophets. How in the world are the writings of the Prophets <u>dependent</u> upon loving God & loving others? The Prophets "hang" on love for their support; they "depend" on the practical functioning of love. Without love, the Prophets "fall" without support.

In what way do the Prophets depend on love? Love is the highest teaching of God. Loving God and loving others is the pinnacle of the teaching, life, and example of Christ. The Prophets, therefore, point forward to the teaching, life, and example of Christ. The Prophets preached the gospel (1 Pet. 1:10-12). The Prophets are dependent upon gospel living (loving God & others). Without gospel living (loving God & others), the Prophets lose their source of suspension. Without being suspended by love, the writings of the Prophets "fall."

**THE ROAD TO EMMAUS**

On the day of the Resurrection, the resurrected Jesus joined alongside two of His disciples who were on their way to Emmaus discussing the recent events concerning the Crucifixion and the reports from earlier in the morning that Jesus had raised.

> And he said to them, "O foolish ones, and slow of heart to believe all that the prophets have spoken! Was it not necessary that the Christ should suffer these things and enter into his glory?" And beginning with Moses and all the Prophets, he interpreted to them in all the Scriptures the things concerning himself. (Luke 24:25-27)

Jesus made their hearts burn by revealing to them the truth of the Scriptures. What did all the Prophets write that the men were foolish and slow of heart to not believe? The Prophets wrote of the sufferings of Christ (Crucifixion) and His subsequent glory (Resurrection & Ascension).

## Ch. 3: Christ Fulfilled the Scriptures and the Prophets

Why would Jesus call them out as being "foolish" and "slow of heart" if what the prophets wrote was to take place upwards of 2000+ years later? If the prophets were writing of Jesus' Second Coming, why would the men have been scolded for not believing what "all the Prophets" wrote? They were foolish and slow of heart because the events that just happened were the fulfillment of what "all that the prophets had spoken."

They should have known. They should have seen it coming. They should have identified that as they were observing "the things that happened in these days" (v.18), that these events were fulfillment of "all that the prophets have spoken."

They were foolish and slow of heart because they didn't connect the dots. They wouldn't be expected to connect the dots to events that would take place at least 20 centuries later, but rather to events that had just taken place. Jesus began by expounding the writings of Moses and then went through "all the Prophets" showing them "in all the Scriptures" the things that were about Him.

Later the same day, Jesus appeared before a larger group of His disciples.

> Then he said to them, "These are my words that I spoke to you while I was still with you, that everything written about me in the Law of Moses and the Prophets and the Psalms must be fulfilled." Then he opened their minds to understand the Scriptures, and said to them, "Thus it is written, that the Christ should suffer and on the third day rise from the dead, and that repentance for the forgiveness of sins should be proclaimed in his name to all nations, beginning from Jerusalem. You are witnesses of these things. (Luke 24:44-48)

Everything written about Jesus in the Law, the Prophets, and the Psalms, He said, was to be fulfilled. Then He proclaimed "thus it is written" (verse 46).

We're accustomed throughout the New Testament that when the phrase "it is written" is written, we're about to read a quotation from the Old Testament. Curiously enough, after stating "it is written" Jesus proceeds to *not* quote any particular Old Testament passage at all. There is no verse in the Old Testament that states "the Christ should suffer and on the third day rise from the dead, and that repentance and forgiveness of sins should be proclaimed in his name to all nations." It's not there! At least it's not there *explicitly*.

When Jesus said "it is written" and then proceeded to not quote a singular Old Testament passage, He advocated that the entire Old Testament, collectively, is writing that "the Christ should suffer and on the third day rise from the dead, and that repentance and forgiveness of sins should be proclaimed in his name to all nations."

Jesus is saying that the point of the entire Old Testament is Himself. The Old Testament preached the gospel of Christ in types, shadows, and pictures; in hidden truths that were later revealed in Christ.

The Holy Scriptures are able to make us wise to know that salvation is through Christ (2 Timothy 3:15). Jesus is unveiling the *mysterion*. The truth that had been hidden for ages was revealed in Jesus' life, death, burial, resurrection, ascension, and multiplication: the mystery of the gospel of Jesus Christ.

## EVERYTHING WRITTEN ABOUT THE SON OF MAN

Before Jesus went to Jerusalem to suffer, He warned His disciples what would happen:

> And taking the twelve, he said to them, "See, we are going up to Jerusalem, and everything that is written about the Son of Man by the prophets will be accomplished. For he will be delivered over to the Gentiles and will be mocked and shamefully treated and spit upon. And after flogging him, they will kill him, and on the third day he will rise." But they understood none of these things. This saying was hidden from them, and they did not grasp what was said. (Luke 18:31-34)

Jesus said that "everything" that the prophets wrote about the Son of Man will be accomplished when Jesus goes to Jerusalem. What was it that was accomplished when He got to Jerusalem? Jesus' Crucifixion and the Resurrection: the key events pertaining to the gospel. Perhaps Jesus was merely using hyperbole when He said "everything". However, put in conjunction with several other similar passages, I'm led to believe that when He said "everything" He meant *everything*!

For about 25 years of my life as a Christian, I might have written it off as hyperbole. In the past few years, however, I now see the Old Testament prophets as having 1st Century fulfillment. Everything that was written about the Son of Man by the prophets was accomplished.

## Ch. 3: Christ Fulfilled the Scriptures and the Prophets

> For I tell you that this Scripture must be fulfilled in me: 'And he was numbered with the transgressors.' For what is written about me has its fulfillment." (Luke 22:37)

Regarding Jesus' first statement of Luke 22:37, it can easily be suggested that only specific Scriptures were fulfilled by Jesus during His First Coming, such as His having been "numbered with the transgressors." But Jesus' second statement of Luke 22:37 indicates that what has been written about Him has its fulfillment in the 1st Century.

Many Christian teachers suggest that what was written about Jesus in the prophets finds its fulfillment in His Second Coming. In other words, they suggest that what was written about Jesus has yet to be fulfilled, but Jesus said what was written about Him "has its fulfillment."

In Acts chapter 10, Peter is speaking to Cornelius about Jesus:

> And he commanded us to preach to the people and to testify that he is the one appointed by God to be judge of the living and the dead. To him all the prophets bear witness that everyone who believes in him receives forgiveness of sins through his name." (Acts 10:42-43)

All the prophets provide testimony ("bear witness") that all who believe in Jesus receives forgiveness of sins. That's the gospel! Did only certain prophets preach the gospel beforehand? "All the prophets" spoke of the coming salvation that was to be offered through the redemptive work of Jesus.

In Acts chapter 13, Paul is preaching to the Israelites:

> "Brothers, sons of the family of Abraham, and those among you who fear God, to us has been sent the message of this salvation. For those who live in Jerusalem and their rulers, because they did not recognize him nor understand the utterances of the prophets, which are read every Sabbath, fulfilled them by condemning him. And though they found in him no guilt worthy of death, they asked Pilate to have him executed. And when they had carried out all that was written of him, they took him down from the tree and laid him in a tomb. (Acts 13:26-29)

*The Mystery of the Gospel*

The rulers and leaders of Jerusalem did not understand that by condemning Jesus they were fulfilling the prophets. Then they carried out "all that was written of him" by crucifying Him. The New Testament teaching of the Old Testament prophets emphasizes that the prophets were writing about the kingdom of God that was ushered in by Jesus' *First* Coming.

Paul shared the testimony of his conversion with King Agrippa and Festus. He continued:

> To this day I have had the help that comes from God, and so I stand here testifying both to small and great, saying nothing but what the prophets and Moses said would come to pass: that the Christ must suffer and that, by being the first to rise from the dead, he would proclaim light both to our people and to the Gentiles." And as he was saying these things in his defense, Festus said with a loud voice, "Paul, you are out of your mind; your great learning is driving you out of your mind." But Paul said, "I am not out of my mind, most excellent Festus, but I am speaking true and rational words. For the king knows about these things, and to him I speak boldly. For I am persuaded that none of these things has escaped his notice, for this has not been done in a corner. King Agrippa, do you believe the prophets? I know that you believe." (Acts 26:22-27)

Paul stated that he said nothing other than what "the prophets and Moses" have already said would come to pass. What did Paul say that the prophets and Moses said would come to pass? "That the Christ must suffer...[and] rise from the dead." That is the primary point and purpose of the Law. That is also the primary point and purpose of the Prophets. The entire Old Testament is about the gospel of Jesus Christ, the message of the gospel hidden in mystery.

Interestingly, Paul also affirmed that the Prophets and the Law indicated that light would be proclaimed to *Gentiles!* The only manner in which Gentiles could see the light of God is through the good news of Jesus.

Paul concluded by appealing to Agrippa that he (Agrippa) professes belief in the prophets. Paul is making the connection that if Agrippa truly believed the prophets as he confessed to do, then Agrippa would also believe in the gospel because what the prophets wrote about was the gospel of Jesus.

## Ch. 3: Christ Fulfilled the Scriptures and the Prophets

**AN APPOINTED DAY**

Paul was given a certain day by the Jewish leaders at Rome to present his case for Christ in their hearing:

> When they had appointed a day for him, they came to him at his lodging in greater numbers. From morning till evening he expounded to them, testifying to the kingdom of God and trying to convince them about Jesus both from the Law of Moses and from the Prophets. And some were convinced by what he said, but others disbelieved. (Acts 28:23-24)

Paul testified to them about the kingdom of God, trying to convince them about Jesus. How did Paul do this? Paul preached Jesus from both the Law and the Prophets. Some of those who heard believed. Paul would not be able to preach the gospel of Jesus from the Prophets unless the Prophets contained the gospel of Jesus.

The prevalent view is that only certain portions of the Old Testament contained prophesies of Jesus, that only select passages were prophetic of the gospel. Some Christians restrict the gospel-related prophetic nature of the Old Testament to passages that are specifically quoted in the New Testament.

It would be quite a limited view the prophetic power of the Old Testament by doing so, however. The more we look throughout the New Testament, the more we find that the Old Testament has been fulfilled. If we limited the prophetic power of the Old Testament to only those passages that are directly quoted in the New Testament, we miss the entire point of the Old Testament.

If being quoted in the New Testament is a prerequisite for an Old Testament passage to be prophetic of the gospel, then it would require the entire Old Testament to be duplicated in the New Testament. That would be altogether redundant!

> For I delivered to you as of first importance what I also received: that Christ died for our sins in accordance with the Scriptures, (1 Corinthians 15:3)

Christ died for our sins in accordance with the Scriptures. Which Scriptures? All of them!

> that he was buried, that he was raised on the third day in accordance with the Scriptures, (1 Corinthians 15:4)

He was raised on the third day in accordance with the Scriptures. Which Scriptures? All of them!

> But now the righteousness of God has been manifested apart from the law, although the Law and the Prophets bear witness to it-- the righteousness of God through faith in Jesus Christ for all who believe. (Romans 3:21-22a)

The Law and the Prophets bear witness to the righteousness of God that has been manifested apart from the law; the righteousness of God through "the faithfulness of Jesus" (NET) for all who believe. The Law and the Prophets bear witness to the gospel message.

> But one of those who stood by drew his sword and struck the servant of the high priest and cut off his ear. And Jesus said to them, "Have you come out as against a robber, with swords and clubs to capture me? Day after day I was with you in the temple teaching, and you did not seize me. But let the Scriptures be fulfilled." (Mark 14:47-49)

What the New Testament teaches us about the Old Testament is that the Old Testament Scriptures were fulfilled by Jesus. Mark quoted Jesus who intimated that the imminent suffering that Jesus was about to experience would "let the Scriptures be fulfilled."

To beat a dead horse even deader, there is one last passage we will address. God had just healed a lame man through Peter. The crowd rushed to Peter; he recognized the opportunity to share the truth of Jesus. While preaching Jesus, Peter made the following pair of statements:

> But what God foretold by the mouth of all the prophets, that his Christ would suffer, he thus fulfilled. ... And all the prophets who have spoken, from Samuel and those who came after him, also proclaimed these days. (Acts 3:18, 24)

## Ch. 3: Christ Fulfilled the Scriptures and the Prophets

God fulfilled what He foretold by the mouth of *all* the prophets, that His Anointed One would suffer (3:18). Peter subsequently said (six verses later) that the prophets, all of the prophets from Samuel on, were proclaiming these very days; the days of the New Covenant era. Days that first took place nearly 20 centuries ago when the kingdom of God was brought into reality through the Crucifixion, Resurrection, Ascension, and Pentecost (and on) are the days that "all the prophets who have spoken" were proclaiming.

When Samuel arrived on the scene, he was regarded as the greatest prophet since Moses. Following Samuel came the great prophets Elijah and Elisha. All 16 prophets who wrote books, from Isaiah to Malachi, followed Samuel. David and the prophetic psalms also followed Samuel. Following Samuel came every relevant prophet, save for Moses who preceded Samuel by about four centuries.

Peter insisted that all the prophets who spoke from Samuel on (basically, *all* of them) proclaimed days (a period of time) that began in our past. Nor does Peter exclude Moses for he quoted Moses prophesying of Jesus in verses 22 and 23. Therefore, Peter is saying that every prophetic utterance, those of Moses and every relevant prophet, was proclaiming the days of the New Covenant era that were ushered in by Jesus.

This is quite in contrast to the view that permeates the modern American church which suggests that the prophets proclaimed the days ushered *out* by Jesus at the *end* of the New Covenant era. In other words, the common view in our land is that the prophets wrote of the Second Coming of Jesus. This is contrary to the teaching found throughout the New Testament that the prophets wrote about the First Coming of Jesus and the New Covenant realities that continue today as the kingdom of God in Christ advances!

# Chapter 4:
# The Old Testament Covenants Foreshadow Christ

The Old Testament covenants contribute significantly to the *mysterion*, the hidden truth that was revealed in Jesus. The covenants point forward to the true kingdom of God found in the gospel message and the realities of the New Covenant. The New Testament teaches us that the purpose served by the Old Testament, including the covenants contained therein, is that it is able to make you wise to know that salvation is through Jesus (2 Tim. 3:15).

**ABRAHAMIC COVENANT**
God promised Abraham four things:
- Seed (Genesis 12:7; 13:15; 24:7)
- Nation (Genesis 12:2)
- Land (Genesis 12:1)
- Blessing (Gen. 12:2)

There was an immediate, temporal, physical fulfillment to God's covenant promises:

Seed → Isaac
Nation → Israel
Land → Palestine
Blessing → Long, wealthy life (Gen. 15:15)

God had delivered on His covenant promises when Israel occupied the Promised Land. This caused Joshua to proclaim:

> Thus the LORD gave to Israel all the land that he swore to give to their fathers. And they took possession of it, and they settled there. And the LORD gave them rest on every side just as he had sworn to their fathers. Not one of all their enemies had withstood them, for the LORD had given all their enemies into their hands. Not one word of all the good promises that the LORD had made to the house of Israel had failed; all came to pass. (Joshua 21:43-45)

All the good promises the Lord made to Israel came to pass. Not one word failed. God delivered on His promises. We should have no reason to anticipate, therefore, that there is any portion of God's promises to Israel's fathers that God has yet to fulfill. He has already fulfilled His promises to Israel and their fathers. "All came to pass."

But the New Testament unveils for us the hidden truth of God's promises to Abraham. It is the mystery of the gospel.

God did indeed promise a seed, a nation, a land, and blessing. He delivered on His promise. Although there was an immediate, temporal, physical fulfillment to God's promises, the New Testament reveals that God's promises to Abraham ultimately are fulfilled in Jesus! Jesus provides the ultimate, eternal, spiritual fulfillment of God's promises to Abraham.

In Paul's letter to the Galatians he addressed three of the four aspects of God's promises to Abraham (seed, nation, and blessing) as they are fulfilled in Jesus. We can go to the writer to the Hebrews for the fourth (land).

### Seed

> Now the promises were spoken to Abraham and to his seed. He does not say, "And to seeds," as referring to many, but rather to one, "And to your seed," that is, Christ. (Galatians 3:16 NASB)

Paul made it clear that the fulfillment of God's promise of a seed to Abraham was Jesus, not Isaac. Isaac served as a picture of the reality that would be revealed in Christ. Isaac was the shadow; Jesus is the substance. God's promise of a seed to Abraham was ultimately Christ. The immediate, temporal, physical fulfillment of Isaac as the seed of promise was not the true form of the reality. The truth of the seed was hidden layers beneath Isaac. In Jesus, the mystery, hidden truth, was revealed.

### Nation

> Know then that it is **those of faith who are the sons of Abraham**. ... so that **in Christ Jesus the blessing of Abraham might come to the Gentiles**, so that we might receive the promised Spirit through faith. ... But the Scripture imprisoned everything under sin, so that **the promise by faith in Jesus Christ might be given to those who believe**. ... And if you are Christ's, then you are **Abraham's offspring, heirs according to promise**. (Galatians 3:7, 14, 22, 29)

## Ch. 4: The Old Testament Covenants Foreshadow Christ

Who are the descendants of Abraham? The Jews thought it was them because of their physical lineage. Jesus seemed to think otherwise:

> "They answered him, 'Abraham is our father.' Jesus said to them, 'If you were Abraham's children, you would be doing the works Abraham did'" (John 8:39).

Clearly, those who are descended from Abraham are not necessarily Abraham's descendants. Abraham's true children are those who are of faith in Christ.

> For not all who are descended from Israel belong to Israel, and not all are children of Abraham because they are his offspring, but "Through Isaac shall your offspring be named." This means that it is not the children of the flesh who are the children of God, but the children of the promise are counted as offspring. (Romans 9:6b-8)

Isaac was the child of promise, as opposed to Ishmael who was Abraham's child according to the flesh:

> For it is written that Abraham had two sons, one by a slave woman and one by a free woman. But the son of the slave was born according to the flesh, while the son of the free woman was born through promise. ... Now you, brothers, like Isaac, are children of promise. But just as at that time he who was born according to the flesh persecuted him who was born according to the Spirit, so also it is now. (Galatians 4:22-23, 28-29)

Isaac was the immediate, temporal, physical fulfillment as the child of promise. This served as a foreshadow of those who would be born of the Spirit in the New Covenant. Those who are in Christ are the true "heirs according to promise", not the physical nation of Israel which also served as a foreshadow.

Paul clarifies in Romans 9:6 the difference between physical Israel and spiritual Israel: not all Israel is of Israel. That is, not all who are of the physical nation of Israel are of the spiritual nation of Israel. The spiritual nation of Israel, those who are born of the Spirit unto faith in Christ, are the true recipients of the promises of God to Abraham. It is not the children of the flesh (ethnic Israel) who are the children of God, but it is the children of the promise (spiritual Israel) who are counted as the offspring/children/descendants of Abraham.

The mystery of the gospel: on the surface it appears God's promises are to a physical nation. The hidden truth of the *mysterion*, however, is revealed through Jesus that God's promises to Abraham are fulfilled to those who abide in New Covenant realities with Christ.

**Blessing**

> Know then that it is those of faith who are the sons of Abraham. And the Scripture, foreseeing that God would justify the Gentiles by faith, preached the gospel beforehand to Abraham, saying, "In you shall all the nations be blessed." So then, those who are of faith are blessed along with Abraham, the man of faith. ... so that in Christ Jesus the blessing of Abraham might come to the Gentiles, so that we might receive the promised Spirit through faith. (Galatians 3:7-9, 14)

Paul declared that when Abraham was being promised "in you shall all the nations be blessed", Abraham was being preached the gospel! The ultimate fulfillment of God's promise of blessing to Abraham is justification for those who have embraced the good news of the kingdom. Abraham was being promised the gospel!

Who receives the blessing promised to Abraham? It is "those who are of faith" (Gal. 3:9); it is Gentiles whom God has purposed to justify (Gal. 3:8). What is the only way any person can possibly ever be justified before God? It is only through Jesus' atoning work; redeemed humans being joined unto Christ. The blessing promised to Abraham came to the Gentiles who are in Jesus by having received the Spirit (Gal. 3:14).

**Land**

God's promise of land to the ethnic nation of Israel was for the purpose of providing her rest. Prior to entering the Promised Land, Moses spoke to the people promising them rest after they possess the land:

> for you have not as yet come to the rest and to the inheritance that the LORD your God is giving you. But when you go over the Jordan and live in the land that the LORD your God is giving you to inherit, and

> when he gives you rest from all your enemies around, so that you live in safety, (Deuteronomy 12:9-10)

After taking the land under Joshua's leadership, the land rested from war:

> So Joshua took the whole land, according to all that the LORD had spoken to Moses. And Joshua gave it for an inheritance to Israel according to their tribal allotments. And the land had rest from war. (Joshua 11:23)

The promise of land was so that the people of God could find rest. This, too, is a foreshadowing of the rest promised to those who abide in Jesus. The Old Covenant people of God were promised a physical place of rest; the New Covenant people of God are promised a spiritual place of rest (in Jesus).

**Rest**

Following a quotation of Psalm 95:7-11 in Hebrews 3:7-11, the writer to the Hebrews warned his readers to take care lest any of them have an unbelieving heart like that of the rebellious wilderness generation (3:12). He then encouraged his readers to:

> exhort one another every day, as long as it is called "today," that none of you may be hardened by the deceitfulness of sin. (Hebrews 3:13)

Why? Because the wilderness generation could not enter God's rest because of unbelief (Heb. 3:16-19). What was it they did not enter? They did not enter the Promised Land. Entering the Promised Land symbolized rest.

Rest could not be had until they were in the land. Also, rest could apparently only be had with belief, foreshadowing New Covenant realities in Christ.

The concept of the Promised Land providing rest is another example of the *mysterion*. Beneath the surface of the promise of rest via entering a certain portion of land was the mystery of the gospel. The hidden truth was that only through faith in Jesus will a person find rest. It is not the kind of rest that would be found by possessing any piece of property; it is rest for our souls as we settle ourselves upon the salvation that comes through Jesus.

Therefore, while the promise of entering his rest still stands, let us fear lest any of you should seem to have failed to reach it. ... For we who have believed enter that rest (Hebrews 4:1, 3a)

The writer of Hebrews observed that even though Joshua led the people to enter the promised land (circa 1400 BC), about 400 years later (circa 1000 BC) David indicated in Psalm 95 that there was a rest yet to be fulfilled (Heb. 4:8). The writer knew that David's use of the term "today" (Ps. 95:7) was not limited to the time of David. The writer read David state "today" and knew it applied to New Covenant realities. Even though Joshua proclaimed that God had delivered on all of His promises ("all came to pass") the writer to the Hebrews knew that the ultimate fulfillment of the land promise was not fulfilled in Joshua (Heb. 4:6-8). It was fulfilled in Jesus.

Observe the phrases written in Hebrews chapter 4 that indicate that the writer knew that the fulfillment of rest (i.e. the land promise) began its true fulfillment in the 1st Century, rather than in Joshua's day:

- "while the promise of entering his rest still stands" (4:1)
- "we who have believed enter that rest" (4:3)
- "Since therefore it remains for some to enter it" (4:6)
- "For if Joshua had given them rest, God would not have spoken of another day later on" (4:8)
- "there remains a Sabbath rest for the people of God" (4:9)
- "Let us therefore strive to enter that rest" (4:11)

| PROMISE | PICTURE | FULFILLMENT |
| --- | --- | --- |
| Seed | Isaac | Jesus |
| Nation | Israel | Believers in Christ |
| Land | Palestine | Salvation rest |
| Blessing | Long, wealthy life | Justification |

God's promises to Abraham were fulfilled in an immediate, temporal, physical manner which foreshadowed the ultimate, eternal, spiritual realities.

God's eternal purpose was to bring into His Kingdom members of every nation through the gospel (Rev. 14:6). God revealed His eternal purpose in the Person of Jesus and those who are in Him (Eph. 3:10-11). Before God's eternal purpose was realized in Jesus, the truth of God's plan was hidden in mystery (Eph. 3:9), such as in God's promises to Abraham. The Abrahamic Covenant consisted of the mystery of the gospel, realizing its ultimate fulfillment in Jesus.

*Ch. 4: The Old Testament Covenants Foreshadow Christ*

**DAVIDIC COVENANT**

The Davidic Covenant profiles very similarly with the Abrahamic Covenant. Just as it was with God's promises to Abraham, God's promises to David saw an immediate, temporal, physical fulfillment that served as a picture of the ultimate, eternal, spiritual realities.

David was promised a son who would sit on his throne and build a house for God. David's son Solomon did indeed reign as king and built a temple for God. King Solomon and his temple serve as the picture of what would later be realized in Jesus. God promised to David:

> When your days are fulfilled and you lie down with your fathers, I will raise up your offspring after you, who shall come from your body, and I will establish his kingdom. He shall build a house for my name, and I will establish the throne of his kingdom forever. I will be to him a father, and he shall be to me a son. When he commits iniquity, I will discipline him with the rod of men, with the stripes of the sons of men, but my steadfast love will not depart from him, as I took it from Saul, whom I put away from before you. And your house and your kingdom shall be made sure forever before me. Your throne shall be established forever.' (2 Samuel 7:12-16)

**Son**

Though Solomon was David's direct descendant, the term son is also often used to refer to descendants several generations later. Jesus was, of course, a descendant of David.

> The book of the genealogy of Jesus Christ, the son of David, the son of Abraham. (Matthew 1:1)

Jesus descended from both David and Abraham, thus their son. Jesus is also considered the son of both David and Abraham not merely because of physical lineage, but also because He was fulfillment of the promises made to the offspring of David and Abraham.

## Throne

Jesus reigns as king over God's kingdom. This was promised through the kingdom God gave to David. Jesus' reign as king of God's kingdom fulfills the promise to David that his descendant would reign on his throne forever.

Mary was comforted with these words by the angel Gabriel:

> And behold, you will conceive in your womb and bear a son, and you shall call his name Jesus. He will be great and will be called the Son of the Most High. And the Lord God will give to him the throne of his father David, (Luke 1:31-32)

Jesus was given "the throne of his father David." Peter also spoke of the throne of David in his speech at Pentecost:

> "Brothers, I may say to you with confidence about the patriarch David that he both died and was buried, and his tomb is with us to this day. Being therefore a prophet, and knowing that God had sworn with an oath to him that he would set one of his descendants on his throne, he foresaw and spoke about the resurrection of the Christ, that he was not abandoned to Hades, nor did his flesh see corruption. (Acts 2:29-31)

Peter knew and declared that the promise to David that his son would reign on his throne was fulfilled by the Resurrected Christ. David's son Solomon is a type, a picture of the reality to be made known in the future, revealed in Jesus: "something greater than Solomon is here" (Matt. 12:42, Luke 11:31). Jesus does not need to wait for an ostensible yet-future-to-us Millennial Kingdom to reign, Peter's words confirm that Jesus' reign began with the coronation of resurrection.

## Temple

Solomon built a house for the Lord, a temple. Solomon's temple represented the dwelling place of God on earth. Of course, God is infinite, without limits, and cannot be contained within a certain space. That said, if someone wanted to "meet God", they would do so by approaching the temple and meeting Him there because the temple represented His dwelling place.

The physical structure of the Old Covenant temple provided a foreshadowing of the New Covenant temple which is a spiritual structure. The New Covenant temple of God is, first and foremost, the Person of Jesus ("destroy this temple,

## Ch. 4: The Old Testament Covenants Foreshadow Christ

and in three days I will raise it up" [John 2:19]). Never has God dwelt on earth in any more real way than in the very Person of Jesus. Jesus is the truest fulfillment of the dwelling place of God on earth.

However, it is not only Jesus who comprises the New Covenant temple. All those who are *in* Jesus are also part of the New Covenant temple of God! After Jesus ascended, the Spirit descended on believers at Pentecost by indwelling them. Since Pentecost, Spirit-indwelt believers are the very dwelling place of God on earth. The New Covenant temple is a spiritual structure comprised of Spirit-born believers who have been immersed into Jesus.

> So then you are no longer strangers and aliens, but you are fellow citizens with the saints and members of the household of God, built on the foundation of the apostles and prophets, Christ Jesus himself being the cornerstone, in whom the whole structure, being joined together, grows into a holy temple in the Lord. In him you also are being built together into a dwelling place for God by the Spirit. (Ephesians 2:19-22)

> Do you not know that you are God's temple and that God's Spirit dwells in you? If anyone destroys God's temple, God will destroy him. For God's temple is holy, and you are that temple. (1 Corinthians 3:16-17)

> Or do you not know that your body is a temple of the Holy Spirit within you, whom you have from God? You are not your own, (1 Corinthians 6:19)

> What agreement has the temple of God with idols? For we are the temple of the living God; as God said, "I will make my dwelling among them and walk among them, and I will be their God, and they shall be my people. (2 Corinthians 6:16)

The dwelling place of God on earth today is in His people! God has made redeemed, former sinners His home! Living stones are being built up as a spiritual house (1 Pet. 2:5).

| PROMISE | PICTURE | FULFILLMENT |
|---|---|---|
| Son | Solomon | Jesus |
| Throne | Kingdom of David | Kingdom of God |
| House | Old Covenant temple | New Covenant temple |

Solomon reigned on his father's throne and built the temple as a dwelling place on earth for God. This was the immediate, temporal, physical fulfillment of God's promises to David.

Jesus, the son of David, reigns on the throne of God's kingdom and He is building a temple as a dwelling place on earth for God. This is the ultimate, eternal, spiritual fulfillment of God's promises to David.

Let's look again at God's promises to David:

| PROMISE | PICTURE | FULFILLMENT |
| --- | --- | --- |
| I will raise up your offspring after you, who shall come from your body, and I will establish his kingdom. (2 Sam. 7:12) | God raised up Solomon, David's offspring, and established his kingdom | God raised up Jesus, David's offspring, and established His kingdom |
| He shall build a house for my name, and I will establish the throne of his kingdom forever. (2 Sam. 7:13) | Solomon built a house for the Lord. | Jesus is building a house for the Lord, and God has established the throne of Jesus' kingdom forever. |
| I will be to him a father, and he shall be to me a son. (2 Sam. 7:14) | Solomon was treated as though a son of God. | God is to Jesus a Father, and Jesus is to God a Son. |
| When he commits iniquity, (2 Sam. 7:14) | Solomon sinned against God by following idols. | Jesus, though having committed no sin, took upon Himself the guilt of sin as though He had committed iniquity. |
| I will discipline him with the rod of men, with the stripes of the sons of men, (2 Sam. 7:14) | Solomon was chastised by God for his sin. | Jesus was beaten, received stripes, and ultimately crucified for bearing the sin of many. |

## MOSAIC COVENANT

There is much that can be said about the Old Covenant, God's promises to Israel through Moses, filling volumes upon volumes. This writing will not sufficiently address the impact of God's covenant to Israel through Moses. The following analysis of this covenant will be in brief overview form, such as a view from over 30,000 feet.

## Ch. 4: The Old Testament Covenants Foreshadow Christ

It is said by some that the Old Covenant and the Law can be distinguished; the Old Covenant being temporary but the Law being eternal. However, it is difficult to distinguish between the Old Covenant and the Law, as though we can try to peel the layers off of one as though it won't impact the other. In fact, the covenant the people of Israel made with God was based on the regulations of the Law, beginning with the Ten Commandments in Exodus chapter 20 and the many rules stipulated in chapters 21-23. Then, in chapter 24, the people committed themselves to obedience:

> Then he took the Book of the Covenant and read it in the hearing of the people. And they said, "All that the LORD has spoken we will do, and we will be obedient." And Moses took the blood and threw it on the people and said, "Behold the blood of the covenant that the LORD has made with you in accordance with all these words." (Exo 24:7-8)

The people covenanted obedience to the laws they were given. It is difficult, therefore, to attempt to delineate between the covenant and the law. They are interconnected.

We've already addressed in a previous chapter that the New Testament teaches that Jesus fulfilled the Law. In so doing He also fulfilled the covenant comprised of those laws.

Jesus brought in a law of love. Moses was the intermediary of a covenant based on works. In contrast, Jesus is the intermediary of a new covenant based on love. Jesus' new covenant brings with it a new law: a law of love.

Jesus taught that the greatest commandment in the Law is based on love (Matt. 22:37-38). The second greatest commandment in the Law is like it because it is also based on love (Matt. 22:39). The law of love that Jesus ushered in with the new covenant fulfilled the Old Covenant and its law:

> Love does no wrong to a neighbor; therefore love is the fulfilling of the law. (Rom 13:10)

> For the whole law is fulfilled in one word: "You shall love your neighbor as yourself." (Gal 5:14)

If you really fulfill the royal law according to the Scripture, "You shall love your neighbor as yourself," you are doing well. (Jas 2:8)

The Old Covenant was not faultless (Heb. 8:10) and was made obsolete (Heb. 8:13). When Jesus came, those who are in His New Covenant are not under the law (Gal. 3:25; Rom. 6:14, 10:4). The law created separation between Jews and Gentiles. The division that caused hostility was killed by Jesus (Eph. 2:14-16).

Jesus fulfilled the Law! (Matt. 5:17, 7:12, 22:40)

# PART II:
# New Testament Evidences of the Mysterion

# Chapter 5:
## New Testament Evidence of the Mysterion

Hidden in the Old Testament is the promise of the New Covenant realized in Jesus ushering in God's kingdom. Reading the Old Testament in the context of the Old Testament alone will lead to a veiled understanding. When we read the Old Testament in the context of Christ, the veil is removed and we can understand the Old Testament in its proper context as a foreshadowing or prefiguration of Christ (see 2 Cor. 3:12-16).

There are several Old Testament passages quoted in the New Testament in a context that is significantly different than the context of the original Old Testament passage. What appears to be the context of an Old Testament passage is said by the New Testament author to be fulfilled very differently. The context of the Old Testament passage is merely the surface-level understanding; the hidden truth is buried deep beneath; the true context being revealed in the gospel of Jesus Christ. What an Old Testament passage appears to be about and what the New Testament says it's really about can be very different.

Let's examine a few prominent examples. We'll begin with Joel 2:28-32.

**JOEL 2**

> "And it shall come to pass afterward, that I will pour out my Spirit on all flesh; your sons and your daughters shall prophesy, your old men shall dream dreams, and your young men shall see visions. Even on the male and female servants in those days I will pour out my Spirit. "And I will show wonders in the heavens and on the earth, blood and fire and columns of smoke. The sun shall be turned to darkness, and the moon to blood, before the great and awesome day of the LORD comes. And it shall come to pass that everyone who calls on the name of the LORD shall be saved. For in Mount Zion and in Jerusalem there shall be those who escape, as the LORD has said, and among the survivors shall be those whom the LORD calls. (Joel 2:28-32)

**Surface-level context:** Events in the natural realm will turn the world upside down.
**Hidden truth:** Events in the spiritual realm will turn the world upside down.

Reading Joel only in the context of Joel may lead us to think that these events are likely to be fulfilled at the end of the world as we know it, particularly the sun being turned to darkness and the moon to blood. After all, there is no record that those events have already happened.

However, the New Testament reveals to us that the description of these cataclysmic events is not meant to speak of physical events. Peter quotes this passage at Pentecost when the Spirit fell upon the apostles and they spoke in other human languages:

> And all were amazed and perplexed, saying to one another, "What does this mean?" But others mocking said, "They are filled with new wine." But Peter, standing with the eleven, lifted up his voice and addressed them: "Men of Judea and all who dwell in Jerusalem, let this be known to you, and give ear to my words. For these people are not drunk, as you suppose, since it is only the third hour of the day. But this is what was uttered through the prophet Joel: (Acts 2:12-16)

"This is what was uttered through the prophet Joel." Then Peter quoted the Joel passage above. Peter informed his hearers that what was happening in front of them is fulfillment of what Joel wrote. God poured out His Spirit on humans.

Peter speaks of wonders in the sky, signs on the earth, blood, fire, smoke, the sun to darkness, the moon to blood, all as he is quoting Joel. Peter indicated that each of these things is fulfilled by the Lord pouring out His Spirit upon men, beginning at Pentecost in Acts chapter 2. Thus, when Joel states "And it shall come to pass afterward...", the "afterward" came to pass in what Peter and the apostles experienced on that day.

Joel also announced that "it shall come to pass that everyone who calls on the name of the LORD shall be saved." When does this happen? When is it when those who call on the name of the Lord shall be saved? The New Testament informs us that it is through the message of the gospel. Only through the gospel of Jesus is any human saved!

> And there is salvation in no one else, for there is no other name under heaven given among men by which we must be saved." (Acts 4:12)

*Ch. 5: New Testament Evidence of the Mysterion*

> For "everyone who calls on the name of the Lord will be saved." (Romans 10:13)

Paul directly quoted Joel 2:32 in Romans 10:13, whereas Peter alluded to it in Acts 4. When Joel wrote in 2:32 "And it shall come to pass", he is prophesying of the coming salvation through Jesus and His gospel message.

Joel 2:28-32 is not end-times prophesy. It is prophetic of the gospel of Jesus Christ and salvation through Him. This is the hidden truth, the *mysterion*, being revealed in the New Testament. The reality of Joel 2:28-32 is the gospel of Jesus.

**AMOS 9**

> "In that day I will raise up the booth of David that is fallen and repair its breaches, and raise up its ruins and rebuild it as in the days of old, that they may possess the remnant of Edom and all the nations who are called by my name," declares the LORD who does this. "Behold, the days are coming," declares the LORD, "when the plowman shall overtake the reaper and the treader of grapes him who sows the seed; the mountains shall drip sweet wine, and all the hills shall flow with it. I will restore the fortunes of my people Israel, and they shall rebuild the ruined cities and inhabit them; they shall plant vineyards and drink their wine, and they shall make gardens and eat their fruit. I will plant them on their land, and they shall never again be uprooted out of the land that I have given them," says the LORD your God. (Amos 9:11-15)

**Surface-level context:** The Lord will restore Israel.
**Hidden truth:** The gospel of Jesus being spread to Gentiles.

This seems incredibly contradictory. Whether the Lord is restoring Israel or Gentiles leads to diametrically opposed viewpoints. Gentiles are non-Israel, Israel is non-Gentile. How can Amos' promise to restore Israel be fulfilled by God restoring non-Israel?

The immediate context of Amos' message is that the tabernacle of David will be restored to a state as it was a couple centuries prior (in Old Covenant Israel). It is a message of hope for the future utilizing the past as precedent. Amos promised the fortunes restored for "my people Israel."

However, James, an Israelite, has a very different perspective. He sees this passage by Amos as being about Gentiles receiving the message of the gospel. At the Jerusalem Council:

> After they finished speaking, James replied, "Brothers, listen to me. Simeon has related how God first visited the Gentiles, to take from them a people for his name. And with this the words of the prophets agree, just as it is written, "'After this I will return, and I will rebuild the tent of David that has fallen; I will rebuild its ruins, and I will restore it, that the remnant of mankind may seek the Lord, and all the Gentiles who are called by my name, says the Lord, who makes these things known from of old.' (Acts 15:13-18)

Why did James quote Amos 9:11-12? James made reference to the Amos passage as evidence that "the prophets agree" that God is taking "from [the Gentiles] a people for His name."

Paul and Peter had just spoken to the crowd, sharing stories of how Gentiles have come to faith (Acts 15:6-12). James confirmed this. Then James thought of a passage of Scripture that prophesies that Gentiles are to come to the Lord. Amos 9:11-12 came to his mind as verification that God's plan is to call Gentiles to Himself.

Raising the tabernacle of David is fulfilled by Jesus, the son of David. Jesus will rebuild the tabernacle of David. Jesus is rebuilding a city for God. We know in the New Testament that Jesus is not building a physical city. He is building a spiritual city, the New Jerusalem. The New Jerusalem is not comprised of brick and mortar; it is a so-called "city" comprised of people. What appears to be the physical rebuilding of cities is fulfilled by Jesus rebuilding for God a spiritual city with spiritual vineyards, spiritual wine, spiritual fruit on a spiritual land.

Regarding any potential concerns of "spiritualizing" the text in Amos, both James and Luke (the author of Acts) will have to be accused of doing the same. James spoke and Luke wrote that the promise to restore Israel from Amos 9 is fulfilled by the gospel of Jesus bringing Gentiles into God's kingdom.

## JEREMIAH 31

> "Behold, the days are coming, declares the LORD, when I will make a new covenant with the house of Israel and the house of Judah, not like

## Ch. 5: New Testament Evidence of the Mysterion

> the covenant that I made with their fathers on the day when I took them by the hand to bring them out of the land of Egypt, my covenant that they broke, though I was their husband, declares the LORD. For this is the covenant that I will make with the house of Israel after those days, declares the LORD: I will put my law within them, and I will write it on their hearts. And I will be their God, and they shall be my people. And no longer shall each one teach his neighbor and each his brother, saying, 'Know the LORD,' for they shall all know me, from the least of them to the greatest, declares the LORD. For I will forgive their iniquity, and I will remember their sin no more." (Jeremiah 31:31-34)

**Surface-level context:** God will make a new covenant with Israel.
**Hidden truth:** God's New Covenant is mediated by Jesus and inaugurated by the Crucifixion.

It appears to be clear that the promise of a new covenant through Jeremiah will be made to the nation of Israel. However, the supposedly clear understanding actually leads to murky and muddy conclusions. Conclusions drawn from what appears to be clear (on the surface) leads to a veiled interpretation. The hidden truth of this passage is revealed in the New Testament: it is about Jesus.

In Hebrews 8:1-5, the writer is describing Jesus as a new and different high priest. The priestly aspects of the old covenant serve as a type or shadow of the reality.

> But as it is, Christ has obtained a ministry that is as much more excellent than the old as the covenant he mediates is better, since it is enacted on better promises. For if that first covenant had been faultless, there would have been no occasion to look for a second. (Hebrews 8:6-7)

Jesus established a new and better covenant being a new and better mediator. The writer then stated that because of the faultiness of the first covenant, God promised a new covenant (Heb. 8:8). God promised this New Covenant in Jeremiah 31:31-34, which the writer quoted in Hebrews 8:8-12.

Some, who are committed to the surface-level interpretation, suggest that the new covenant promised by Jeremiah is yet to be fulfilled by Christ because of their adamancy to demand that the promises are made to physical Israelites. There is a lot that can be said in response to this view, but at this point I will suffice by referring again to the writer to the Hebrews two chapters later.

In chapter 10, verses 11-14, the writer to the Hebrews addressed Jesus' offering as a one-time sacrifice for sins. This is undoubtedly in reference to the Crucifixion. The writer then quoted a portion of Jeremiah's promise again (Heb. 10:16). The writer prefaced the re-quotation by stating that "the Holy Spirit also bears witness to us" (10:15). In other words, the Holy Spirit bears witness that Jesus' Crucifixion offered a one-time sacrifice for sin because after the promise of writing "my laws on their hearts", the Holy Spirit added "I will remember their sins and their lawless deeds no more" (10:17). The writer concluded the thought by stating "Where there is forgiveness of these, there is no longer any offering for sin" (10:18).

The writer confirmed that it was indeed the Holy Spirit who spoke through Jeremiah, and when the Holy Spirit did speak this promise through Jeremiah the promise was fulfilled by Jesus' one-time sacrifice for sin. Therefore, suggesting that the promise of a new covenant to Israel through Jeremiah that is still yet to be fulfilled is in opposition to the Holy Spirit. God has confirmed that the promise of the new covenant given by Jeremiah was fulfilled when Jesus ushered in His New Covenant at the last supper, culminating in the Crucifixion. In no other way than Jesus' Crucifixion is there any forgiveness for sins.

## PSALM 8

> what is man that you are mindful of him, and the son of man that you care for him? Yet you have made him a little lower than the heavenly beings and crowned him with glory and honor. You have given him dominion over the works of your hands; you have put all things under his feet, (Psalm 8:4-6)

**Surface-level context:** Mankind has dominion over Creation
**Hidden truth:** Jesus has dominion over Creation

Psalm 8 is saturated with Creation speak. Verses one through three mention God's name being majestic over the earth, His glory is above the heavens, babies and infants are newly created beings, He formed the heavens, and He set the moon and stars in their place; all displaying the essence of beginnings. Then, in verse 4, the psalmist David, brings man into the picture. David reminisces that

## Ch. 5: New Testament Evidence of the Mysterion

Adam was given dominion over the animals (8:6-8, cf. Genesis 1:28). Then in verse 9 the psalm ends as it began.

It would be quick and easy to determine that Psalm 8 takes us back to the Creation account of Genesis 1. However, the writer to the Hebrews brings Psalm 8 *forward* to the *new* creation.

The first chapter of Hebrews establishes Jesus as superior to the angels because of apparent angel worship that had been taking place. The same stream of thought carries over into chapter 2. In verse 5, the writer declared that it was not angels to whom God has subjected the world to come. The evidence provided is a testimony from "a certain place." That "somewhere" is Psalm 8, quoting verses 4-6. The writer then added his commentary on Psalm 8 pertaining to Jesus:

> Now in putting everything in subjection to him, he left nothing outside his control. At present, we do not yet see everything in subjection to him. But we see him who for a little while was made lower than the angels, namely Jesus, crowned with glory and honor because of the suffering of death, so that by the grace of God he might taste death for everyone. (Heb. 2:8b-9)

Whereas David was writing of Creation 3000 years in his rear-view mirror, the writer to the Hebrews refers to God giving to Jesus "the world to come" (2:5) and uses Psalm 8 as evidence that God is giving to Jesus the consummation of the new creation. David appears to have the old creation in mind; the New Testament author views Psalm 8 with the new creation in mind.

When David wrote of man being crowned with glory and honor, the Holy Spirit revealed through the writer to the Hebrews that the "son of man" of Psalm 8:4 is Jesus and it is He who is crowned with glory and honor because of willingly suffering the Crucifixion.

David also wrote of mankind having authority over God's creation, but we know it is Jesus who has been given "all authority in heaven and on earth" (Matt. 28:18) and all things have been put under the feet of Jesus (1 Cor. 15:27).

On the surface, Psalm 8 is looking back at Creation, but it finds its fulfillment in its future Messiah.

All four of these passages (Joel 2:28-32, Amos 9:11-15, Jeremiah 31:31-34, and the 8th Psalm) have a very different Old Testament context from how the New Testament writers incorporate each passage through the lens of Jesus. In each passage, there is a hidden truth beneath the surface. What each of these passages have in common is that they find their fulfillment in the gospel of Jesus Christ. This is the mystery of the gospel; truths hidden for ages are realized in Jesus (Eph. 3:9-11).

These passages are not alone. We're just getting our feet wet.

# Chapter 6:
# More New Testament Evidence of the Mysterion

Last chapter we examined large passages of Old Testament text that were quoted in the New Testament. Each of them was said to be fulfilled in the New Covenant in a way very different from what the original context would appear. Most New Testament quotations of the Old Testament are not large chunks, but often single statements.

In this chapter, we'll examine some New Testament passages in which the writer quoted multiple portions of Old Testament text. Each Old Testament passage has a very different original context than how the New Testament writer identified them to find their fulfillment.

**MATTHEW 2**

Matthew provided some interesting quotations in the 2nd chapter of his gospel account. He referred to the Old Testament on four occasions in chapter 2. The first is rather straightforward; it gets increasingly curious with each passing reference.

The chapter begins with the wise men approaching Herod, looking for the newborn king of the Jews. Herod gathered the scholars and they informed him that the Messiah would be born "in Bethlehem of Judea" and referred to Micah's prophecy in 5:2, the first of Matthew's four quotations in the chapter.

After Herod realized the wise men never returned to him to inform him where Jesus was born, he got furious. Threatened that he might lose his own regional throne, he attempted to eliminate this newly born king by eradicating all boys ages two and under. Of course, Jesus was already in Egypt because the Lord gave Joseph advance notice and instructions.

Matthew wrote that Jesus was in Egypt "and remained there until the death of Herod. This was to fulfill what the Lord had spoken by the prophet, 'Out of Egypt I called my son'" (2:15). Matthew's second Old Testament quotation in this chapter is the second half of Hosea 11:1:

> When Israel was a child, I loved him, and out of Egypt I called my son.

**Surface-level context:** In its infancy, the nation of Israel was called out of Egypt.
**Hidden truth:** In Jesus' infancy, God loved Him, and He was called out of Egypt.

*The Mystery of the Gospel*

As Hosea wrote he was looking back at the exodus which had happened about 700 years prior. Matthew read Hosea 11:1 and looked *forward* about 700 years in Hosea's future to the life of Jesus. Matthew wrote of Jesus' journey to Egypt and declared "this was to fulfill what the Lord had spoken by the prophet."

Did we even suspect that Hosea was writing of anything to which there would be future fulfillment? There is nothing in Hosea 11:1 that suggests that the content is something that will be fulfilled in the future. Unlike Micah 5:2 in which Micah clearly promises something that will take place in his future, Hosea 11:1 is written with Hosea's *past* in mind. Even though there doesn't appear to be anything in Hosea 11:1 that suggests a future fulfillment, Matthew saw that Hosea 11:1 found its fulfillment in Jesus.

Matthew knew that the truth of God's kingdom inaugurated via Jesus is hidden in the Old Testament text. Matthew understood the *mysterion*, the mystery of the gospel. Matthew read the Old Testament and saw it as typifying Christ. When Matthew read "when Israel was a child, I loved him, and out of Egypt I called my son", he saw God declaring "when Jesus was a child, I loved Him, and out of Egypt I called My Son."

When Matthew explained Herod's killing of boys age two years or less, he stated "then was fulfilled what was spoken by the prophet Jeremiah." According to Matthew, there is an Old Testament prophecy of Herod's slaughter of baby boys.

> Thus says the LORD: "A voice is heard in Ramah, lamentation and bitter weeping. Rachel is weeping for her children; she refuses to be comforted for her children, because they are no more." (Jeremiah 31:15)

**Surface-level context:** The Israelite women of Ramah are mourning the loss of their children as a result of the Babylonian invasion.
**Hidden truth:** Herod murdered baby boys around 1st Century Bethlehem.

Imagine a person living prior to Christ reading Jeremiah. When that person gets to the passage stating "Rachel is weeping for her children", the person exclaims "I know how this is going to be fulfilled! There's going to be a future day when a regional king will be threatened by the birth of the Messiah and he will kill all baby boys in that region ages two years and under!" That person would

## Ch. 6: More New Testament Evidence of the Mysterion

be declared insane! Yet that's exactly what Matthew informs us is the fulfillment of that passage.

The immediate context of Jeremiah's writing pertains to the destruction of Jerusalem, and surrounding region, at the hands of the Babylonians. Ramah was a town located in the tribe of Benjamin. The reference to Rachel is likely because she was Benjamin's mother, the true love of Jacob (the progenitor of Israel). Her weeping in this passage may be symbolic of the fact that she died after giving birth to Benjamin. The weeping of Rachel for her children in Jeremiah 31:15 brings the sadness of her death in childbirth forward to the time and context of Jeremiah as members of that region are being killed or carried away into captivity in Babylon.

Matthew saw in Jeremiah 31:15 a hidden truth. He saw that truth as being realized in the 1st Century AD. If not for Matthew's quotation of Jeremiah 31:15, there is not a person who would suspect that Jeremiah 31:15 had anything to do with the coming of the New Covenant era. Matthew, however, understood the *mysterion*.

Matthew's fourth and final reference to the Old Testament in chapter 2 is most curious:

> And he went and lived in a city called Nazareth, so that what was spoken by the prophets might be fulfilled, that he would be called a Nazarene. (Matthew 2:23)

Question: which prophets spoke that the Messiah would be called a Nazarene? Answer: none of them. No prophet wrote that he would be called a Nazarene! The term Nazarene cannot be found in the entire Old Testament. Nor is the town of Nazareth ever mentioned.

There are a couple views to explain what may have been Matthew's intention. Identifying which is true is beyond the scope of this writing. To briefly summarize, one view states that Nazarene was a term of scorn and derision. Nazareth was viewed as a humble, inconsequential, even worthless town. That Nazareth was looked down upon is substantiated by Nathanael wondering if anything good could come out of Nazareth (John 1:46). According to this view, Matthew associated Jesus' having been a Nazarene to suggest that the prophets spoke that Jesus would receive scorn and derision, such as is stated by Isaiah in 53:3 ("despised and rejected by men").

The other view suggests the term Nazareth is derived from the Hebrew word *netse*, meaning branch, used in Isaiah 11:1 ("a branch from" the roots of Jesse). Thus, when Matthew referred to Jesus as a Nazarene, according to this view his intention was to suggest that the prophets spoke that Jesus would be the branch of Jesse, i.e. the son of David.

Regardless of which view is true of Matthew's intentions (perhaps both?), Matthew clearly stated that the prophets spoke it and that Jesus fulfilled it. By not quoting a single particular passage, Matthew lumped all the prophets into a single collective and associated all of them as having spoken that the Messiah would be called a Nazarene. He acknowledged that all of the prophets spoke that Jesus would (1) receive scorn and be reviled by men (fulfilled by the Crucifixion), and/or (2) fulfill the promise as the descendant of David, the branch of Jesse.

By lumping "the prophets" into a single group, he affirmed that the purpose of the prophets' writings was Jesus. Matthew is further validating that the overall content of what the prophets spoke was fulfilled in Jesus. The hidden truth contained in all of the prophets as a collective entity is the gospel of Jesus Christ.

**HEBREWS 2**

We've previously looked at Hebrews chapter 2 in relation to Psalm 8. Jesus was "made a little lower than the angels" and "crowned with glory and honor" (2:9). The writer continued to express that Jesus was crowned with glory and honor "because of the suffering of death, so that by the grace of God he might taste death for everyone."

Picking up where that left off, the writer to the Hebrews remarked that it was fitting that Jesus would bring many sons to glory (2:10). Of the sons Jesus is bringing to glory, He is the founder of their salvation, making them perfect through His suffering. Just as Jesus was crowned with glory and honor because of His suffering unto death, so too does His suffering unto death crown many others with glory and honor. Jesus is bringing with Him those who are sanctified because He and they are united into one (2:11). Therefore, Jesus is not ashamed to call us brothers and sisters. The writer then ascribed Jesus as the one expressing the words of Psalm 22:22:

> I will tell of your name to my brothers; in the midst of the congregation I will praise you: (Psalm 22:22)

*Ch. 6: More New Testament Evidence of the Mysterion*

**Surface-level context:** David is crying out for deliverance from his suffering (see Ps. 22:19-21) and will then praise God in the midst of his brothers.
**Hidden truth:** It is Jesus crying out for deliverance from His suffering and will then praise God in the midst of *His* brothers.

The writer attributed the words of Psalm 22:22 directly to Jesus. The writer stated "…he is not ashamed to call them brothers, saying… (quotes Psalm 22:22)" as if to say it is Jesus who will tell of His Father's name. Jesus will do so to His brothers and sisters in the midst of the congregation of heaven. The writer understood Psalm 22 to contain the *mysterion*; the hidden truth of the psalm is that it is about Jesus.

The writer provided two more quotes to prove the point. The first is of an uncertain reference: "I will put my trust in Him" (2:13a). Certainly, it sounds like psalm-speak, but the precise source is uncertain. The second quote is from Isaiah:

> Behold, I and the children whom the LORD has given me… (Isaiah 8:18a)

**Surface-level context:** Amidst the impending doom to come at the hand of the Assyrians, Isaiah and his children are proclaimed to provide testimony of the Lord.
**Hidden truth:** Evidence that Jesus is not ashamed to call us brothers.

That sounds absolutely ridiculous! How can the surface-level context of Isaiah 8:18 and the use of the passage by the writer to the Hebrews appear so incongruous? Without having the book of Hebrews as support, if anyone were to read Isaiah chapter 8 (in particular verses 11-18) and suggest that verse 18 had anything to do with the suffering of Jesus and His subsequent glory, that person would be run out of town on a rail. Yet the writer to the Hebrews does exactly that! The writer used that portion of Isaiah to validate the point that Jesus is bringing many sons to glory and He is not ashamed to call us brothers.

What a mystery! What a hidden truth! To read the Old Testament without seeing Christ in and throughout every part of it is to read it with a veiled understanding (see 2 Cor. 3:14).

## ROMANS 9

In Romans chapter 9, Paul is exalting God as sovereign over all creation, bringing all things to pass by the counsel of His will. Paul stated in verse 6 that not all of physical Israel consists of spiritual Israel. He later asked a rhetorical question that implies that a potter has power over his clay (9:21), just as God has power over His creation (9:20). Paul then remarked that those who experience God's mercy and the riches of His glory (i.e., spiritual Israel) include not only Jews but also believing Gentiles (9:23-24). Paul substantiated this fact that God is calling Gentiles into spiritual Israel by consecutively quoting two passages from Hosea. The first:

> and I will sow her for myself in the land. And I will have mercy on No Mercy, and I will say to Not My People, 'You are my people'; and he shall say, 'You are my God.'" (Hosea 2:23)

**Surface-level context:** The Lord will restore Israel.
**Hidden truth:** Spiritual Israel includes Gentiles.

Hosea's wife left him for other men. In Hosea chapter 2, the Lord uses Hosea's adulterous wife to portray a picture of Israel's adultery to the Lord. The Lord will bring judgment upon Israel. In verse 14 the mood shifts; the Lord will *restore* Israel.

Paul informed us that God's intention all along was to bring Gentiles into this restored Israel. Throughout the Old Covenant era, the general sentiment was that Gentiles were not loved by God. In Christ, believing Gentiles are now loved by God. Formerly, Gentiles were not God's people. In Christ, believing Gentiles have become God's people.

> Yet the number of the children of Israel shall be like the sand of the sea, which cannot be measured or numbered. And in the place where it was said to them, "You are not my people," it shall be said to them, "Children of the living God." (Hosea 1:10)

**Surface-level context:** Israel and Judah shall be gathered together (see Hosea 1:11)
**Hidden truth:** The gathering together of God's people consists of Gentiles.

## Ch. 6: More New Testament Evidence of the Mysterion

Both Hosea quotations serve as Paul's evidence that Gentiles are called into God's people; they will be called sons of the living God. The Old Testament portrays that the focus of God's love is upon the physical nation of Israel. The New Testament reveals that the focus of God's love is on a spiritual nation, initially among the Jews at Jerusalem but then largely consisting of Gentile converts.

These are just the first two of five Old Testament quotations utilized by Paul in the last nine verses of chapter 9 (9:25-33). The third quotation Paul attributed to Isaiah, although Hosea used the same phrase in the first half of 1:10 ("the children of Israel shall be like the sand of the sea") while Paul had already just quoted the second half of Hosea 1:10.

> For though your people Israel be as the sand of the sea, only a remnant of them will return. (Isa 10:22a)

**Surface-level context:** Only a remnant of Israel will return amidst decreed destruction.
**Hidden truth:** The majority of ethnic Israel served as vessels of wrath prepared for destruction. (see Rom. 9:22)

The hidden truth in this instance is not all that different from the surface-level context of the original text. The reason this may cause a big stir, however, is because this is very different than the predominant teaching of the modern American church. I don't want to belabor the point here & now because that's for a different discussion on another day, but Paul is establishing the point that Gentiles are among those who are promised blessing as the remnant of Israel, whereas a majority of ethnic Israel suffered the judgment of destruction.

Paul confirmed that this is his intended teaching by his fourth consecutive quotation from the Old Testament:

> Unless the LORD of hosts had left to us a very small remnant, we would have become like Sodom, we would have been made like Gomorrah. (Isa 1:9 NKJV)

**Surface-level context:** God is furious with Judah. (see Isaiah 1:1-25, especially verses 7-11)
**Hidden truth:** If not for God saving a small remnant, all of Israel would meet the same end as did Sodom & Gomorrah.

All of this talk about Israel facing judgment is within the context that Paul is establishing the fact that believing Gentiles are vessels of mercy to whom have been made known the riches of God's glory (Rom. 9:23-24). He continued to contrast Gentiles and Israel in the verses that immediately follow:

> What shall we say, then? That Gentiles who did not pursue righteousness have attained it, that is, a righteousness that is by faith; but that Israel who pursued a law that would lead to righteousness did not succeed in reaching that law. Why? Because they did not pursue it by faith, but as if it were based on works. They have stumbled over the stumbling stone, (Rom 9:30-32)

By pursuing a law of works, Israel failed to attain unto righteousness. Righteousness can be found only in Jesus. Believing Gentiles have attained unto the righteousness of Jesus through faith. The Jews stumbled over Jesus on their path toward works-based righteousness (which can never be attained).

> therefore thus says the Lord GOD, "Behold, I am the one who has laid as a foundation in Zion, a stone, a tested stone, a precious cornerstone, of a sure foundation: 'Whoever believes will not be in haste.' (Isa 28:16)

**Surface-level context:** God is laying a foundation for hope.
**Hidden truth:** Israel tripped over that hope (Jesus) and were offended by it (Him).

Paul phrases the verse a little differently:

> as it is written, "Behold, I am laying in Zion a stone of stumbling, and a rock of offense; and whoever believes in him will not be put to shame." (Rom 9:33)

## Ch. 6: More New Testament Evidence of the Mysterion

Israel was offended by Jesus. Because they did not believe in Him, they were ultimately put to shame. Their unbelief caused them to stumble over the stumbling stone (Rom. 9:32). Though Isaiah 28:16 revealed God's promise of hope, even the surface-level context shows that Isaiah 28:16 is God's response to the rebellious leaders of Jerusalem (Is. 28:14-15). Therefore, Jerusalem stumbled and believing Gentiles will not be put to shame, just as Isaiah prophesied, because Jesus is the stone, the tested stone, the precious cornerstone, the sure foundation.

### JOHN 19

In John's description of the Crucifixion he referred to four Old Testament passages. The first three are from the Psalms.

> they divide my garments among them, and for my clothing they cast lots. (Psalm 22:18)

**Surface-level context:** David feels overwhelmed by the wicked.
**Hidden truth:** The Crucifixion of Jesus.

When David wrote Psalm 22, he was in a state of desperation. From his opening words "my God, my God, why have you forsaken me?" to "I am...scorned by mankind and despised by the people" (v. 6). He feels mocked, encompassed by bulls, attacked by a lion, poured out like water, his bones feel out of joint, his heart has melted like wax, and his strength is dried up. Evildoers encircle him, have pierced his hands and feet, and they stare and gloat over him.

Then David indicated that they have treated him so poorly that they have stripped him of his clothing and distributed them to others. They have cast lots for his clothing while he is left naked. Meanwhile, as John is describing the Crucifixion:

> so they said to one another, "Let us not tear it, but cast lots for it to see whose it shall be." This was to fulfill the Scripture which says, "They divided my garments among them, and for my clothing they cast lots." So the soldiers did these things, (John 19:24)

There is nothing in Psalm 22 that implies that there will be a futuristic fulfillment. That's the amazing thing about Old Testament prophecy! We often think that only that which is written in a futuristic manner is prophetic of Christ, leaving the rest of the Old Testament limited to its original context.

Psalm 22:18 is yet another example that the Scriptures do not need to be presented in a futuristic manner in order to be prophetic of Jesus. David wrote indicative statements one millennia prior to Jesus, and yet John acknowledged that what happened to Jesus is fulfillment of a non-futuristic writing of David. Jesus didn't merely fulfill certain prophesies that provided a clearly futuristic fulfillment. The entire Old Testament was prophetic of Jesus!

> They gave me poison for food, and for my thirst they gave me sour wine to drink. (Psalm 69:21)

**Surface-level context:** David treated poorly by his adversaries.
**Hidden truth:** The Crucifixion of Jesus.

Psalm 69 is very similar in nature to Psalm 22. David is lamenting how he has been mistreated by his adversaries. Yet John distinctly declared (John 19:28-29) that what David wrote was experienced by Jesus in purposeful fulfillment of the Scriptures.

> He keeps all his bones; not one of them is broken. (Psalm 34:20)

**Surface-level context:** The Lord delivers the righteous from affliction.
**Hidden truth:** The Crucifixion of Jesus.

David exalted God in that the Lord delivers the righteous out of all his afflictions (Ps. 34:19). This includes the one who is righteous keeping all his bones with not one of them broken (34:20). We might think that David is referring to himself as the one who is righteous. However, this righteous one of whom David is writing is Jesus. John agrees:

> For these things took place that the Scripture might be fulfilled: "Not one of his bones will be broken." And again another Scripture says, "They will look on him whom they have pierced." (John 19:36-37)

## Ch. 6: More New Testament Evidence of the Mysterion

The Zechariah passage John quoted in 19:37 is a bit different from the setting of the Psalms from which John quoted.

> "And I will pour out on the house of David and the inhabitants of Jerusalem a spirit of grace and pleas for mercy, so that, when they look on me, on him whom they have pierced, they shall mourn for him, as one mourns for an only child, and weep bitterly over him, as one weeps over a firstborn. (Zech 12:10)

**Surface-level context:** God pouring out a spirit of grace.
**Hidden truth:** The Crucifixion of Jesus.

The writings of the prophets can be complicated; I won't be able to do justice to this Zechariah passage in this space. Suffice to say that the Lord states through Zechariah that He will pour out grace upon the inhabitants of Jerusalem. We know that God's grace comes through the gospel of Jesus Christ. We also know that those who do receive God's grace are members of the New Jerusalem.

John sees in this Zechariah passage the Crucifixion. Thus, this promise of grace is to spiritual Jerusalem, those who have received the gospel message. When we, who have received God's grace, look upon Jesus, Him whom they have pierced, we shall mourn for Him as one mourns for an only child (the only begotten Son of God).

Just five verses later in Zechariah (13:1), "On that day" (the same day as the Crucifixion as portrayed in Zech. 12:10) "there shall be a fountain opened for the house of David and the inhabitants of Jerusalem, to cleanse them from sin and uncleanness." There is only one way in the history of the world, both history past and history future, that anyone, anywhere, anyhow receives cleansing from sin. That is only through the sacrificial atonement of Jesus, God's Anointed One.

Zechariah's writings may not appear on the surface to be promises of the coming gospel of Jesus, but John declared that Jesus does indeed fulfill what Zechariah wrote.

With each of these New Testament passages (Matthew 2, Hebrews 2, Romans 9, John 19), we see evidence that the Old Testament finds its fulfillment in Jesus and His gospel message, even if the original context doesn't appear to be Messianic, nor even futuristic.

# Chapter 7:
# Evidence of the Mysterion in Paul's Writings

Paul understood the *mysterion* better than anyone. Perhaps Matthew, Luke, the writer to the Hebrews, as well as other apostles and early church leaders learned the *mysterion* from Paul. Or maybe the Spirit revealed these truths to the other writers as well.

We certainly won't be able to address every New Testament quotation of an Old Testament passage. We will, however, continue to look at several New Testament quotations of an Old Testament passage that appears to have a very different context on the surface than how the New Testament author applies it. This chapter, we'll look at more examples of the *mysterion* in Paul's writings, beginning with his letters to the Corinthians.

## 1 CORINTHIANS

In Paul's letters to the Corinthians, he devotes significant space writing to defend his apostleship. In chapter 9 of 1st Corinthians he is sharing some of his rights. He has the right to eat and drink (9:4). He has the right to take a believing wife (9:5). He has the right to refrain from working for a living (9:6). Despite having these rights, Paul declined to either take a believing wife or refrain from working for a living.

He implied that soldiers receive provisions, a planter of a vineyard gets to eat of the fruit, and a shepherd gets some of the flock's milk (9:7). He acknowledged that he did not say these things out of human authority, for the Law says the same:

> You shall not muzzle an ox when it is treading out the grain. (Deut. 25:4)

**Surface-level context:** An ox shall be allowed to eat while it is treading out the grain.
**Hidden truth:** Those who proclaim the gospel have the right to get their living by the gospel. (see 1 Cor 9:14)

Deuteronomy 25:4 is a straightforward command. When oxen were treading the grain, they were not to be muzzled. Muzzling an ox would prevent it from eating while treading. The Law dictated care for the creature while it is working.

Paul doesn't simply use Deuteronomy 25:4 as a metaphor. He explicitly ascribes the Lord's intentions for this commandment to be fulfilled directly to those who partake in the New Covenant.

> For it is written in the Law of Moses, "You shall not muzzle an ox when it treads out the grain." Is it for oxen that God is concerned? Does he not certainly speak for our sake? It was written for our sake, because the plowman should plow in hope and the thresher thresh in hope of sharing in the crop. (1Co 9:9-10)

"Is it for oxen that God is concerned?" Paul implied that God's purpose for that commandment isn't because God is most concerned for oxen; it is because God is most concerned with laborers for the gospel.

"Does he not certainly speak for our sake?" Paul seemed to expect that his readers already know that Deuteronomy 25:4 speaks to those in their present day, to apostles and laborers of the gospel. He wrote that God is speaking, not about oxen, but about the labors of Paul and others like Paul.

"It was written for our sake." Paul answered his own hypothetical question confirming that Deuteronomy 25:4 was indeed written for the sake of Paul and his contemporaries.

Surely, God would want owners of animals to care well for their livestock, but He's a bit more concerned with the message of good news regarding His kingdom. Deuteronomy 25:4 contains the mystery of the gospel.

## 2 CORINTHIANS

Isaiah 49 is saturated with restoration language. Because of Israel's disobedience, God will judge the nation. God also promised to do a work of restoration. God declared that He will glorify Himself in the work He does with Israel: "You are my servant, Israel, in whom I will be glorified" (49:3). The Lord plans "to bring Jacob back to him; and that Israel might be gathered to him" (49:5). He will "raise up the tribes of Jacob" and "bring back the preserved of Israel" (49:6). The Lord is "the Redeemer of Israel" (49:7). Prisoners will "come out" (49:9) and not suffer any need (49:10). In the midst of all this restoration speak, the Lord says:

> Thus says the LORD: "In a time of favor I have answered you; in a day of salvation I have helped you" (Isaiah 49:8a)

## Ch. 7: Evidence of the Mysterion in Paul's Writings

The Lord promises that He will do this work of restoration at a special time. There will be a period of time when God helps Israel by providing her salvation.

**Surface-level context:** The Lord promises to restore Israel.
**Hidden truth:** Through the reconciling work of Jesus, the Lord restores a spiritual nation.

In Paul's 2nd letter to the Corinthians, he describes the work of reconciliation performed by Jesus in His death and resurrection (5:14-21). Through the events of the gospel, Jesus has reconciled sinners to God. This culminates in the commonly-called 'great exchange' presented in 5:21; our sin was put upon Jesus in exchange for His righteousness being put upon us.

The following verse (6:1) Paul wrote: "Working together with him, then, we appeal to you not to receive the grace of God in vain." Then he quoted a portion of Isaiah 49:8 (in 6:2). Paul made absolutely clear that when this time of favor took place was when God answered Israel. He made it utterly undeniable that when this day of salvation occurred was when God would help Israel.

> Behold, now is the favorable time; behold, now is the day of salvation. (2 Cor. 6:2b)

The reconciling work of Jesus (5:21), the grace of God (6:1), and God's promise to restore Israel (Isaiah 49:8) all come together at the same time. The time of God's favor and the day of His salvation is "now." It began in the 1st Century AD and it continues to this day. The time of God's favor and the day of His salvation are *still* "now."

God's promises to restore Israel through the prophets were not fulfilled by a past event pertaining to the ethnic nation of Israel. God's promises to restore Israel are not to be fulfilled by a future event pertaining to the ethnic nation of Israel. God's promises to restore Israel are fulfilled currently to a spiritual nation, those for whom Jesus performed the work of reconciliation. God's promises to restore Israel are fulfilled via the gospel of Jesus Christ.

The gospel was in Isaiah 49, hidden in mystery. The hidden truth of Isaiah 49 was realized in the grace of God through the death, burial, and resurrection of Jesus Christ.

Later in the same chapter of 2nd Corinthians, Paul quoted from Leviticus 26, which begins with a few commandments from the Lord (26:1-2). The Lord then issued an "if…then…" condition (26:3-4). If Israel is obedient, then they will receive a multitude of blessings. The "then" begins in verse 4 and the listing of blessings continues through verse 12. In verse 13, the Lord concludes the thought with a statement about His identity and what He has accomplished on Israel's behalf: "I am the Lord your God…"

The last promises mentioned in this passage are in verses 11 & 12:

> I will make my dwelling among you, and my soul shall not abhor you. And I will walk among you and will be your God, and you shall be my people. (Leviticus 26:11-12)

**Surface-level context:** The Lord promises to be the God of Israel and make His home among them, pending obedience.
**Hidden truth:** The Lord dwells in believers in Christ.

Amidst all the difficulties that were going on in the church at Corinth, Paul's encouragement to them is to remind them of their identity in Christ. He contrasted their Christ-identity with the ways of the world in the form of questions (2 Cor. 6:14-16a). The final question he asked was "what agreement has the temple of God with idols?" He responded to that question with a statement about the identity of believers: "for we are the temple of the living God."

Who does Paul say is the temple of the living God? It is 1st Century believers to whom Paul is writing, of course. What does the temple represent? The temple represents the dwelling place of God on earth. The physical structure of the Old Covenant temple symbolically represented the dwelling place of God on earth, foreshadowing Jesus. Never has God dwelt on earth in any more real way than in the very Person of Jesus: "Destroy this temple, and in three days I will raise it up" (John 2:19).

## Ch. 7: Evidence of the Mysterion in Paul's Writings

However, Jesus is no longer on earth. He has ascended into heaven to the right hand of the Father. Shortly after Jesus ascended, God again dwelt on earth, this time through the Spirit, beginning at Pentecost.

Paul reassured the Corinthian believers (however many or few of them were actually regenerate believers) that they "are the temple of the living God." Then Paul provided evidence that they are indeed the dwelling place of God on earth (i.e. temple) by quoting from the Scriptures:

> What agreement has the temple of God with idols? For we are the temple of the living God; as God said, "I will make my dwelling among them and walk among them, and I will be their God, and they shall be my people. (2 Corinthians 6:16)

Paul quoted from Leviticus 26:11-12 to provide proof that Christ-indwelt believers are the fulfillment of God's promises to Israel! Also note that "dwelling" in Leviticus 26:11 means "tabernacle," as in "I will make my tabernacle among you." In the same way, John wrote that the Word became flesh and tabernacled among us (John 1:14).

After Paul quoted from Leviticus 26:11 (2 Cor. 6:16), he quoted from Isaiah 52 (6:17). Then he added that God promised "I will welcome you, and I will be a father to you, and you shall be sons and daughters to me" (6:18). We know that New Covenant believers are considered sons and daughters of God (Rom. 8:14-17; Gal. 4:4-7). Paul listed several promises in verses 16 through 18. In the next verse, he confirmed that these promises are for believers in Christ:

> Since we have these promises, beloved, let us cleanse ourselves from every defilement of body and spirit, bringing holiness to completion in the fear of God. (2 Cor. 7:1)

"Since we have these promises..." Paul wrote that he and believers in Corinth have these promises; hence "we." Believers today have these promises too. These promises *include* Leviticus 26:11. Paul confirmed that Christians possess the promise offered by God in Leviticus 26:11. Believers are now indwelt by the living God! The blessing promised in Leviticus 26:11 is possessed by the restored Israel in the New Covenant; a spiritual Israel (1 Pet. 2:9), a new people group (Eph. 2:15).

The promise of Leviticus 26:11 was conditional upon Israel's obedience. Israel was not obedient. The only one who has ever been truly obedient is Jesus. Jesus is the lone Israelite who was faithful and obedient. Jesus is the true recipient of all of God's promises (2 Cor. 1:20).

All of God's promises to Israel are given to the only Israelite who has ever been perfectly obedient: Jesus. Because Jesus now makes His tabernacle within a redeemed portion of fallen humanity, this redeemed portion of fallen humanity can claim ownership to the promises made to Israel. This claim can only be made through Jesus. Jesus is the true recipient; all those who are in Jesus are recipients of these promises with Him (Gal. 3:29).

Leviticus 26 contains hidden truths of the gospel!

## GALATIANS

> And if a man has committed a crime punishable by death and he is put to death, and you hang him on a tree, his body shall not remain all night on the tree, but you shall bury him the same day, for a hanged man is cursed by God. You shall not defile your land that the LORD your God is giving you for an inheritance. (Deuteronomy 21:22-23)

**Surface-level context:** Laws regarding execution.
**Hidden truth:** The Crucifixion of Jesus.

Chapter 21 is one of many in the book of Deuteronomy that list various laws and regulations for the people of Israel. Verses 22 & 23 appear to be no different, describing the instructions of how to handle a man who has been punished with death.

Paul saw something more. Paul understood that Jesus fulfilled the Law; and he knew this meant all of the Law. Jesus' fulfillment of the Law also includes fulfilling what was written regarding the handling of a man who was punished with death.

Jesus was punished by death and hanged on a tree. His body did not remain all night on the tree but was buried the same day. All this is because "a hanged man is cursed by God" (Deut. 21:23).

Paul quoted this passage in his letter to the Galatians:

## Ch. 7: Evidence of the Mysterion in Paul's Writings

> Christ redeemed us from the curse of the law by becoming a curse for us--for it is written, "Cursed is everyone who is hanged on a tree"-- (Galatians 3:13)

The argument could be offered that Jesus didn't fulfill Deuteronomy 21:22-23 as much as the regulations pertaining to Deuteronomy 21:22-23 were faithfully and carefully carried out by those who crucified Him. This argument could be valid if it was the Jews who performed the Crucifixion. However, it was Rome who performed capital punishment by crucifixion. It was Roman soldiers and Roman officials who performed the Crucifixion with no knowledge or concern about what the Law of this despised-to-them Jewish people dictated.

Jesus didn't hang on a tree because the Jews were following the mandate of the Law in Deuteronomy 21:22-23. In fact, Israel's standard form of capital punishment was by stoning. That Jesus was put to death on a tree is actually an outlier of Jewish practice.

The statement in Deuteronomy 21:23 that "a hanged man is cursed by God" is a foreshadowing of Jesus. Jesus suffered the curse of God. Jesus was cursed by taking the guilt of sin upon Himself. Jesus became "a curse for us" (Gal. 3:13).

Just a few verses prior, Paul made a tremendous statement that would shock an Israelite and draw his fury:

> Know then that it is those of faith who are the sons of Abraham. And the Scripture, foreseeing that God would justify the Gentiles by faith, preached the gospel beforehand to Abraham, saying, "In you shall all the nations be blessed." So then, those who are of faith are blessed along with Abraham, the man of faith. (Galatians 3:7-9)

Paul quoted from Genesis 12:3, when God initially called Abraham. Paul announced that the promise Jews had been counting on for centuries was fulfilled very differently than they expected: through the gospel of Jesus. Many Christians today still count on these promises to be fulfilled to ethnic Jews. To the contrary, Paul taught that the promises made to Abraham were fulfilled in Jesus!

> Now the LORD said to Abram, "Go from your country and your kindred and your father's house to the land that I will show you. And I will make of you a great nation, and I will bless you and make your name great, so that you will be a blessing. I will bless those who bless you, and him who dishonors you I will curse, and in you all the families of the earth shall be blessed." (Genesis 12:1-3)

**Surface-level context:** God is making promises to Abraham and his descendants.
**Hidden truth:** Abraham was being preached the gospel.

In Galatians 3:8, Paul wrote that when Abraham was being promised "in you shall all the nations be blessed" God was purposing to justify Gentiles. Abraham was being preached the gospel!

God's ultimate purpose in His promises to Abraham was not Israel-centered. God's ultimate purpose in His promises to Abraham was Christ-centered. Again, Abraham was being preached the gospel. The Scripture foresaw that God would justify Gentiles. How are Gentiles justified? Only by the gospel of Jesus.

God's promises to Abraham found their ultimate fulfillment in the gospel of Jesus Christ. What Abraham was promised came in the form of the *mysterion*.

## EPHESIANS

The 68th psalm is about God wiping out His enemies. From the very first verse ("God shall arise, his enemies shall be scattered; and those who hate him shall flee before him!"), it is pronounced that it is the Lord who will be victorious!

God will drive away the wicked who will perish like wax in a fire (68:2), whereas the righteous will sing praise to God (68:3-6). God is victorious in battle (68:7-14).

Then David questioned the mountains of Bashan why they look with hatred at the mount where God desires to make His abode to dwell forever (68:15-16). God's chariots are innumerable and the Lord is among them (68:17). And then, addressing God:

> You ascended on high, leading a host of captives in your train and receiving gifts among men, even among the rebellious, that the LORD God may dwell there. (Psalm 68:18)

## Ch. 7: Evidence of the Mysterion in Paul's Writings

**Surface-level context:** The Lord is mighty in battle.
**Hidden truth:** Jesus gives gifts to men.

In the first 3 chapters of Paul's letter to the Ephesians, he described the big picture of God's work on earth to bring humans into His kingdom. This is according to His eternal purpose (3:11). His eternal purpose is fulfilled in Jesus through the gospel.

In chapter 4, Paul transitioned from the big picture of God's blessings upon His redeemed people and zoomed in to the life and activity of those who have received these blessings. Paul's thesis statement for the second half of his letter, in response to the blessings described in the first 3 chapters, is to "walk in a manner worthy of the calling to which you have been called" (4:1). Paul mentioned five components to doing so (4:2-3) and then issued a creed of seven "one" declarations (4:4-6) which support whom it is we are to maintain the unity of the spirit in the bond of peace (4:3). Paul's next words:

> But grace was given to each one of us according to the measure of Christ's gift. Therefore it says, "When he ascended on high he led a host of captives, and he gave gifts to men." (Ephesians 4:7-8)

God gave grace to each one of us (believers). The grace we were given is in accordance to the measure of Christ's gift. Paul then stated that Christ's giving of gifts is why Psalm 68:18 said what it said. "Therefore it says," he wrote. When Jesus ascended on high, He led a host of captives (redeemed by His blood), and gave gifts to men (through the Spirit, beginning at Pentecost).

The surface-level context of Psalm 68:18 would indicate that the ascending is in reference to God leading chariots that are prepared for battle to the mount of His dwelling place. Paul said that it's about Jesus. It is about Jesus' ascension, His giving of gifts, and His dwelling place (which is Jesus abiding in His people).

Before Paul proceeded to address the giving of gifts by Jesus in verse 11, he interjected a parenthetical thought regarding the matter of ascending (4:9-10). Paul noted in his parenthetical thought that when Psalm 68:18 referenced "ascending", it was speaking of Jesus who ascended. Before Jesus could ascend to heaven, He first had to descend from heaven to earth, where He stayed for 33 years.

Also note that the English translations of Psalm 68:18 indicate God *received* gifts among men. Paul makes the point that Jesus is the *giver* of those gifts. The gifts Paul records as being given to men pertain to the functions of apostles, prophets, evangelists, and shepherd/teachers (4:11). Thus, Psalm 68:18 has a very different interpretation, based on New Testament revelation, than what appears on the surface.

There are many other Old Testament quotations by Paul that apply a different fulfillment in the New Covenant than what the surface-level interpretation of an Old Testament passage would suggest. Explore them and discover the *mysterion* for yourself!

# Chapter 8:
# Evidence of the Mysterion by Various New Testament Authors

Last chapter we examined several passages in which Paul quoted from the Old Testament and applied New Covenant-related fulfillment to Old Testament passages that appear on the surface to have a very different context. This chapter will examine passages of other New Testament writers who do the same.

Matthew supplied a tremendous number of Old Testament quotations. Let's look at just a few more of them as we further unveil examples of Matthew's understanding of the *mysterion*.

## MATTHEW 1

Matthew recorded that, after discovering that Mary was with child, Joseph received a dream in which an angel reassured him that this was God's doing and she would bear a son who will save His people from their sins (Matt. 1:18-21). Then Matthew wrote "All this took place to fulfill what the Lord had spoken by the prophet" (Matt. 1:22) and he quoted from Isaiah:

> Behold, the virgin shall conceive and bear a son, and shall call his name Immanuel. (Isaiah 7:14b)

**Surface-level context:** The Lord will give King Ahaz a sign.
**Hidden truth:** The birth of Jesus.

We are so familiar with this passage being a prophecy of Jesus that we don't really know or appreciate the context in Isaiah. There is nothing about the Isaiah passage that suggests that this child who will be born will be the Messiah! We read this portion of Isaiah and we immediately understand its New Covenant fulfillment. The hidden truth of Isaiah 7:14 does not surprise us. We're more likely to be surprised by the immediate context of the original passage.

Syria and Israel had joined forces and were about to attack Jerusalem where Ahaz, king of Judah, was located. Ahaz heard of it and became terrified. The Lord sent Isaiah to Ahaz to give Ahaz a message of comfort. The Lord then told Ahaz to ask the Lord for a sign. Ahaz would not do it. Isaiah proclaimed that the Lord will give Ahaz a sign anyway. The sign would be that a "virgin shall conceive and bear a son, and shall call his name Immanuel."

The Hebrew term translated "virgin" does not necessarily mean a woman who has never had sexual intercourse. It means a young maiden, likely old enough to marry and possibly even newly married. We know that it is true of Mary the mother of Jesus that she had never had sexual intercourse prior to being with child, but Isaiah announced that a young maiden shall conceive and bear a son.

Isaiah's wife does exactly that; she bears a son (8:3). Isaiah declared that the son will be named "Immanuel" to symbolize that "God is with us." God informed Isaiah that the name of his son is Maher-shalal-hash-baz. (Probably because Bob was taken.)

Isaiah's young maiden did conceive and she bore a son. Maher-shalal-hash-baz means "the spoil speeds, the prey hastens" to signify the doom to come upon Syria and Israel (8:4, where Damascus and Samaria represent, respectively, Syria and Israel). The birth of Maher-shalal-hash-baz appears to be fulfillment of the sign given to Ahaz to comfort him about the desolation that will occur to the two kings whom he fears (7:14-25).

Of course, we all know that the fulfillment of that promise is ultimately Jesus. This is an example in which we all already know the hidden truth. Perhaps we didn't realize how hidden it really was.

**MATTHEW 4**

After successfully resisting the temptation of the devil, Jesus went to Galilee. Though nearby Nazareth was where He grew up, He spent most of His earthly ministry in Capernaum, which is located on the Sea of Galilee. Before the northern tribes were scattered in the 8th Century BC, that region is where the tribes of Zebulun and Naphtali settled. Matthew wrote that Jesus went to Capernaum "so that what was spoken by the prophet Isaiah might be fulfilled" (4:14). Then he quoted from Isaiah 9, beginning with the last portion of verse 1 and all of verse 2:

> ...the land of Zebulun and the land of Naphtali, but in the latter time he has made glorious the way of the sea, the land beyond the Jordan, Galilee of the nations. The people who walked in darkness have seen a great light; those who dwelt in a land of deep darkness, on them has light shone. (Isa 9:1b-2)

## Ch. 8: Evidence of the Mysterion by Various New Testament Authors

**Surface-level context:** Although rebellious Judah will find herself in darkness, the land of Zebulun and Naphtali will see a great light.
**Hidden truth:** Jesus is that great light.

The hidden truth of Isaiah 9:1b-2 makes perfect sense to us when we look at it from the New Testament perspective. If we attempt to walk in the Old Testament context, however, it would not seem so clear.

We've previously looked at portions of Isaiah chapters 7 and 8. As chapter 8 comes to a close, it states that rebellious Israel will be "greatly distressed...hungry...enraged...[and] speak contemptuously against...God" (8:21). They will behold "distress and darkness, the gloom of anguish. And they will be thrust into thick darkness" (8:22).

The Lord then promised hope for her (Israel) who was in anguish (9:1a). The Lord had formerly brought into contempt the land of Zebulun and the land of Naphtali. In 9:2, the Lord promised a great light in that region. Jesus is that great light. The people in that region, they "have seen a great light [Jesus]...on them has light [Jesus] shone."

Because we know that Matthew quoted Isaiah 9:2 and informed us that it was fulfilled in Jesus, this may not seem extraordinary to us. However, if Matthew had not quoted Isaiah 9:2, would we not see a more immediate context to this promise? After all, the message continues to proclaim judgment upon Israel (9:8-10:4) and then judgment upon Assyria after God has used Assyria to judge Israel (10:5-19).

Without Matthew's quotation, would you think it to be in err to propose that Isaiah 9:2 was looking forward to Jesus? Perhaps you would think suggesting such would be looking too deeply into the text and say that suggesting that it's about Jesus is inserting something that isn't there. However, that's exactly what the New Testament writers did. They saw Jesus everywhere in the Scriptures, even in passages that may look like it would be reading into the text to apply it to Jesus.

Behold the mystery of the gospel. You can find it hidden throughout the Old Testament, even where it may look like it doesn't belong.

### MATTHEW 15

Matthew loved the book of Isaiah; he quoted it throughout his writing. In Matthew 15, Matthew quoted Jesus who quoted from Isaiah.

The scene begins with Pharisees and scribes approaching Jesus. They have come all the way from Jerusalem to the Sea of Galilee to meet Him. (About 75 miles!) They challenge Jesus that His disciples break the tradition of the elders by not washing their hands. Jesus rebuked them because their adherence to tradition caused them to make void the word of God (15:6). Jesus said, "You hypocrites! Well did Isaiah prophesy of you, when he said:" and then Jesus quoted a portion of Isaiah 29:13.

> And the Lord said: "Because this people draw near with their mouth and honor me with their lips, while their hearts are far from me, and their fear of me is a commandment taught by men, (Isaiah 29:13)

**Surface-level context:** 6th Century BC Jerusalem is refusing to heed the Lord.
**Hidden truth:** 1st Century AD leaders of Jerusalem have made void the word of God to adhere to their traditions.

In Isaiah 29, Jerusalem is being scolded for their rebellion to the Lord. They have disregarded Him and Jerusalem is promised ruin. In verse 13, the Lord said that He would do this because they draw near with their mouth and honor Him with their lips, meanwhile their hearts are far from Him and their best attempt at worshipping Him is to follow man-made commandments.

This passage is speaking about Isaiah's contemporaries. Note in verse 13 the addressing of "this people." This is being addressed to 6th Century BC Jerusalem. There is nothing that denotes any reference to any future fulfillment of people who draw near with their mouth and lips but have a heart that is far from Him.

However, Jesus tells 1st Century Jerusalem that Isaiah spoke about *them*! "Well did Isaiah prophesy of you." Of *you!* Jesus said that Isaiah prophesied about *Jesus'* contemporaries. The Old Testament provided a foreshadowing of 1st Century realities relating to Jesus. Matthew well understood this.

### EXAMPLES OF THE *MYSTERION* IN ACTS
As recorded in Acts chapter 1, Jesus ascended to heaven (1:9). The disciples then went to Jerusalem where they were joined by many others (1:12, 15). Peter stepped up and spoke to the community:

## Ch. 8: Evidence of the Mysterion by Various New Testament Authors

> "Brothers, the Scripture had to be fulfilled, which the Holy Spirit spoke beforehand by the mouth of David concerning Judas, who became a guide to those who arrested Jesus. For he was numbered among us and was allotted his share in this ministry." ... "For it is written in the Book of Psalms, "'May his camp become desolate, and let there be no one to dwell in it'; and "'Let another take his office.' (Acts 1:16-17, 20)

Peter proclaimed that David prophesied about Judas, quoting David in two places: Psalm 69:25 and Psalm 109:8. Peter acknowledged that these passages, possibly among others, had to be fulfilled by the betrayal of Judas.

> May their camp be a desolation; let no one dwell in their tents. (Psalm 69:25)

**Surface-level context:** David is overwhelmed by his persecutors.
**Hidden truth:** Judas was to betray Jesus.

Psalm 69 is a psalm of deep desperation. We will look at Psalm 69 in greater depth in a later portion of this book. For now, we will examine the immediate context of this verse.

David is sick and tired of being treated poorly by those who hate him without cause (69:4). He feels under attack perpetually and is crying out to God for deliverance from his persecutors (69:14). David even prays to God that devastating things will happen to his persecutors in response to what they have done to him (69:22-28). It is in this portion of the psalm that Peter references as evidence that Judas' betrayal of Jesus had to happen in order for the Scriptures to be fulfilled.

The immediate context pertains to those who persecute David. Peter thinks of David's expressions and sees his expressions fulfilled in the 1st Century by the persecutors of Jesus. There is nothing in the immediate context of David's expressions that indicates there is anything Messianic in this passage. But Peter knew that all of the Scriptures are Messianic and he recognized that Jesus lived out what David expressed.

Observe Peter's use of a singular pronoun: *his* camp. All the English translations of Psalm 69:25 state *their* camp. Luke recorded Peter's speech with a

Greek pronoun that is singular, not plural. Whether the singular pronoun was used by Peter in his speech or only in Luke's writing of the text, ultimately the devastation that David prayed against his persecutors was seen by Peter and/or Luke to be fulfilled by those who persecuted Jesus, specifically Judas. More importantly, the Holy Spirit revealed that David's expressions pertaining to his persecutors in Psalm 69 were fulfilled by the persecutions pertaining to Jesus.

Peter's other quotation is from Psalm 109:18 with a very similar context. David is crying out because of his persecutors. Psalm 109 is regarded as an imprecatory psalm, a psalm invoking judgment or calamity upon one's enemies or the enemies of God. Peter, Luke, and the Holy Spirit agree that David's expressions are ultimately fulfilled by Judas' mistreatment of Jesus.

> May his days be few; may another take his office! (Psalm 109:8)

**Surface-level context:** David wishing for God to bring retribution to his enemies.
**Hidden truth:** Judas' share in the ministry will be replaced by another.

### ACTS 2:25-28
In Peter's sermon in Acts 2, after quoting from Joel 2, he proclaimed Jesus of Nazareth who did mighty works, was crucified, and raised from the dead (Acts 2:22-24). Peter provided scriptural evidence and quoted from Psalm 16:

> I have set the LORD always before me; because he is at my right hand, I shall not be shaken. Therefore my heart is glad, and my whole being rejoices; my flesh also dwells secure. For you will not abandon my soul to Sheol, or let your holy one see corruption. You make known to me the path of life; in your presence there is fullness of joy; at your right hand are pleasures forevermore. (Psalm 16:8-11)

**Surface-level context:** David is proclaiming his trust in the Lord.
**Hidden truth:** God raised Jesus from the dead.

David wrote this in the first person. He did not speak of another person to come. David proclaimed *his* trust in the Lord: "...*I* shall not be shaken...*my* heart is glad...*my* flesh dwells secure..."

## Ch. 8: Evidence of the Mysterion by Various New Testament Authors

Peter asserted that David wrote of Jesus: "For David says concerning him..." (2:25). David stated "You will not abandon my soul to Sheol, or let your holy one see corruption" (Ps. 16:10). David rested assured that God would not leave him uncared for.

Peter shared to his listeners with great confidence that David is dead and buried (2:29). Acknowledging David as a prophet, Peter said that David foresaw the resurrection of Christ and thus spoke about it (2:30-31). Peter announced that when David said "you will not abandon my soul to Sheol or let your holy one see corruption" he foresaw the resurrection of the coming Anointed One. It is Jesus who was not abandoned to the grave! It is Jesus whose flesh would not decay. Jesus was raised from the dead! Praise Jesus!

Peter assured his listeners that David's body is decaying. It is Jesus, God's holy one, whose body did not see corruption. Peter knew that David was not merely expressing himself. The inspiration of God's Spirit expressed Jesus *through* David.

All too often, we mistake the Psalms as being merely an expression of the human author. We then find ways to apply the experience of the human author to our experiences. This can be beneficial and comforting for us to do, but it is missing the primary point.

It is true that the human author pens the words in response to real circumstances. Ultimately, however, the writings are the Holy Spirit's expression of Jesus. Instead of reading the psalms merely from a David-centered perspective, or even me-centered, let's read the psalms with a Jesus-centered perspective. In a later portion of the book, we'll perform a few exercises of reading Psalms from a Jesus-centered perspective.

**ACTS 4**

Peter and John spent a night in prison because they were preaching Jesus (4:1-3). After being threatened and released, they shared their experience with their friends (4:23). The response of the people was that they praised God and corporately expressed everything beginning from the second half of verse 24 all the way through verse 30. In the midst of this corporate expression was another quotation from a psalm.

> And when they heard it, they lifted their voices together to God and said, "Sovereign Lord, who made the heaven and the earth and the sea and everything in them, who through the mouth of our father David, your

servant, said by the Holy Spirit, "'Why did the Gentiles rage, and the peoples plot in vain? The kings of the earth set themselves, and the rulers were gathered together, against the Lord and against his Anointed'-- …" (Acts 4:24-26)

They indicated that David wrote Psalm 2 "by the Holy Spirit" and quoted the psalm's first two verses:

> Why do the nations rage and the peoples plot in vain? The kings of the earth set themselves, and the rulers take counsel together, against the LORD and against his Anointed, saying, (Psalm 2:1-2)

**Surface-level context:** The rulers of the earth take counsel against God.
**Hidden truth:** Herod, Pilate, along with other Gentiles and the peoples of Israel, took counsel against Jesus.

Psalm 2 appears to be like a summit of world leaders gathering together to take counsel against the Lord. The believers in Acts 4 understood that they saw Psalm 2:1-2 play out before their eyes. They exclaimed:

> for truly in this city there were gathered together against your holy servant Jesus, whom you anointed, both Herod and Pontius Pilate, along with the Gentiles and the peoples of Israel, to do whatever your hand and your plan had predestined to take place. (Acts 4:27-28)

What the believers were indicating was that when David wrote Psalm 2, the Holy Spirit was expressing these realities pertaining to Jesus:

- The Gentiles (Herod, Pilate, etc.) raged against Jesus; the peoples (among both Gentiles and Israel) plotted in vain against Jesus (see Ps. 2:1).
- The kings of the land and the rulers took counsel together against Jesus (see Ps. 2:2).
- They determined "Let us separate God from His Anointed One and cast away their cords so that they may not be rejoined" (see Ps. 2:3).

## Ch. 8: Evidence of the Mysterion by Various New Testament Authors

- God laughs because He knows He has a plan of resurrection and scoffs at them (see Ps. 2:4).
- Then God will speak to them in His wrath and terrify them with the knowledge that He will set His King on Zion, His holy hill (see Ps. 2:5-6); as a result, Roman and Jewish leaders will suffer the King's holy wrath.
- In so doing, Jesus affirms the decree that God said to Him "You are my Son; today I have begotten you" (see Ps. 2:7).
- Jesus will have as his heritage a people from among all nations to be His possession (see Ps. 2:8).
- Those who are not among His heritage, Jesus will break and dash in pieces like a potter's vessel (see Ps. 2:9).
- The kings and rulers are therefore warned to serve the Lord with fear and rejoice with trembling (see Ps. 2:10-11).
- "Kiss the Son, lest he be angry, and you perish in the way, for his wrath is quickly kindled. Blessed are all who take refuge in (Jesus)" (Ps. 2:12).

Psalm 2: the gospel of Jesus Christ!

Also, observe the verb tenses of Psalm 2:1-2 compared with Acts 4:25-26:
- "Why do the nations rage" vs. "Why *did* the Gentiles rage"
- "the rulers take counsel together" vs. "the rulers *were* gathered together"

The believers in Acts 4 treated the events of Psalm 2 as having taken place in the past tense. What David wrote is Psalm 2 was fulfilled in their immediate past. They were filled with the Holy Spirit; the place shook. God was moving in that room in a mighty way, providing validation that their perspective that the events that happened to Jesus were fulfillment of Psalm 2. The believers in that room were greatly encouraged, knowing that God is victorious over the threats of those who set themselves against God's Anointed (Jesus):

> And now, Lord, look upon their threats and grant to your servants to continue to speak your word with all boldness, while you stretch out your

hand to heal, and signs and wonders are performed through the name of your holy servant Jesus." (Act 4:29-30)

Praise the Lord! May we all be encouraged to proclaim Jesus with all boldness despite a world that sets itself against Him!

## EXAMPLES OF THE *MYSTERION* IN HEBREWS

The writer to the Hebrews came out of the gate in chapter 1 and tackled the false teaching that was going on in Jewish circles that involved the worship of angels. The writer made it clear that the angels are not to be worshipped and it is Jesus who is to be worshipped, being superior to the angels.

In verse 5, the writer quoted Psalm 2:7 as speaking of God to Jesus. Incidentally, this further confirms that the believers in Acts 4 correctly viewed Psalm 2 as being about Jesus.

> I will tell of the decree: The LORD said to me, "You are my Son; today I have begotten you. (Psalm 2:7)

**Surface-level context:** David will tell of God's decree.
**Hidden truth:** Jesus is telling of God's decree.

It appears on the surface that it is David who will tell of the decree of God, writing in the first person ("I will tell...said to me..."). The decree is that the Lord declared "You are my Son; today I have begotten you." But the writer to the Hebrews introduced that quote by stating "to which of the angels did God ever say" and then quoted the statement made in the second half of Psalm 2:7.

Therefore, it is God who said to Jesus "You are my Son; today I have begotten you." This means that when David wrote "I will tell of the decree: the Lord said to me," it is actually what Jesus is expressing. The proper reading of Psalm 2:7 is to read it from the perspective of Jesus: "Jesus will tell of the decree: the Lord said to Jesus, 'You are my Son.'"

Just a few verses later (1:8-9), the writer quoted from Psalm 45:6-7 and attributed those words as God speaking of Jesus.

> Your throne, O God, is forever and ever. The scepter of your kingdom is a scepter of uprightness; you have loved righteousness and hated

*Ch. 8: Evidence of the Mysterion by Various New Testament Authors*

> wickedness. Therefore God, your God, has anointed you with the oil of gladness beyond your companions; (Psalm 45:6-7)

**Surface-level context:** David is exalting God.
**Hidden truth:** God is exalting Jesus.

It is God the Father lavishing praise to God the Son. Jesus' throne is forever and ever. The scepter of Jesus' kingdom is a scepter of righteousness. Jesus loved righteousness and hated wickedness. Therefore, God the Father has anointed Jesus "with the oil of gladness beyond your companions." Jesus is to be greatly esteemed above all His human companions!

The same applies to the quotation from Psalm 102 in Hebrews 1:10-12:

> Of old you laid the foundation of the earth, and the heavens are the work of your hands. They will perish, but you will remain; they will all wear out like a garment. You will change them like a robe, and they will pass away, but you are the same, and your years have no end. (Psalm 102:25-27)

**Surface-level context:** The psalmist is exalting God.
**Hidden truth:** God is exalting Jesus.

Of old Jesus laid the foundation of the earth, and the heavens are the work of Jesus' hands. They will perish, but Jesus will remain; they will wear out like a garment. Jesus will change them like a robe, and they will pass away, but Jesus is the same (see Heb. 13:5), and Jesus' years have no end.

In chapter 10, the writer to the Hebrews addressed Jesus' one-time sacrifice for sin. Prior to quoting from Psalm 40, the writer indicated that what Psalm 40:6-8 states is what Christ said when He came into the world (Heb. 10:5-7).

> In sacrifice and offering you have not delighted, but you have given me an open ear. Burnt offering and sin offering you have not required. Then I said, "Behold, I have come; in the scroll of the book it is written of me: I delight to do your will, O my God; your law is within my heart." (Psalm 40:6-8)

**Surface-level context:** David wants to give God more than just burnt offering, but to do the will of God.
**Hidden truth:** Jesus will offer Himself as a sacrifice, delighting to do the will of God.

First note of interest, the psalm states "you have given me an open ear" whereas the writer to the Hebrews wrote "a body you have prepared for me." The Psalms are translated to English from the Hebrew Masoretic Text; the writer to the Hebrews quoted from the Septuagint (the Greek translation of the Old Testament). Why the Hebrew text and the Septuagint differ is a discussion to be had elsewhere. It's possible that the difference isn't as great as appears from a cursory view. Regardless, the writer to the Hebrews clearly took David's words and made them Jesus' expression.

Sacrifices and offerings God has not desired, but a body God has prepared for Jesus; in burnt offerings God has taken no pleasure. Then Jesus said, 'Behold, I have come to do Your will, O God, as it is written of Me in the scroll of the book.'"

In the scroll of God's eternal purpose, it is written of Jesus to have a body prepared for sacrifice: the holy, one-time sacrifice for sin. Jesus came to do His Father's will. Hebrews 10:5-7 confirms that David's expression in Psalm 40:6-8 is not limited to David; but it reflects Christ's purpose when He came into the world.

There are more examples in the New Testament of the *mysterion* than these listed in this and previous chapters. You'll also find examples of the *mysterion* in Peter's writings and in John's writings. Experience the sense of discovery by exploring some of these on your own. You, too, can reveal the mystery of the gospel by taking layers off the surface of the Old Testament writings. Without seeing Jesus hidden throughout the Old Testament, we read it with a veil over our understanding. But when we see Jesus foreshadowed in the Scriptures, the veil is removed (see 2 Cor. 3:14-16).

# PART III:
# Discovering the Mysterion in the Old Testament

# Chapter 9:
# Discovering the Mysterion in the Old Testament: An Example (Joshua 7)

In Part 1, we looked at the New Testament teaching on how Jesus, His apostles, and the New Testament authors utilized the Old Testament; from a Christocentric perspective. In Part 2, we saw several examples of quotations from the Old Testament in the New Testament that reveal that there was more to the Old Testament than appears on the surface.

In this Part 3, we will survey the Old Testament, walking through it and peeling back the layers to reveal the hidden truth of Jesus beneath the surface. There is no possible way to address every aspect of seeing Christ in the Old Testament. That pursuit is inexhaustible.

We will journey through the Old Testament looking at select passages that foreshadow Jesus. There are many passages that we could address but will not. Even some of the passages we will address could go deeper than we will go. This is merely an exercise of whetting your appetite to perceive Christ throughout the Old Testament Scriptures.

In this portion, we will not limit ourselves to Old Testament passages that are quoted in the New Testament. Some suggest that only those Old Testament passages that are explicitly quoted in the New Testament have New Covenant applications, leaving the entirety of the unquoted portions of the Old Testament to stand in their original context and no more. I believe we will discover that the Old Testament displays pictures, types, and shadows of Jesus and the realities of abiding in Him well beyond the passages that are quoted in the New Testament.

If it was necessary for the New Testament to quote an Old Testament passage for an Old Testament passage to find its fulfillment in Christ, then nearly the entire Old Testament would be quoted in the New Testament, making the New Testament largely redundant and the Bible nearly double in size.

Before we begin at Genesis chapter 1 and the Creation account, we'll start with an example to give us a taste of what we'll find. We'll first look at Joshua chapter 7.

## JOSHUA 7

Israel had just won its first victory in the conquest for the Promised Land by defeating Jericho (Joshua chapter 6). Israel was instructed that the silver and gold and finest vessels be put in the treasury of the house of the Lord (6:19); everything else was to be devoted to destruction (6:18, 21).

After the victory over Jericho, "the LORD was with Joshua, and his fame was in all the land" (6:27). The problem is that a man named Achan took some of the things from Jericho and secretly kept them for himself (7:1).

The next city for them to conquer was the city of Ai. Joshua sent scouts to examine Ai (7:2). The scouts return suggesting that conquering Ai will be easy, and they shouldn't bother to send all their troops, only a portion (7:3).

Three thousand men of Israel went up to Ai, and they were surprisingly defeated (7:4). In response to this defeat, Joshua fell on his face before the Lord and pleaded on behalf of both the nation and the Lord's great name (7:6-9).

The Lord responded to Joshua by encouraging him to "Get up!" (7:10). The Lord also revealed to Joshua that Israel departed Jericho with some of the things that had been devoted to destruction; therefore, Israel will be devoted to destruction unless the devoted things are destroyed (7:11-12).

Then the Lord told Joshua that the next morning they'll have a form of a lottery, but it won't at all be random. The Lord will identify who has taken the devoted things, and that man and all that he has will be burned with fire (7:13-15).

The next morning the Lord identified Achan as the transgressor (7:16-18). Joshua confronted Achan (7:19). Achan fessed up and told them where he hid the stuff (7:20-21). Joshua sent messengers and they find the stuff right where Achan told them it was (7:22-23). The chapter concludes:

> And Joshua and all Israel with him took Achan the son of Zerah, and the silver and the cloak and the bar of gold, and his sons and daughters and his oxen and donkeys and sheep and his tent and all that he had. And they brought them up to the Valley of Achor. And Joshua said, "Why did you bring trouble on us? The LORD brings trouble on you today." And all Israel stoned him with stones. They burned them with fire and stoned them with stones. And they raised over him a great heap of stones that remains to this day. Then the LORD turned from his burning anger.

*Ch. 9: Discovering the Mysterion in the Old Testament: An Example (Joshua 7)*

> Therefore, to this day the name of that place is called the Valley of Achor. (Jos 7:24-26)

There. You have all now been preached the gospel of Christ in the form of the *mysterion* from Joshua chapter 7.

How so? Any idea?

The account regarding Achan is reminiscent of Romans 5:19, which states: "For as by one man's disobedience many were made sinners, so by one man's obedience many will be made righteous." The context of Romans chapter 5 is that Paul is contrasting Jesus with Adam. Just as Adam's disobedience resulted in many others being made sinners, so too does Christ's obedience unto death result in many being made right before God.

In Joshua chapter 7, Achan serves as a picture of both Adam and Jesus. Achan represented Adam in that by the sin of one man, the entire nation was guilty before God: "the people of Israel broke faith/committed a trespass/acted unfaithfully" (7:1). And verse 11: "Israel has sinned." An entire people group was deemed guilty and devoted to destruction because of the action of one man.

Later in verse 1: "the anger of the Lord burned against the people of Israel." The Lord's anger burned against an entire population of people, because of the sin of one man. In this way, Achan is symbolic of Adam.

In addition, by the death of Achan, God's anger was appeased. In verse 26 following the stoning of Achan: "Then the Lord turned from His burning anger." With the death of Achan, an entire people group was vindicated before God. In this way, Achan serves as symbolic of Jesus: a representative death on behalf of a nation. Just as Jesus' death appeased God's wrath for a spiritual nation of believers, Achan's death appeased God's wrath for an entire physical nation.

In chapter 8, Israel made a second attempt at the city of Ai. This time they took it easily, for the Lord was with them, just as He had been with them at Jericho.

Achan sinned, the entire nation suffered defeat at Ai. Achan was put to death, a whole people group was vindicated as God's wrath was appeased. They returned to right standing before God and went on to victory.

Adam sinned, humanity earned God's wrath. Jesus provided a substitutionary death, an entire people group was justified as God's wrath was appeased.

Redeemed humanity is restored to right standing before God and we will reign victoriously with Him forever.

The mystery of the gospel of Jesus Christ, here in Joshua chapter 7.

## VALLEY OF ACHOR

"Now, Chuck" you may be thinking, "you're taking this a little too far...seeing something that's not really there...you're reading too much into it."

Perhaps. But I don't think so. At least not in this case.

The location of the stoning of Achan was the Valley of Achor. The Valley of Achor is mentioned 5 times in the Old Testament; twice right here in the closing verses of chapter 7 and once more in Joshua, in chapter 15, used simply as a landmark when defining boundaries of the land allotted to the tribe of Judah. The Valley of Achor is then mentioned twice more in the Prophets.

In Isaiah chapter 65, the Lord promised a future for those who are his:

> I will bring forth offspring from Jacob, and from Judah possessors of my mountains; my chosen shall possess it, and my servants shall dwell there. Sharon shall become a pasture for flocks, and the Valley of Achor a place for herds to lie down, for my people who have sought me. (Isa 65:9-10)

Clearly, we have shepherding language here. "A pasture for flocks" and "a place for herds to lie down." How is it that God shepherds His people? We know that God shepherds his people through the Great Shepherd, Jesus. Isaiah wrote that the Valley of Achor pointed forward to a future shepherding of God's people.

The final mention of the Valley of Achor is found in Hosea chapter 2. In Hosea chapter 1, Hosea's wife acts unfaithfully and bears children from other men. She represents unfaithful Israel.

In chapter 2, verse 2, speaking of Israel, the Lord says "she is not my wife, and I am not her husband." The Lord continues from there to scold Israel for her unfaithfulness; until verse 14, the turning point of the chapter. For the rest of chapter 2 the Lord reveals that there will be a day when He will betroth unto himself a bride.

> "And in that day, declares the LORD, you will call me 'My Husband,' and no longer will you call me 'My Baal.' ... And I will betroth you to me

> forever. I will betroth you to me in righteousness and in justice, in steadfast love and in mercy. I will betroth you to me in faithfulness. And you shall know the LORD. (Hos 2:16, 19-20)

Who is it that the Lord betroths? Of course, it is the bride of Christ. Believers are betrothed to God "in righteousness and in justice, in steadfast love and in mercy."

Now go back to verse 14, the turning point of the chapter. These are the verses immediately preceding the promise of the Lord betrothing unto Himself a bride:

> "Therefore, behold, I will allure her, and bring her into the wilderness, and speak tenderly to her. And there I will give her her vineyards and make the Valley of Achor a door of hope. And there she shall answer as in the days of her youth, as at the time when she came out of the land of Egypt. (Hos 2:14-15)

Hosea brings all this bad news to Israel, and then recalls the Valley of Achor and it makes him think of "a door of hope."

How is it that the Valley of Achor provides a door of hope in Hosea's future, and the promise of God's shepherding of His people in Isaiah's future? What is it about a dead man's bones beneath a huge pile of rocks that provides hope, and the tender care of a shepherd?

Both Isaiah & Hosea look back at the Valley of Achor, and what they see at the Valley of Achor causes them to look forward to the coming Christ; the husband and shepherd of God's people.

The hidden truth of the Valley of Achor is that it serves as a foreshadowing of Christ. Achan served as a foreshadowing of Jesus by suffering a representative death that appeased the anger of the Lord on behalf of a nation.

The mystery of the gospel: hidden throughout the Old Testament, realized in Christ.

# Chapter 10:
# Discovering the Mysterion in Genesis

We will certainly not be able to address every nuance of the *mysterion* in the Old Testament. There is more there than any of us can possibly ever fully comprehend. There is more for me to learn every time I read the Old Testament. We'll only select certain passages to address. The evidence of the *mysterion* is far from limited to the select passages we do address.

**THE LIGHT OF CREATION**

The Creation account; let's start at the beginning with "In the beginning...":

> In the beginning, God created the heavens and the earth. The earth was without form and void, and darkness was over the face of the deep. And the Spirit of God was hovering over the face of the waters. And God said, "Let there be light," and there was light. (Genesis 1:1-3)

John's gospel account famously begins with Creation language. Creation is on John's mind from his very first words: "In the beginning" (John 1:1). Creation language continues in verse 3: "All things were made through him, and without him was not any thing made that was made." In Jesus was "life" and "the life was the light of men" (1:4). John described Jesus as light in much the same way as was described the entrance of light upon the earth in the Creation account:

> The light shines in the darkness, and the darkness has not overcome it. ... The true light, which gives light to everyone, was coming into the world. (John 1:5, 9)

John referred to Jesus as the "true" light. The light of the Creation account was a foreshadowing of Jesus. Jesus is the "true" light with the light of the Creation account being a precursor to Jesus. Just as Jesus was the "true" Jonah and the "true" Solomon (Matt. 12:41-42; Jonah and Solomon serving as precursors to Jesus), so too is Jesus the "true" light of the Creation account.[3]

---

[3] For understanding Jesus as the "true" light in contrast to the light of creation, I am indebted to friend Patrick Rauh and his yet unpublished epic manuscript tentatively titled *The Picture of Scripture*.

It's as though God said "Let there be My Son", and there was His Son. "Let there be My Word," and there was God's Word. "Let there be My Message, My Expression to mankind," and there was God's Expression to mankind. God's Expression to mankind became flesh and dwelt among us.

We all know that God created light by saying "Let there be light." What was there before light? Before light there was darkness. Darkness preceded light.

Just as darkness preceded light, evening preceded morning. "There was evening and there was morning" (Gen. 1:5, 8, 13, 19, 23, 31). The Jewish day began at sundown and ended at the next sundown. Therefore, if half of every 24 hours was daylight, the first 12 hours of a day on the Jewish calendar was darkness; the next 12 hours was light. The day began when darkness arrived. Evening preceded morning just as darkness preceded light.

Not only did evening precede morning and darkness precede light, Crucifixion preceded Resurrection. The daily setting and rising of the sun give us a visible picture displaying the Crucifixion and Resurrection of Jesus. Because evening preceded morning according to the Jewish calendar, the sun having set (darkness) precedes its rising (light).

Every time the sun sets it symbolizes the Anointed One of God going to the grave. The sun rises to bring newness. It brings a new day. It brings light. It brings warmth. It brings life. Every morning the birds chirp as they sing their praises to the rising of the sun. The rooster crows to announce that the sun has risen. Darkness has not overcome it, the sun rises victorious.

Before there was light, there was darkness. Through the darkness the Spirit of God hovered over the earth. Then the decree came forth for there to be light. And there was light. "Light," God exclaimed, "come forth!"

Before Jesus was raised, He was in the grave. The Spirit of God hovered over Jesus' dead body. Then the decree came forth for Jesus to be raised. And He was raised. "Jesus," God exclaimed, "come forth!"

The Spirit of God Who hovered over the face of the waters is the same Spirit of God who raised Jesus from the dead:

> If the Spirit of him who raised Jesus from the dead dwells in you, he who raised Christ Jesus from the dead will also give life to your mortal bodies through his Spirit who dwells in you. (Rom 8:11)

*Ch. 10: Discovering the Mysterion in Genesis*

The same Spirit of God who raised Jesus from the dead is the same Spirit of God who raises dead sinners unto life!

Just as darkness preceded light, evening preceded morning, and Crucifixion preceded Resurrection, so too does spiritual deadness ("You were dead in trespasses and sins" [Eph 2:1]) precede spiritual life ("But God ... even when we were dead in our trespasses, made us alive together with Christ" [Eph 2:4-5]).

Paul used Creation language to describe the work of regeneration:

> For God, who said, "Let light shine out of darkness," has shone in our hearts to give the light of the knowledge of the glory of God in the face of Jesus Christ. (2 Cor. 4:6)

By His grace, God has given life to those who were dead. God shined light where there had only been darkness. We dwelled in darkness. God looked upon our deadness and proclaimed "Let light shine out of darkness" and there was light. The Spirit gave life to us, imparting to us "the light of the knowledge of the glory of God in the face of Jesus Christ."

Jesus raising Lazarus from the dead foreshadowed both Jesus' resurrection and the believer's conversion. Just as the Creator spoke life into existence, Jesus spoke life into Lazarus' dead body. And Lazarus was raised. "Lazarus," Jesus exclaimed, "come forth!"

Before we were alive with Christ, we were dead in our trespasses. The Spirit of God hovered over our spiritual deadness. Then the decree came forth for dead sinners to be given life by His grace. And they were given life by His grace. "Child," God exclaimed, "come forth!"

When we think of the creation of light, we may often think of the light provided by the sun. But the sun, moon, and stars were not created until the 4th day. Then what is the significance of the light that was created on the 1st day?

We can read that God said "Let there be light" and know that there was light. Or, we can read that God said "Let there be light" and see Jesus, see His Resurrection, even see the enlightenment our own conversion.

> ...And God saw that the light was good. (Gen 1:4a)

## BE FRUITFUL AND MULTIPLY

Adam and Eve were commissioned by God to "be fruitful and multiply" (Gen. 1:28). The purpose for being fruitful and multiplying was to fill the earth and exercise dominion over the rest of Creation.

In what is commonly referred as the Great Commission, Jesus commanded the apostles to go and make disciples (Matt. 28:19). The great commission of the Old Testament era was to be fruitful and multiply *physically*. The great commission of the New Testament era is to be fruitful and multiply *spiritually*.

The Old Testament era provided a physical picture of the spiritual realities of the New Testament era. The physical preceded the spiritual; "But it is not the spiritual that is first but the natural, and then the spiritual" (1 Cor 15:46). It is a pattern we see throughout the Scriptures.

Physical → Spiritual
Adam → Jesus
Old Testament era → New Testament era
Picture → Fulfillment
Be fruitful and multiply → Go and make disciples

The relationship between Adam and Jesus established the pattern:

> Thus it is written, "The first man Adam became a living being"; the last Adam became a life-giving spirit. ... The first man was from the earth, a man of dust; the second man is from heaven. (1 Cor. 15:45, 47)

Thus, the great commission of each era shares a relationship in this pattern. The physical picture of the Old Testament great commission corresponds to the spiritual reality of the New Testament great commission.

Better yet, the spiritual fulfillment of being fruitful and multiplying in the New Testament is the work of Jesus! Yes, it is believers in Jesus whom He uses to perform His work, but it is actually Jesus who is being fruitful and multiplying.

Adam was the one commissioned to be fruitful and multiply in the Old Testament era. Jesus is the One whose mission it is to be fruitful and multiply in the New Testament era.

First of all, in the verse immediately preceding Jesus' issuing the great commission, He said, "All authority in heaven and on earth has been given to

## Ch. 10: Discovering the Mysterion in Genesis

me" (Matt. 28:18). Remember, Adam was issued the great commission of the Old Testament era so that he would exercise dominion over the earth. Here Jesus has been given all authority so that *He* may exercise dominion over the earth. The dominion of Jesus' kingdom will expand as Jesus is fruitful and multiplies Himself on the earth.

Secondly, we see Psalm 8 connect the first Adam and the last Adam (Jesus). The writer to the Hebrews makes it clear to us that Psalm 8, on the surface appearing to speak of Adam and his posterity (mankind), was actually depicting Jesus (Heb. 2:5-9).

Thirdly, how is it that Jesus is fruitful and multiplies? After all, aren't we the ones commanded to go and make disciples?

> Truly, truly, I say to you, unless a grain of wheat falls into the earth and dies, it remains alone; but if it dies, it bears much fruit. (John 12:24)

Jesus used the grain of wheat as imagery of His death and Resurrection. The context of Jesus' statement was that He was preparing His disciples for these events that were about to take place in Jerusalem (see John 12:23, 27).

In order for wheat to grow, we need a grain of wheat. Not only must the grain of wheat be dead, it must also be buried. If the grain of wheat is not dead and buried, it will not produce wheat. Hold a grain of wheat in your hand, six months later you still have a grain of wheat, but no wheat stalks. The grain of wheat must be buried; it can only produce fruit after having been dead and buried.

Once the grain of wheat has been buried, it comes to life. A stalk of wheat rises from where it had been buried and bears forth much fruit.

What does a grain of wheat produce? More wheat. Does it produce inferior wheat? No, it produces more of the same as what it was. The DNA of the wheat continues to produce the same DNA. Wheat produces wheat. All created things were made according to its kind. Each kind produces more of its kind.

So it is with Jesus. Jesus was dead and buried. Jesus rose from the place where He was buried and He bears forth much fruit. He bears fruit through the Spirit. If the seed of the Spirit is planted into a human, the human is born anew, and Jesus dwells in the human, thus having multiplied Himself.

since you have been born again, not of perishable seed but of imperishable, through the living and abiding word of God; (1 Peter 1:23)

Like the seed of wheat that produces more wheat, the seed of the Spirit produces more of its kind (Gal. 5:22-23). We are to bear the image of Jesus so that He might be the firstborn among many brothers (Rom. 8:29). Christ is the "firstfruits" (1 Cor. 15:20, 23). However, *we* also are said to have the firstfruits of the Spirit (Rom. 8:23; James 1:18).

What Jesus is doing in believers is producing more of Himself (i.e., more "wheat"). Jesus is multiplying on earth. Believers in Jesus comprise His body and we are His fullness (Eph. 1:22-23). The fullness of Jesus is being revealed in His body, in those in whom He dwells (Col. 2:9-10). Each kind produces more of its kind. Jesus produces more of Himself.

> Abide in me, and I in you. As the branch cannot bear fruit by itself, unless it abides in the vine, neither can you, unless you abide in me. I am the vine; you are the branches. Whoever abides in me and I in him, he it is that bears much fruit, for apart from me you can do nothing. (John 15:4-5)

The fruit that a believer bears is Jesus' fruit. It is not the believer's own fruit; without Him we "can do nothing." It is the DNA of the vine that determines what kind of fruit its branches produce. The vine does not produce any fruit itself, the branches of the vine produce the fruit. Believers are branches that abide in the vine of Jesus producing *His* fruit.

We can read God's commission to the first Adam to "be fruitful and multiply" and merely see that Adam and his posterity are to reproduce more humans. Or, we can read God's commission to the first Adam to "be fruitful and multiply" and see a picture of the last Adam, who is a life-giving spirit, multiplying Himself by indwelling humans and producing His fruit in their lives.

Praise Jesus!

## CAIN, ABEL, & SETH

Three children of Adam and Eve are named in the Bible. We know Adam and Eve had other children because Genesis 5:4 tells us outright that Adam "had other sons and daughters." However, only three are named.

*Ch. 10: Discovering the Mysterion in Genesis*

Why, then, aren't any of the other children named in the Genesis account? Why are only three of them named? These three children of Adam and Eve are the only three named because they are the only three necessary to tell the story of the gospel. Cain, Abel, and Seth provide a picture, a foreshadowing, of Jesus.

Cain was born first. Just as darkness preceded light and Adam preceded Jesus, so too did Cain precede Abel.

Abel was a shepherd. Jesus said "I am the good shepherd" (John 10:11). Abel's sacrifice was acceptable to the Lord. The one sacrifice throughout the history of the world that the Lord found most acceptable was the fragrant offering of the sacrifice of Jesus (Eph. 5:2).

Cain was jealous, so he killed Abel. Cain was a persecutor of the righteous. Jesus' parable of the tenants exposes the jealousy of the Jews who killed Him (Matt. 21:38, 45). (Incidentally, the tenants worked the ground [Matt. 21:33] just as Cain "worked the ground" [Gen. 4:2]). Abel was commended as righteous by God. However, we know that none are righteous (Rom. 3:10) except Jesus. He is the only One who is truly righteous. For the rest of us, we can only be righteous because of Jesus' righteousness.

> By faith Abel offered to God a more acceptable sacrifice than Cain, through which he was commended as righteous, God commending him by accepting his gifts. And through his faith, though he died, he still speaks. (Heb 11:4)

The writer to the Hebrews states that though Abel died "he still speaks" because Abel's blood was crying from the ground (Gen. 4:10). Though Jesus died, He still speaks! Jesus' blood still speaks as it provides atonement for sinners.

We know that Jesus did not remain in the grave. To the contrary, Abel's blood did remain in the ground. However, the Lord provided a replacement.

> And Adam knew his wife again, and she bore a son and called his name Seth, for she said, "God has appointed for me another offspring instead of Abel, for Cain killed him." (Gen 4:25)

Seth was a replacement for Abel. Whereas Abel suffered death, Seth served as a substitute. It's as though Adam and Eve were given another Abel, a replacement for the first Abel.

Abel had no documented children. Seth had many children (Gen. 5:7). Likewise, Jesus had no children while living on earth. After He was raised, however, He gave birth to many sons and daughters of God by being fruitful and multiplying.

Abel represents the crucified Christ. Seth represents the resurrected Christ. Cain represents the persecutors of Christ. Cain, Abel, and Seth: the only three named children of Adam and Eve. Together, they tell the story of the gospel.

| Picture | Fulfillment |
|---------|-------------|
| Cain | Persecutors of Christ |
| Abel | Crucified Christ |
| Seth | Resurrected Christ |

## THE FLOOD

The Flood did many things. One of them was to foreshadow salvation through Jesus.

Eight persons entered the ark and were saved from the flood waters. Those who were saved from the flood waters were saved by being immersed into the ark. The Lord sealed the ark, safely shutting them in (Gen. 7:16).

At the final day, judgment will come upon the world. Only a remnant will be saved, those who have been sealed by the Holy Spirit. The Holy Spirit seals us in our immersion into Jesus.

Peter wrote of the days of Noah while the ark was being prepared, and mentioned that only a few, a remnant of eight persons, were saved (1 Pet. 3:20). He wrote that baptism "corresponds to this" (1 Pet. 3:21). There are two very interesting points to make about Peter's statement.

First, Peter uses the word *antitypos*, from which we derive 'antitype.' The New King James Version even translates it "antitype." An antitype is the fulfillment of what a type foreshadows. For example, the light of Creation was a type (picture); Jesus, the true light, is the antitype (fulfillment).

Don't be confused into thinking that the "anti" prefix of antitype is bad or negative, as though it means "in opposition to." The type is the shadow, the antitype is the true form of the realities (see Heb. 10:1; the law was a type, Jesus is the antitype). Peter's use of the term *antitypos* indicates that what Noah experienced was a type; the baptism Peter is referring to is the antitype.

## Ch. 10: Discovering the Mysterion in Genesis

Second, the word "baptism" is translated from the Greek word *baptisma*. We can clearly see that the word baptism is derived from *baptisma*. However, the meaning of *baptisma* is "immersion", not "baptism." The word baptism came from *baptisma*, but *baptisma* should be translated "immersion." So much doctrine and confusion has resulted from respectively translating *baptisma* and *baptizo* as "baptism" and "to baptize" instead of the actual meanings "immersion" and "to immerse."

Imagine the clarity and deeper understanding we would have of our union with Jesus if Romans 6:3 had been translated this way: "Do you not know that all of us who have been immersed into Christ Jesus were immersed into his death?" Instead, the translation to baptism confuses the proper understanding of Romans 6:3. Translating Peter's use of *baptisma* as baptism also confuses our understanding of what Peter is writing.

Peter stated that the antitype of immersion "now saves you." Peter even makes clear that he is not writing about water baptism: "not as a removal of dirt from the body." It is not the ritual of baptism that saves. It is immersion into Jesus that saves. How does this antitype of immersion that saves happen? "Through the resurrection of Jesus Christ" (1 Pet. 3:21).

Therefore, with these two points in mind, we know that what Noah experienced served as a type. Immersion into Jesus is the antitype. The ark represents immersion into Jesus, and the Holy Spirit seals us into that immersion. The Lord used the saving of eight persons from the great flood to provide a picture of salvation that comes by being immersed into Jesus.

### CIRCUMCISION

God made promises to Abraham.[4] God instructed Abraham that to keep covenant with God, every male in his household must be circumcised. God's covenant promises were passed down and confirmed to Abraham's son Isaac and Isaac's son Jacob. Jacob's sons constitute the foundation of the nation of Israel, with whom God's covenant promises were further confirmed.

Circumcision in the Old Covenant was the entry point to becoming a member of God's covenant people. All males who were physically born into the physical nation of Israel were circumcised to reflect that they had been born into God's community. Being born into God's community identified an individual as a

---

[4] See chapter 4 for more discussion regarding God's promises to Abraham.

descendant of Abraham and a recipient of the promises made to him. Any Gentile who wanted to convert to Judaism had to be circumcised before he would be granted access into the community of God's people. Circumcision was the entry point to the Old Covenant.

Circumcision in the Old Covenant corresponds to regeneration in the New Covenant. Regeneration means 'to be newly created', also in terms of forming new animal or plant tissue. Spiritual regeneration is the act of God to make a person a new creation through the enlightenment of the Spirit. Regeneration is the point of our conversion when we are made alive (i.e., made new). Regeneration is the entry point to the New Covenant, when sinners are made alive in Christ; circumcision served as its foreshadow.

In the Old Covenant, circumcision meant everything. You were either "in" or you were "out" and it depended on whether or not you had been circumcised as a member of God's people. In the New Covenant, circumcision no longer means anything (Gal. 5:6).

> For neither circumcision counts for anything, nor uncircumcision, but a new creation. (Galatians 6:15)

What matters now is whether a person has been regenerated, been made a "new creation." You are either "in" or "out" based on whether or not you are a result of God's supernatural intervention that raises a sinner from spiritual death unto spiritual life. God's New Covenant community is comprised of individuals who have been regenerated, or spiritually circumcised.

> For no one is a Jew who is merely one outwardly, nor is circumcision outward and physical. But a Jew is one inwardly, and circumcision is a matter of the heart, by the Spirit, not by the letter. His praise is not from man but from God. (Romans 2:28-29)

A true Jew (member of God's community) is one who has been circumcised inwardly, spiritually.

Paul reminded the Ephesian believers that because of their Gentile background they were not citizens of Israel, but rather aliens and strangers to the covenants of promise (2:12). It was those of "the circumcision" (i.e., Jews) who

## Ch. 10: Discovering the Mysterion in Genesis

referred to the Gentiles as "the uncircumcision." The Jews were adhering to the physical picture (physical circumcision) but the Gentiles, who have been brought near by the blood of Jesus (2:13), have experienced the spiritual circumcision that made them "no longer strangers and aliens" but "fellow citizens with the saints and members of the household of God" (2:19). Believers in Jesus are of the true circumcision. "We are the circumcision" (Ph. 3:3).

This spiritual circumcision Paul addressed to the Colossians:

> In him also you were circumcised with a circumcision made without hands, by putting off the body of the flesh, by the circumcision of Christ, (Colossians 2:11)

Circumcision → Regeneration
Entry point to the Old Covenant → Entry point to the New Covenant
Physical picture → Spiritual reality

Circumcision was the shadow that found its fulfillment in the regeneration life of a heart converted to Christ.[5]

### ABRAHAM & ISAAC

We're most familiar with Abraham's near sacrifice of Isaac being a foreshadowing of Jesus in the fact that God provided a lamb of sacrifice as a substitute for Isaac. The ram that got caught in the thicket served as a type of Jesus. Just as the ram was sacrificed as a substitute for Isaac, so too was Jesus sacrificed as a substitute

---

[5] On a related note, one's view of circumcision impacts one's view of how to implement baptism. There is significant dispute in the church pertaining to the implementation of baptism. One side connects baptism to circumcision, the other side connects baptism to faith. Over the course of my Christian life, I have spent time on each side of that fence. I have seen the Biblical case for connecting baptism to faith, and consequently advocated that view for a significant time. I have also seen the Biblical case for connecting baptism to circumcision, and consequently advocated that view for a time.

The baptism issue was resolved for me by understanding that the New Covenant correlation to circumcision is regeneration. For me, it was not a matter of figuring out what to properly correlate to baptism (faith or circumcision). Realizing that the New Covenant correlation to Old Covenant circumcision is regenerated life in Christ was conclusively determinative.

for us. But did we know that, before the ram served as a picture of Jesus' sacrifice, Isaac also served as a picture of Jesus?

God commanded to Abraham to:

> "Take your son, your only son Isaac, whom you love, and go to the land of Moriah, and offer him there as a burnt offering on one of the mountains of which I shall tell you." (Gen 22:2)

First of all, we know full well that Isaac wasn't Abraham's only son. He had Ishmael long before he had Isaac, and Ishmael was still alive at this time. Three times in Genesis chapter 22 God referred to Isaac as Abraham's "only son." Why would God do this? Certainly, God is not ignorant, nor forgetful that Abraham had a previous son. Why does God repeatedly refer to Isaac as Abraham's "only son"? God told Abraham to offer as a sacrifice his "only son" whom he greatly loved to represent God's offering of His only begotten Son whom He greatly loved.

Ishmael was Abraham's firstborn son; Isaac was Abraham's "only" son. Incidentally, Israel was God's "firstborn son" (Ex. 4:22); Jesus is God's "only" son (John 3:16). Ishmael and Israel were born into bondage; Ishmael from the slave girl Hagar, Israel into the bondage of the law. Hagar corresponds to Old Covenant Jerusalem, in bondage. In contrast, Isaac and Jesus were born of promise. Isaac, born of Sarah who corresponds to the New Covenant, was a type of Jesus. (See Galatians 4:22-31.)

In Genesis 22, God told Abraham to go the land of Moriah and offer Isaac on the mountain the Lord tells him. The mountain where the Lord told Abraham to go is the same location where Solomon's temple was built nearly 1000 years later. That temple provided a type of Jesus. That same temple hosted a great multitude of sacrifices and procedures, each of which also served as a picture of Jesus.

Isaac was to foreshadow Jesus by being offered as a sacrifice at the same location that will later provide innumerable sacrifices that also foreshadow Jesus. Not only so, but Isaac also carried the wood on his back en route to the location of his sacrifice (Genesis 22:6) just as Jesus carried the wood on His back en route to the location of His sacrifice (John 19:17).

## Ch. 10: Discovering the Mysterion in Genesis

Isaac went all the way to laying on the wood to be offered as a sacrifice. At the moment Abraham was about to accomplish the offering, the Lord spoke to Abraham and told him to stop. At this point, the analogy of Isaac representing Jesus shifts as the goat then symbolizes Jesus and Isaac represents us, the ransomed.

As a result of Abraham's willingness to sacrifice Isaac, God promised:

> I will surely bless you, and I will surely multiply your offspring as the stars of heaven and as the sand that is on the seashore. And your offspring shall possess the gate of his enemies, and in your offspring shall all the nations of the earth be blessed, because you have obeyed my voice." (Gen 22:17-18)

As a result of Jesus' willingness to provide Himself as a ransom, His offspring shall surely be multiplied as the stars of heaven and the sand on the seashore (Gal. 3:29). Jesus' offspring will consist of members from all nations of the earth because He was obedient to the voice of His Father, doing all that God gave Him to do (John 17:4).

Better yet, Galatians 3:16 informs us that Abraham's offspring is singular, and it is Christ. Let us restate Genesis 22:17-18 and insert Jesus for each occasion of "your offspring":

> ...I will surely multiply Jesus as the stars of heaven and as the sand that is on the seashore. And Jesus shall possess the gate of his enemies, and in Jesus shall all the nations of the earth be blessed, because Jesus obeyed God's voice...

**THE LIFE OF JOSEPH**

The events pertaining to Joseph foreshadow Jesus in two phases of Joseph's life. First of all, let's get to know Joseph.

Joseph was the 11th of 12 sons of Jacob. Joseph was Jacob's favorite son because he was the firstborn of Jacob's true love, Rachel. For this reason, Joseph's 10 older brothers were jealous of Joseph and they hated him. To show Jacob's love for Joseph he made him in a robe of many colors.

Joseph was a shepherd boy and at age 17 he had a dream that indicated that his brothers would bow down to him. That made his brothers despise him even more. He had another dream. This time the sun, moon, and stars were bowing down to him; the eleven stars being his brothers and the sun and moon representing his father and mother. His brothers' hatred for him intensified.

One day, Jacob sent Joseph to where his brothers had been pasturing Jacob's flock. His brothers saw him coming and they conspired against him to kill him. When Joseph got to them, they stripped him of his robe and threw him in a pit to leave him for dead.

Before we discuss Joseph any further, let's examine a pattern that can be seen throughout the Old Testament. This recurring pattern looks something like the diagram to the right, somewhat reminiscent of a cardiogram. From where the line starts at the left, it suddenly drops to the bottom and then rises to settle at a plane higher than where it began. This diagram reflects the events pertaining to the gospel of Jesus Christ.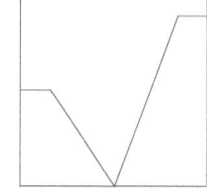

The plane on which the line begins at the left represents Jesus' earthly life. Death and burial sent Him to the depths of the grave. Then sprung forth resurrection life as Jesus lives again at a higher plane in His resurrected body than where He began. Sometimes the pattern we find in the Old Testament is cyclical, which means it doesn't necessarily reflect being raised to a higher plane. Take the recurring cycle of the Judges, for example.

Nonetheless, the consistent part of the pattern is that there is a depth to low places followed by an ascent to places of restoration (or beyond). This is a pattern that we can see throughout the Old Testament, even in the narratives, like in the life of Joseph for example.

Let's revisit what we've seen thus far about Joseph. Joseph was Jacob's favorite son. Jacob gave him a glorious robe, as if to say "this is my beloved son, with whom I am well pleased" (Matt. 3:17). Joseph, a shepherd (like Jesus the Great Shepherd), wore this colorful robe to display the glory of his father's love for him (see John 17:24). Although it's true that Joseph's brothers would one day be bowing before him to plead for his favor, it's ultimately Jesus whom all mankind will bow before (Phil. 2:10).

Joseph was sent out to the field where his brothers were, and "his own [brothers] received him not" (John 1:11 KJV). They threw Joseph into the pit as good as dead (which was to serve as his grave), just as Jesus went to the grave.

## Ch. 10: Discovering the Mysterion in Genesis

But Joseph's brother Judah spoke up, and Joseph was lifted up out of the grave; Joseph would live again!

Joseph's brothers stained the robe with goat blood to make it look like a wild animal devoured him. The stained robe arrived to Jacob, symbolizing the glory of the Father (which is His Son) having been marred with blood.

Of course, Joseph's second chance at life began as a slave, which isn't what we would call glorious living. Therefore, Joseph's rising out of the pit unto newness of life is where the first portion of Joseph's life resembling Jesus ends. The second portion of Joseph's life that resembled Jesus began as Joseph was being taken off to Egypt.

Joseph was sold as a slave in Egypt to Potiphar. Like Jesus, Joseph was an alien in his new land which was not his previous habitat. Like Jesus, Joseph was given glory in his homeland, the glory given to him by his father. However, Joseph had become a slave in Egypt, and, having been emptied of the glory he had previously known, like Jesus, he took the form of a servant (see Ph. 2:7).

Joseph began the Egypt portion of his life in bondage. Similarly, Jesus was born under the law (Gal. 4:4).

Recognize the continued similarities between Joseph and Jesus in Genesis 39:2-6. The Lord was with Joseph. All that Joseph did was blessed by God. Joseph found favor in the sight of his master. Therefore, like Jesus, Joseph "increased in wisdom...and in favor with God and man" (Luke 2:52).

Joseph was put in charge of all that his master had. Likewise, Jesus said to His Father, "...you have given [me] authority over all flesh..." (John 17:2a).

Like Jesus, Joseph was falsely accused of a crime he didn't commit (Gen. 39:7-20); both receiving accusations based on false testimonies that left them naked and shamed (Gen. 39:15; Luke 18:32). Just as Jesus went to the depths of the grave as a result of the false accusations, so too did Joseph go to the depths of prison.

After a series of circumstances, Pharaoh "brought [Joseph] out of the pit" (Gen. 41:14; cf. Gen. 37:28). Pharaoh praised Joseph that there are none as wise as him (41:39) and granted him authority over his kingdom. Pharaoh gave Joseph his signet ring, clothed him in fine linen and put on him a gold chain necklace. Joseph was given the kingdom's #2 chariot to designate that he was second in command and the people were called to "bow the knee" to him.

Then Pharaoh gave Joseph a bride. She birthed two sons to Joseph.

Joseph called the name of the firstborn Manasseh. "For," he said, "God has made me forget all my hardship and all my father's house." The name of the second he called Ephraim, "For God has made me fruitful in the land of my affliction." (Genesis 41:51-52)

Finally, when the famine came, all the people came to Joseph to receive grain so that they might live.

Before Joseph arrived, Egypt was already established as the greatest kingdom in the world as they knew it. After the famine came, Egypt's prominence was even more definitive. All the neighboring countries and foreign lands were so deprived by the famine that they sold what they had to Egypt in exchange for food. Wealth of the entire surrounding region funneled into Egypt under Joseph's control. Egypt got richer while everyone else around it got poorer.

Without question, Pharaoh was the most powerful man in the world; the ruler of the world's greatest kingdom. Joseph was given authority over everything Pharaoh had. Joseph entered his service to the most powerful man in the world at the age of 30. With Pharaoh's signet ring, being his right-hand man, Joseph's decisions and power made him the most influential man in the world.

Jesus entered His service to God, His public ministry beginning at His baptism, at the age of 30. He has since been the most influential Person in the world.

After Jesus was brought out of the pit of the grave, "all authority on heaven and earth was given to [Him]" (Matt. 28:18). Jesus ascended to sit at the right hand of the most powerful One in the universe. God is omnipotent, omniscient, and sovereign over all creation. To God belong all glory and honor and power (Rev. 4:11). Pharaoh's bestowing of glory and authority in his kingdom to Joseph is symbolic of God the Father's bestowing of glory and authority in His kingdom to Jesus (cf. Dan. 7:13-14).

Jesus is the One to be praised as being most wise, there are none as wise as Him. To Jesus has been given the signet ring of God's kingdom. God said to Jesus, "You shall be over my house" (cf. Gen. 41:40). When Jesus appeared to John, He was "clothed with a long robe and with a golden sash around his chest" (Rev. 1:13). All the people will "bow the knee" to Jesus (Phil. 2:10).

After Jesus ascended to the right hand of God, at Pentecost God the Father began the process of giving Jesus a bride. Jesus' bride is still being formed 2000

## Ch. 10: Discovering the Mysterion in Genesis

years later. Just as Pharaoh gave Joseph a bride, God the Father is giving Jesus a bride.

Joseph had two sons. Manasseh means "making to forget." Ephraim means "making fruitful."

The glory given the ascended Jesus made him to no longer recount the suffering He experienced. Rather, Jesus was "made to forget" all his hardship. Jesus endured the cross, despising the shame, because of the joy that was set before Him (Heb. 12:2). Through His joy of having been raised and ascended and now securing for Himself a bride, Jesus has "forgotten" (figuratively) the anguish of His suffering.

God has made Jesus to be "fruitful" in the land of His affliction. Jesus was afflicted and suffered on earth. This same earth is where Jesus is being fruitful and multiplying Himself by indwelling a bride that is being prepared for Him.

Sin brings death. Famine brings death. Just as famine was spread all around the land, sin has been spread like a spiritual famine throughout the world. Just as people came to Joseph to be nourished and live (Gen. 41:56-57), only by coming to Jesus may a person be truly nourished and live (John 10:10).

Jesus alone provides nourishment that gives life (John 6:33). Joseph gave bread so that people might live, victorious over the famine. Jesus gives bread from heaven that people may live, victorious over sin.

Jesus gives bread from heaven. Jesus *is* the bread from heaven. Jesus gives of Himself so that we may have life. Despite our sin, which brings death, Jesus gives life. Despite the famine, which brought death, Joseph provided life and sustenance.

Jesus has opened the storehouses, and He gives life! Praise Jesus!

These listed examples have been among the most central themes to the metanarrative of Genesis. There may be more specific details available to consider upon further unpeeling of each layer, as well as many other cases that could be identified as containing the hidden truth of Christ, yet were unmentioned in this chapter, such as the persons of Enoch, Melchizedek, and Jacob. It is not possible to exhaust every detail of God's glorious *mysterion*.[6]

---

[6] These topics and others are presented with great detail in a fascinating work by Samuel Mather titled *The Figures or Types of the Old Testament By Which Christ and the Heavenly Things of the Gospel Were Preached and Shadowed to the People of God of Old*, published in 1705.

# Chapter 11:
# Discovering the Mysterion in the Wilderness

The first several chapters of Exodus play more of a role of the *mysterion* in terms of the metanarrative of the history of Israel than in the minutiae of the text. Let's observe the overarching storyline.

## THE EXODUS

After Joseph and his brothers settled in Egypt, their descendants were put into arduous service by the Egyptians. After Israel had spent more than 400 years in Egypt, the Lord called Moses to go before Pharaoh to ask to let Israel go. The Lord performed many signs and wonders through Moses and the plagues. The last of these signs and wonders was the killing of the firstborn in Egypt while the Israelites participated in the Passover.

The Israelites were led out to the Red Sea. When they saw the Egyptian armies approaching, they felt trapped and were fearful. They cried "Is it because there are no graves in Egypt that you have taken us away to die in the wilderness?" (Ex. 14:11). They considered themselves as good as dead & buried. Of course, the Lord parted the sea. Israel passed through to the other side of the sea to enter new life, freed from bondage while the enemy is destroyed.

Israel was led to Mount Sinai. Moses went up the mountain for 40 days. He returned to give the Law to the people. They have already been led astray into idolatry. As a consequence, 3000 men died (Ex. 32:28).

The Jewish feast of Pentecost was a celebration of the giving of the Law, the Law being the agent of the Old Covenant. Of course, on the celebration of Pentecost following Jesus' ascension was the day the Lord gave to the people the Spirit, the agent of the New Covenant. On the day that the Law, the ministry of death (2 Cor. 3:7), was given 3000 men died. On the day that the Spirit was given, the ministry of life, 3000 men were saved.

Before the outpouring of the Spirit on Pentecost, the resurrected Jesus appeared for 40 days. Prior to that was His substitutionary atonement via His death, burial, and resurrection. Before that, He performed many signs & wonders in the form of miracles. Prior to Christ's earthly ministry there were more than 400 silent years between Malachi and John the Baptist. There was no recorded revelation from God during those 400 years, just as there was no recorded revelation from God in the 400 years between Joseph and Moses.

Following the giving of the Law at Mount Sinai, Israel wandered the wilderness. These 40 years served as a transition period between Egypt and the Promised Land. In these 40 years, they were no longer in bondage to Egypt. However, the attitude of those who were in Egypt remained among them. There were grumblers and complainers to the extent that out of more than 600,000 men who entered the wilderness at least age 20, only two of them saw the Promised Land; the rest died off in the wilderness. It was a whole new generation who was led by Joshua to enter the Promised Land. All but two men who entered the Promised Land were either born in the wilderness or were youths when they entered the wilderness.

Following the giving of the Spirit at Pentecost, there was a 40-year transition period until the Old Covenant ways died off with permanence. A mindset of the prior ways of bondage to the Law was still among them. The old ways continued, in err, after the giving of the Spirit. Although the veil was torn at Jesus' Crucifixion, the sacrifices continued, Old Covenant practices remained; until, that is, the Lord brought an end to the Old Covenant people and their Old Covenant practices in AD 70 via the Roman armies' destruction of Jerusalem. The "old" generation continued after AD 30 until the 40-year transition period ended with Jerusalem's destruction in AD 70. Just as there was a 40-year transition period until the final removal of the ways of those who came out of Egypt, there was a 40-year transition period from the time the Old Covenant was fulfilled by Jesus until the Old Covenant practices were done away with for good.

| Order of Events | Old Covenant | New Covenant |
|---|---|---|
| 400 "Silent" Years | Joseph to Moses | Malachi to John the Baptist |
| Signs & Wonders | Performed through Moses | Performed by Jesus |
| Atonement | Passover | Crucifixion of Jesus |
| Burial | As good as dead (Ex. 14:11) | Burial of Jesus |
| New Life | Passing through the Red Sea | Resurrection of Jesus |
| 40 Days | Moses on Sinai | Resurrected Jesus on earth |
| Agent of the Covenant | The Law | The Spirit |
| 3000 men | 3000 killed | 3000 saved |
| 40 Years of Transition | Until Promised Land | Until AD 70 |

Israel's exodus from Egypt foreshadows our deliverance from sin through Jesus. Israel's slavery in Egypt represents the bondage of our slavery to sin. We

*Ch. 11: Discovering the Mysterion in the Wilderness*

were delivered from that bondage by a great work wrought by God. Just as the Passover provided deliverance for the people of God and the crossing of the Red Sea on dry ground was God's miraculous intervention to provide victory over their bondage to Egypt, the Crucifixion provided deliverance for the people of God (setting the captives free) and the Resurrection was God's miraculous intervention to provide victory over our bondage to sin (newness of life).

Dear sisters and brothers, our bondage to sin is a victory that has been won! Israel's flight from Egypt foreshadows our freedom from sin. We have been delivered and are no longer in the grip of sin's bondage. We are free from the bondage to sin!

The words of encouragement offered by Moses when Israel looked at the Egyptian armies could be shared to us today when we are discouraged by looking at our sin: "Fear not, stand firm, and see the salvation of the Lord, which he work[ed] for you [on the day of the Crucifixion and Resurrection]. For [the bondage to sin that] you see today, you shall never see again" (Ex. 14:13).

The victory is already secure! The battle we fight against sin has already been won! We have been cleansed by the blood of Jesus and have been raised to new life with Him. Let us walk in that cleansing and in that life this very day!

When we look upon our sin, let us remember that Jesus has already fought the victory over our sin. We may rest securely in the Blood and Life of Jesus. Jesus has done it all! "It is finished."

"The Lord will fight for you, and you have only to be silent" (Ex. 14:14).

**PASSOVER**

The Passover is possibly the most widely-known foreshadowing of Jesus in the Scriptures. Most Christians do already see the Passover as a depiction of Jesus; it would be a rare Christian who does not see the Passover as depicting Jesus' atoning work. What might surprise people is the extent to which the rest of the Old Testament foreshadows Jesus much like the commonly accepted Passover account does. Because of the widespread acceptance that the Passover foreshadowed Jesus, we won't spend all that much time on it.

Each Israelite household was to take a lamb without blemish and kill it (Ex. 12:1ff). The blood of the lamb was to be placed on the doorposts of the house. They were to eat unleavened bread and bitter herbs. When the Lord saw the blood, He passed over that house and did not kill the firstborn.

Jesus is the true Lamb of God (John 1:29). He was without blemish. Jesus was sacrificed so that His blood would cover us. Only by being covered by the blood of God's sacrificial lamb, Jesus, can a person's sins be passed over.

Leaven represents sin. Jesus was without sin. They ate unleavened bread to represent Jesus' sinlessness.

The bitter herbs represent suffering. The Israelites suffered bitterly in their slavery to Egypt; Jesus suffered bitterly in His path to and on the Cross.

The Passover meal is only to be shared by those in covenant with God; no outsider, or foreigner, shall eat of it (Ex. 12:42). Only the slaves who have been circumcised may eat the meal (i.e., only the regenerate partake in the spiritual Passover). They were not to break the bones of the Passover lamb, just as Jesus, the true Passover Lamb (1 Cor. 5:7), was sacrificed without any of His bones being broken.

Jesus is the Passover Lamb of God who has been sacrificed to take away the sins of the world. Praise Jesus!

**MANNA**

When Israel sojourned the wilderness, the Lord provided for the sustenance of His people by giving them manna. The Lord called it "bread from heaven" (Ex. 16:4).

Each morning, manna appeared on the ground. Each person was to collect a jar full of manna for each person of their family. If they tried to store it, the next morning it spoiled. Each day's manna was sufficient for that day. Today's manna was not good for tomorrow; tomorrow's manna would be sufficient for tomorrow's need. Amazingly, all were adequately filled each day with no lack, no waste, and no leftovers.

Certainly, God was pleased to provide for His people in the wilderness, but the manna predominately served as a *mysterion*. The hidden truth of the manna is that it foreshadowed Jesus. Jesus is the true manna, the true bread from heaven.

> Our fathers ate the manna in the wilderness; as it is written, 'He gave them bread from heaven to eat.'" Jesus then said to them, "Truly, truly, I say to you, it was not Moses who gave you the bread from heaven, but my Father gives you the true bread from heaven. For the bread of God is he who comes down from heaven and gives life to the world." They said to him, "Sir, give us this bread always." Jesus said to them, "I am the

## Ch. 11: Discovering the Mysterion in the Wilderness

> bread of life; whoever comes to me shall not hunger, and whoever believes in me shall never thirst. (John 6:31-35)

Eating of the manna provided sustenance for the day. Eating of the "true bread from heaven" provides perfect sustenance. The sustenance that Jesus provides causes one to no longer hunger nor thirst. The sustenance that Jesus provides gives life! He shares His divine life with those who feast upon Him. Those who eat the true bread from heaven shall never die.

> I am the bread of life. Your fathers ate the manna in the wilderness, and they died. This is the bread that comes down from heaven, so that one may eat of it and not die. I am the living bread that came down from heaven. If anyone eats of this bread, he will live forever. And the bread that I will give for the life of the world is my flesh." (John 6:48-51)

Jesus gave His own body so that we may have life! His body was the bread that was broken for us (1 Cor. 11:23-24).

Those who depend on the Bread of Life for their sustenance are fully satisfied. Like the manna, there is no lack, there is no spoil. The bread from heaven is perfectly sufficient!

> This is the bread that came down from heaven, not like the bread the fathers ate, and died. Whoever feeds on this bread will live forever." (John 6:58)

Jesus is perfectly sufficient for each person who eats of Him. From feasting upon Jesus, we receive of His life which is Divine life and eternal life. Praise Jesus! The true manna!

### WATER FROM THE ROCK

As Israel continued its wilderness journey, they came to Rephidim, where there was no water for the people. They grumbled against Moses, blaming him for bringing them to the wilderness to kill them. Moses appealed to God and God, of course, had a plan to provide for them. Moses struck the rock and water came out of it for the people to drink.

The rock was Christ. How do I know this? "...the Rock was Christ" (1 Cor. 10:4). That's how.

Paul wrote that they "all drank the same spiritual drink" and that the drink came from a spiritual rock. It was spiritual drink and a spiritual rock. Of course, there was a physical drink and a physical rock. The physical drink nourished the physical bodies of the people. The physical drink came from a physical rock. But Paul indicates that there is more to the story.

Paul does not state that Christ was the physical rock; he states that they drank from a spiritual rock and the spiritual rock was Christ. Paul is making the point that this is another example of the *mysterion*. "These things took place as examples (*typos*) for us" (1 Cor. 10:6). Israel was nourished by water from the rock so that *we* (believers in Christ) could see Israel's experience as a foreshadow of the nourishment we receive from Jesus. The physical water and rock was a type; Jesus is the fulfillment.

The rock was struck, from it came water to nourish God's people. Jesus was struck, from the crucifixion came the provision for God's people.

Jesus contrasted the physical water that nourishes people physically with the spiritual water that nourishes people spiritually.

> Jesus said to her, "Everyone who drinks of this water will be thirsty again, but whoever drinks of the water that I will give him will never be thirsty again. The water that I will give him will become in him a spring of water welling up to eternal life." (John 4:13-14)

Jesus provides living water, of which the rock at Rephidim served as a picture. The hidden truth of the water flowing from the rock is the truth of Jesus.

Praise Jesus!

## A HOLY NATION

Israel was led to the wilderness of Sinai, and they camped next to the mountain (Ex. 19:1-2). This is the message that the Lord told Moses to give to Israel:

> You yourselves have seen what I did to the Egyptians, and how I bore you on eagles' wings and brought you to myself. Now therefore, if you will indeed obey my voice and keep my covenant, you shall be my treasured possession among all peoples, for all the earth is mine; and you

## Ch. 11: Discovering the Mysterion in the Wilderness

> shall be to me a kingdom of priests and a holy nation. These are the words that you shall speak to the people of Israel." (Exo 19:4-6)

God recalls to Israel what He has done for her. Then God assures them that all they have to do is obey God's voice and keep His covenant. Upon doing so, their reward would be that they will be God's treasured possession. They will be "a kingdom of priests" to God, and a "holy nation."

One problem: we all know that Israel failed to obey God's voice and keep His covenant. That's where the *mysterion* comes in. More particularly, that's where Jesus comes in.

Jesus is the only one who has truly been obedient to God and kept covenant with Him (John 14:31). Ultimately, it is Jesus who is God's most "treasured possession among the peoples," and all those who are immersed into Jesus are also God's treasured possession.

> But you are a chosen race, a royal priesthood, a holy nation, a people for his own possession, that you may proclaim the excellencies of him who called you out of darkness into his marvelous light. (1Pe 2:9)

Peter wrote these words to believers in Jesus. Those whom God has transferred from the kingdom of darkness into the kingdom of His Son (Col. 1:13) are His treasured possession.

What appeared on the surface to be a promise to a physical nation is actually fulfilled in Jesus and, by extension, to a spiritual nation who has been united with Jesus. God's kingdom of priests is not a physical nation, it is a spiritual nation. God's holy nation is not an ethnic people, it is a spiritual people, a spiritual nation of people who have been made holy by the atoning work of Jesus.

Israel disobeyed God and broke covenant with Him. Thus, it is not ethnic Israel that receives the blessing of being God's treasured possession. It is a spiritual nation who are a royal priesthood, a holy nation, God's treasured possession. We observe God's words to ethnic Israel at the foot of Mount Sinai and in them we can see the *mysterion* that the promises are fulfilled in those who make their encampment at Mount Zion.

> For you have not come to what may be touched, a blazing fire and darkness and gloom and a tempest and the sound of a trumpet and a voice whose words made the hearers beg that no further messages be spoken to them. For they could not endure the order that was given, "If even a beast touches the mountain, it shall be stoned." Indeed, so terrifying was the sight that Moses said, "I tremble with fear." **But you have come to Mount Zion** and to the city of the living God, the heavenly Jerusalem, and to innumerable angels in festal gathering, and to the assembly of the firstborn who are enrolled in heaven, and to God, the judge of all, and to the spirits of the righteous made perfect, and to Jesus, the mediator of a new covenant, and to the sprinkled blood that speaks a better word than the blood of Abel. (Heb 12:18-24)

The writer to the Hebrews presents Mount Sinai as the physical picture, Mount Zion as the spiritual reality. God's promise of Exodus 19:5-6 is fulfilled in a spiritual nation, those who make their abode in Jesus.

## THE TABERNACLE & ITS FURNISHINGS

The Lord led Moses up Mount Sinai where He revealed to him the Law. Part of what was revealed to Moses was the construction of a tabernacle and its furnishings. The Lord had Moses take a collection of items "from every man whose heart moved him" (Ex. 25:2). This was to make for the Lord "a sanctuary, that I may dwell in their midst" (Ex. 25:8).

Ultimately, it is Jesus who is the sanctuary of the Lord, the dwelling place of God among men. Those who are immersed into Jesus are also members of the sanctuary of the Lord. Believers today are the dwelling pace of God among men.

The wilderness tabernacle has everything to do with Jesus and those who partake in Him. A sanctuary was provided by all whose heart moved to contribute. This is a picture of the kingdom of God displayed in New Covenant realities! All those whose hearts are moved within them today (through the moving of the Spirit), are taking part in constructing the New Covenant tabernacle. We as a people are a sanctuary unto the Lord, a holy people so that the Lord may dwell in our midst.

There is great detail given on how to precisely construct the tabernacle and the elements contained within it. All of it shows the precision with which Jesus is constructing His New Covenant tabernacle.

## Ch. 11: Discovering the Mysterion in the Wilderness

There is much more that could be said about the elements of the tabernacle and their Christological connections than I will be able to address here. I will merely highlight a few key points.

The blue, purple, and scarlet yarns of the tabernacle display the beauty of Jesus. The ark of the covenant, the table for bread, and the altar of incense were made of wood overlaid by pure gold; the wood symbolizing humanity and the pure gold symbolizing divinity. Together, the overlaying of gold upon the wood shows us Jesus; the purity of divinity being overlaid upon humanity.[7]

The items contained within the ark each depict Jesus. The manna, of course, represents Jesus. Aaron's staff that budded represents Jesus; life coming from that which did not have life (i.e., the Resurrection). The tablets of the covenant also represent Jesus, the true lawgiver, giving the law of love (John 15:12).

The bread on the table represents Jesus, the true bread. The light from the lampstand represents Jesus, the true light. Both the bread and the oil for the light were to be offered in perpetuity, representing the sustaining life of Jesus.

Note that the elements contained within the Holy Place were overlaid with pure gold; however, the elements just outside the Holy Place were made of bronze: the bronze altar and the bronze basin.

The altar is where sacrifices were performed. Of course, the sacrifices represent the one-time sacrifice of Jesus.

The basin was for washing. Whether entering the Holy Place or approaching the altar to perform a sacrifice, the priest first needed to wash his hands and feet. This washing represents the purity of Jesus that allowed Him to be the perfect sacrifice and be the One worthy to enter into the holy places once for all. More so, the basin also represents the cleansing of the forgiveness of sins for God's New Covenant priesthood of all believers. By Jesus we are cleansed and may enter the Holy Place.

Gold is regarded as more valuable than bronze. Gold exceeds bronze in purity. Only in the Holy Place was there gold, and only gold could be seen in the Holy Place.

Bronze was outside the tabernacle. The altar and the basin represent the removal of sin. The ugliness of sin and the ugliness of the brutality of the sacrifice that atoned for sin remained outside the sanctuary. Cleansing and an atoning

---

[7] See Milt Rodriguez' *The Community Life of God: Seeing the Godhead as the Model for All Relationships* (2009).

sacrifice are necessary to partake in the sanctuary of God. The Holy Place of God is reserved for those who have entered via washing and atonement. The bronze elements outside the sanctuary represent the atoning and cleansing work that must be accomplished before one may partake in the purity of divinity as the dwelling place of God.

The priestly garments were "for glory and for beauty" (Ex. 28:2). The fabric and the stones display the glory of Jesus and the beauty of Jesus.

On two black stones that the priests wore were written the names of the sons of Israel. Jesus promised to the one who overcomes a white stone with a new name written on it (Rev. 2:17).

On the front of the turban was a plate of gold with the engraving "Holy to the Lord" (Ex. 28:36). It is Jesus' holiness that makes Him "accepted before the Lord" (Ex. 28:38). Only by our being in Jesus and having His righteousness bestowed upon us may we also be considered "Holy to the Lord" and be acceptable before Him.

The veil that separated the Holy Place from the Most Holy Place represents the body of Jesus; the curtain was His flesh (Heb. 10:19). The Most Holy Place is where the ark was kept. Only the high priest could enter the Most Holy Place to offer a sacrifice on behalf of the nation, and that only one time per year. When the veil was torn in two at the Crucifixion of Jesus, access to the Most Holy Place had been opened up because Jesus entered into it one time on behalf of His holy nation so that we may enter into it through Him. When Jesus' body was broken, so too was the veil.

> Therefore, brothers, since we have confidence to enter the holy places by the blood of Jesus, by the new and living way that he opened for us through the curtain, that is, through his flesh, and since we have a great priest over the house of God, let us draw near with a true heart in full assurance of faith, with our hearts sprinkled clean from an evil conscience and our bodies washed with pure water. Let us hold fast the confession of our hope without wavering, for he who promised is faithful. (Heb 10:19-23)

*Ch. 11: Discovering the Mysterion in the Wilderness*

From all these things we are to receive encouragement! From this knowledge we are to have confidence to enter the holy places! We have full assurance knowing that our hearts have been sprinkled clean!

May we, therefore, draw near with a true heart, holding fast to the confession of our hope without wavering. Why? Because He who promised is faithful!

Praise Jesus!

**THE LEVITICAL SYSTEM**
The Levitical system is entirely saturated with pictures of Jesus. All the various forms of sacrifices: the burnt offerings, the grain offerings, the peace offerings, the sin offerings, the guilt offerings; they each point forward to the atoning work of Jesus.

We see in the Levitical system an emphasis on matters pertaining to holiness, cleansing, and purity. Jesus is the personification of them all. The ritualism of the Old Covenant practices of atonement and purification are realized spiritually in the New Covenant by Jesus' work of atonement and His purification of His people.

Not long ago, my 11-year old son decided he would read Leviticus and look for pictures of Jesus. He came back not much later indicating that he had found one. He only had to go as far as the third verse of the book.

> "If his offering is a burnt offering from the herd, he shall offer a male without blemish. (Leviticus 1:3a)

He says, "'A male without blemish.' That's Jesus."

To provide an exhaustive examination of the sacrifices depicting Jesus' one-time offering for sin would be both overwhelming and redundant. Amidst all the purification rites and offerings, we also find a couple examples of the *mysterion* pertaining to the people of God:

> "Thus you shall keep the people of Israel separate from their uncleanness, lest they die in their uncleanness by defiling my tabernacle that is in their midst." (Lev 15:31)

The Old Covenant people of God were to remain clean because the Lord's tabernacle was in their midst. The New Covenant people of God are to remain clean because they *are* the Lord's tabernacle!

> You shall be holy to me, for I the LORD am holy and have separated you from the peoples, that you should be mine. (Lev 20:26)

The Old Covenant people of God were to be holy because the Lord is holy. Peter quoted this verse and applied it to the New Covenant people of God:

> but as he who called you is holy, you also be holy in all your conduct, since it is written, "You shall be holy, for I am holy." (1Pe 1:15-16)

Jesus' fulfillment of the Levitical system could be summarized as such:

> For if the blood of goats and bulls, and the sprinkling of defiled persons with the ashes of a heifer, sanctify for the purification of the flesh, how much more will the blood of Christ, who through the eternal Spirit offered himself without blemish to God, purify our conscience from dead works to serve the living God. (Hebrews 9:13-14)

### THE FEASTS OF THE LORD

In Leviticus chapter 23 is a brief description of the feasts Israel was to perform to the Lord. The first holy convocation mentioned is the weekly Sabbath (Lev. 23:3), the second is the annual Passover (Lev. 23:4-8), and the third is the Feast of Firstfruits (Lev. 23:9-14). Observe how these holy celebrations interconnect when viewed in the context of Jesus.

In the Creation account, God created in six days and rested on the seventh. God's resting on the seventh day provided the impetus for the Sabbath and its day of rest. The spiritual fulfillment of Sabbath rest in the New Covenant is resting in the finished work of Jesus for all who believe (Heb. 4:1-10, 14-16).

The Passover, also addressed previously in this chapter, featured stipulations that determined a lamb of sacrifice be selected on the tenth day of the first month of the Jewish calendar. Four days later, on the fourteenth day of the month, at twilight, the Passover was celebrated.

## Ch. 11: Discovering the Mysterion in the Wilderness

The day following the Passover began the Feast of Unleavened Bread, which lasted seven days. Leaven represents sin. Unleavened bread represents the removal of sin. Seven is the number of completion or perfection. The seven days of unleavened bread represents the perfection of the removal of sin. Only in the Crucifixion of Jesus can sin be completely removed.

Jesus entered Jerusalem at Passion Week on the first day of the week. Four days later, at twilight, Jesus celebrated the Passover meal with His disciples. During that last supper, Jesus broke the bread that represented His broken body and they drank the cup of the New Covenant which represented His shed blood. The following day Jesus was crucified. On the seventh day of the week, Jesus was in the grave. He rested, doing no earthly work. On the eighth day, Jesus rose to become the firstfruits of the new creation (1 Cor. 15:20).

God created the original creation in six days. He rested on the seventh day. He began the work of the new creation on the eighth day (the Resurrection of Jesus).

Circumcision took place on the eighth day. Circumcision was symbolic of New Covenant circumcision of the heart (i.e., regeneration, being made a new creation [see Gal. 6:15]). God's continued work of a new creation, by regenerating a person as spiritually alive, was foreshadowed by circumcision, which took place on the eighth day. The eighth day represents the new creation (Resurrection & regeneration).

Consider Jesus' Passion Week in reverse chronological order. On the eighth day of Passion Week, Jesus was raised as the firstfruits of the new creation. On the seventh day of Passion Week, Jesus rested. On the fifth day of Passion Week, Jesus performed the Passover meal. Four days earlier Jesus entered Jerusalem as God's chosen Passover Lamb, the same day that the Jews selected their lambs for the Passover meal.

Now let's incorporate the Feast of Weeks (Lev. 23:15-22). The Feast of Weeks took place seven sevens (i.e., weeks), plus one day, following the Feast of Firstfruits. Thus, from the Feast of Firstfruits to the Feast of Weeks was 50 days, from which the term Pentecost was derived.

The first instruction mentioned regarding the Feast of Weeks was to "present a grain offering of new grain to the Lord" (Lev. 23:16). On the day of Pentecost following Jesus' ascension, He first began indwelling humans (i.e., presenting a new grain to the Lord).

Recall Jesus' words in John 12:24 regarding grain falling to the earth and dying (signifying His death and burial). If the grain dies and is buried in the ground "it bears much fruit." Grain produces more grain by multiplying more of its kind.

In the New Covenant fulfillment of the Feast of Weeks, Jesus presented a new grain to the Lord by bearing much fruit. Jesus began multiplying on earth. Jesus is the firstfruits of the new creation (see 1 Cor. 15:20, 23). By multiplying, Jesus was adding to the new creation, according to *His* kind.

> Of his own will he brought us forth by the word of truth, that we should be a kind of firstfruits of his creatures. (Jas 1:18)

We, too, who are in Christ, are firstfruits of the new creation along with Jesus (see also Rom. 8:23 & Rev. 14:4). This is because we are a result of Jesus multiplying, producing more of His kind, more of the new creation.

Praise Jesus!

| Theology | Passion Week | Date of month | Passover | Days of Creation | |
|---|---|---|---|---|---|
| Jesus selected as lamb | Jesus entered Jerusalem | Sunday 10th | Select lamb | Day 1 | First Creation |
| | | Monday 11th | | Day 2 | |
| | | Tuesday 12th | | Day 3 | |
| | | Wednesday 13th | | Day 4 | |
| Jesus is our Passover Lamb | Last Supper | Thursday 14th | Meal | Day 5 | |
| Removal of sin | Crucifixion | Friday 15th | Feast of Unleavened Bread ↓ | Day 6 | |
| Sabbath | Grave | Saturday 16th | | Day 7 | Rest |
| Firstfruits | Resurrection | Sunday 17th | | Day 8 | New Creation |

**THE YEAR OF JUBILEE**

The Lord declared that every seventh year was to be a Sabbath year for the land so that the land could be given rest from its labors (Lev. 25:3-4).

With seven representing fullness, completion, perfection, what could be more full, complete, or perfect than to have *seven* sevens? Therefore, for every seven seventh-year Sabbaths there was reason for celebration! A jubilee, if you will.

## Ch. 11: Discovering the Mysterion in the Wilderness

After the completion of every seven sevens, every 50th year was a year of jubilee (Lev. 25:8ff).

The year of jubilee was consecrated to proclaim liberty throughout the land to all its inhabitants. It was a year of restoration. Each inhabitant of the land was to return to their property and their clan in the year of jubilee.

If you sold land to someone else, in the year of jubilee you'd get it back. If you bought land from someone else, in the year of jubilee you'd have to give it back. Thus, the value of the sale of the land was dependent upon how many years remained until the next jubilee. If there were many years until the next jubilee, the price was great. If the years remaining were few, the price was less.

If a person fell under hard times, they could sell property knowing it would eventually be restored to him in the year of jubilee. If the times were so hard for a man that he had to offer himself as a servant, in the year of jubilee he and his family were freed from the hired service. They could return to their clan and had the possession of their fathers restored to them. The crux of the jubilee, therefore, was a celebration of restoration.

The Prophets are saturated with restoration language. Isaiah in particular wrote of the restoration to be had by experiencing the true jubilee:

> The Spirit of the Lord GOD is upon me, because the LORD has anointed me to bring good news to the poor; he has sent me to bind up the brokenhearted, to proclaim liberty to the captives, and the opening of the prison to those who are bound; to proclaim the year of the LORD's favor, (Isa 61:1-2a)

The jubilee can thus be summarized as "good news to the poor." The brokenhearted are healed in the jubilee. Liberty is proclaimed to captives! Those who have been bound are released and the eyes of the blind opened (see Septuagint). This was all to proclaim the year of the Lord's favor; His blessing of restoration in the year of jubilee.

A long time ago, there was a man who was raised Jewish, accustomed to attending the synagogue every Sabbath. One day he stood up to read in the very synagogue where he had grown up. He took the scroll of Isaiah, searched for and found the part where Isaiah wrote of the jubilee. He read it, gave the scroll back to the attendant, and sat down. Everybody stared at him. To break the awkward silence, the man said "Today this Scripture has been fulfilled in your hearing."

If you weren't already familiar with Luke 4:16-21, you are now. Jesus proclaimed Himself the fulfillment of the jubilee.

Jesus is the One upon whom the Spirit of the Lord rests. Jesus is the One anointed to bring good news to the poor (in spirit). Jesus is the One who was sent to heal the brokenhearted. Jesus proclaims liberty to those who are held captive (to sin). Jesus opens wide the door of freedom that has imprisoned people. Jesus opened the eyes of the blind (physically) and continues to do so (spiritually).

The year of jubilee proclaimed the Lord's favor or blessing. Ultimately, the Lord's favor or blessing is upon Jesus, God's Anointed One. The "year of the Lord's favor" is fulfilled in a Person. The true jubilee is the Person of Jesus. Jesus is the hidden truth of the semi-centennial celebration.

After seven sevens of Sabbaths was the ultimate Sabbath, the jubilee Sabbath, the Sabbath of restoration. On the surface, Israel was to celebrate every 50th year with great jubilee. The *mysterion* of the jubilee is that sinners are set free in Jesus.

Praise Jesus!

**THE BRONZE SERPENT**

On many occasions, the Israelites complained about their circumstances in the wilderness. On one such occasion, the Lord sent poisonous serpents that bit people; many of them died (Numbers 21:4-6). The people pleaded to Moses for relief, having confessed their sins. The Lord told Moses to make a serpent and set it on a pole, promising that all who look at it will live.

> So Moses made a bronze serpent and set it on a pole. And if a serpent bit anyone, he would look at the bronze serpent and live. (Numbers 21:9)

We have all been bitten by sin. Jesus was lifted up (on the Cross). Anyone who looks upon Him (in faith) has life. Jesus explained this very thing to Nicodemus:

> No one has ascended into heaven except he who descended from heaven, the Son of Man. And as Moses lifted up the serpent in the wilderness, so must the Son of Man be lifted up, that whoever believes in him may have eternal life. (John 3:13-15)

## Ch. 11: Discovering the Mysterion in the Wilderness

The very next verse is John 3:16. Certainly, you already know John 3:16. You may even know that John 3:16 was spoken by Jesus in connection to Moses' lifting of the bronze serpent. Had you realized that the most popular verse in the Bible came as a direct result of Jesus revealing the *mysterion*? Jesus revealed to Nicodemus the hidden truth of what was described in Numbers 21:9, that it was about Him (cf. John 5:39).

Many believers admit to having a difficult time reading through certain portions of the Pentateuch (the first five books, the books of the Law). Perhaps delight could be introduced to such readings by utilizing a perspective that peels back the layers to reveal the hidden truths that are contained therein. Read not with a veiled perspective, but as unveiled by viewing the Pentateuch through the lens of Christ (2 Cor. 3:14-16).

# Chapter 12:
# Discovering the Mysterion in the Narratives

**THE CONQUEST**

Throughout the narratives in the Old Testament, sometimes the *mysterion* is in the details, other times it is simply in the grand overarching storyline. Take the Conquest, for example.

Joshua's leading of God's Old Covenant people into the Promised Land is a foreshadowing of God's New Covenant people entering salvation rest through Jesus. Jesus leads us into the place of God's blessings just as Joshua led Israel into the place of God's blessings. Israel was a physical nation that was promised physical blessings; those of us who are in Jesus consist of a spiritual nation to whom is promised spiritual blessings.

Joshua's role of leading the great conquest of the Promised Land provided a shadow of Jesus, whose role is to lead a victorious conquest over sin into God's eternal Promised Land. Even the name Joshua was derived from the same as Jesus' Aramaic name, Yeshua, which means "the Lord saves."

Most of the book of Joshua contributes to the overarching narrative of the Scriptures that depict the victorious work of Jesus. But as we've seen previously, Joshua chapter 7 provides a picture of Jesus' atoning work in the details of a specific account.

Attempting to identify every account which provides details that depict Jesus are far too numerous to exhaust. I will also acknowledge that I am not able to identify or appreciate every such account. The *mysterion* runs far too deep to fully grasp every occurrence. The primary point, whether or not we can see Jesus in the details of the historical narratives, is to understand that the Scriptures do exactly what Jesus said they do. The Scriptures testify about Jesus (John 5:39). This includes the book of Joshua.

**THE JUDGES**

The time period of the judges depicts a cyclical pattern. This pattern is widely understood: Israel falls away from the Lord to follow other gods, the Lord brings oppression, the people cry out to the Lord for deliverance from their oppression, the Lord provides a deliverer (a judge) to defeat the oppression, and finally the people have rest (3:11, 30; 5:11; 8:28). Until, that is, the next time they fall away, and then the whole cycle starts over again.

Each instance of this pattern reflects the overarching narrative of the gospel message: man (Adam) fell into sin resulting in spiritual oppression (bondage to sin), we have a desperate need for God's deliverance, God sent a deliverer (Jesus) to defeat the oppression of sin, and those who have been delivered find rest.

Every time the book of Judges repeats the cycle, it is repeating a foreshadowing of the gospel message. Each judge whom God raised up to deliver His people are emblematic of Jesus. Jesus is the two-edged sword of Ehud (chapter 3) and the tent peg of Jael (chapter 4). Jesus is the broken jars that, after having been smashed, cast forth light that puts the enemy into confusion (chapter 7). Jesus is the strong man who broke the ropes that appeared to have him bound until the Spirit of God came upon him to provide him new life and victory over his enemy (15:13-15). The same strong man's greatest accomplishment came at the occasion of his death (16:30).

Israel went to war with the tribe of Benjamin (20:19ff). On the first day, Judah (Jesus' tribe) suffered defeat. On the second day, the defeat continued and there was also much weeping and a solemn tone. But victory came *on the third day*!

## THE BOOK OF RUTH

Although the Book of Ruth is named after Ruth, it is Boaz who depicts Jesus. Ruth, his bride, depicts the bride of Jesus.

Boaz was "a worthy man" (Ruth 2:1). With eager anticipation, Boaz fulfilled his role as a kinsman redeemer. Boaz means "fleetness" and Ruth means "friend." Boaz acted swiftly, with fleetness of foot, to redeem Ruth, who in marriage would become his dearest friend. He was to spread his covering over her, for he is a redeemer (3:9). Likewise, Jesus, who "for the joy that was set before him" (Heb. 12:2), provided a covering for us by redeeming us, and He calls us friend (John 15:13-15).

Ruth was of a foreign land, a stranger to the people of Boaz. Jesus reached out to a people unlike Himself and made them His bride. Although she was a Gentile, who the Jews generally viewed as filthy, unclean, and unholy, Ruth was deemed to be "a worthy woman" (3:11). We are all born in a filthy, unclean, unholy state before God; those who have been reconciled by Jesus are now deemed righteous, even "worthy" (2 Thess. 1:5, 11; Rev 3:4).

Naomi's husband was named Elimelech, which means "My God is King." Boaz redeemed Ruth as well as Elimelech's inheritance (4:9-10). Jesus redeemed an inheritance in the name of God who is king!

*Ch. 12: Discovering the Mysterion in the Narratives*

Naomi was not a barren woman but the death of her husband and two sons made it as though she was barren because there was none to carry on her inheritance. When Ruth conceived by Boaz, the women treated it as though Naomi's womb had been reopened:

> Then the women said to Naomi, "Blessed be the LORD, who has not left you this day without a redeemer, and may his name be renowned in Israel! He shall be to you a restorer of life and a nourisher of your old age, for your daughter-in-law who loves you, who is more to you than seven sons, has given birth to him." (Ruth 4:14-15)

The Lord has not left us without a redeemer. He has given us Jesus! The name of Jesus is renowned among God's people! Jesus is to us a restorer of life!

Lord Jesus, spread Your covering over Your servants, for You are a Redeemer!

**BARRENNESS**
There is a pattern that can be seen throughout the Old Testament of a barren womb that gives birth to a child of promise. When a child is born from a womb previously regarded as barren, the barrenness of the womb is emphasized to project the theme of something coming out of nothing. More so, something *special* coming out of nothing.

In God's creation, something came out of nothing. There was darkness (which is not a thing, but the absence of a thing [light]) to which God said "Let there be light." Behold, there was light. Something came out of nothing.

As the book of 1 Samuel continues the narrative from Judges, Hannah had no children; "the Lord had closed her womb" (1 Sam. 1:5). The Lord had purpose in making Hannah's womb barren. The Lord gave a significant trial to Hannah so that something special would come from her womb. Because of her barrenness, Hannah prayed that if the Lord would provide her a son, she would devote him to be set apart for the Lord's purposes (1 Sam. 1:11).

The Lord opened her womb and she gave birth to Samuel. Samuel served as the 13th and final of the national judges over Israel. He was highly regarded as a man of God and arguably led Israel toward righteousness more than any of the previous judges.

In addition, Samuel served as priest, following the instruction provided in his upbringing by Eli. Samuel also served as prophet, first distributing God's message as a young boy. Thus, Samuel foreshadowed Jesus (who is the ultimate fulfillment of the Old Testament offices of prophet, priest, and king) by serving as prophet, priest, and ruler (judge, i.e. king).

Samuel was regarded as the greatest leader Israel had since Moses died, which was nearly 400 years prior. And it all happened because the Lord brought an ordinary, Israelite woman to a place of miserable desperation because of the barrenness of her womb. God used a barren womb to produce great things!

Of course, Sarah was also barren (Gen. 11:30). Ultimately, she gave birth to the child of promise, Isaac. Isaac's wife Rebekah was barren (Gen. 25:21) and she gave birth to twins. Her two boys, Jacob and Esau, become the foundation of two nations; one of them had confirmed to him the promises God made to Abraham. Rebekah's child of promise, Jacob, also had a wife who was barren (Rachel, Gen. 29:31). Rachel ultimately gave birth as well, and her firstborn was Jacob's most beloved son, Joseph.

Each of the wives of the patriarchs were barren, yet eventually had children. More notably, the children they did have (Isaac, Jacob, and Joseph, in particular) were special offspring, each in their own way providing a foreshadowing of Jesus.

Manoah's wife was barren (Judges 13:2-3) but ultimately gave birth to a special, set apart individual, Samson, who delivered Israel from oppression via great and mighty works. The last prophet of the Old Testament era, John the Baptizer, was born from a womb that was formerly barren (Luke 1:7), proof that nothing is impossible with God (Luke 1:36-37). This too is the significance of Naomi's "barren" womb being revitalized via Ruth (see above); and just a couple generations from Ruth came David, who was symbolic of Jesus.

Isaiah spoke of the blessing that comes from a barren womb giving birth to life:

> "Sing, O barren one, who did not bear; break forth into singing and cry aloud, you who have not been in labor! For the children of the desolate one will be more than the children of her who is married," says the LORD. (Isa 54:1)

*Ch. 12: Discovering the Mysterion in the Narratives*

Life coming from a womb that had been barren depicts something coming out of nothing. A barren womb that gives birth to new life forecasts a theme that has recurring New Covenant fulfillment.

First, a barren womb giving birth to life symbolizes the miracle incarnation of Jesus. Mary, the mother of Jesus, was not barren, but her virgin womb produced the Anointed One of God. From a virgin womb came life; something came from nothing. And it was something very special that came from nothing. Although the life that was produced from barren wombs in the Old Testament accounts occurred as a result of natural relations, the specialness of the blessed womb depicts the miracle birth that was to come in the womb of Mary.

Secondly, something coming from nothing depicts the Resurrection of Jesus. As life came from the dead womb of Hannah and other barren women, the resurrected life of Jesus emerged from the grave, a place that is barren of life.

Thirdly, something coming from nothing depicts the regenerating work of the Spirit to make a sinner alive in Jesus. Our hearts are born in a spiritually barren state. Only the miracle birth of regeneration can bring a person out of spiritual deadness unto spiritual life.

The barrenness of a women's womb in the Old Testament that eventually gave birth to children was more than simply a case of God showing His power over Creation. It was God prefiguring New Covenant realities in Jesus.

Praise Jesus!

**THE ANOINTING**

After the people of Israel requested a king to rule over them, Samuel followed the Lord's instructions to anoint Saul as Israel's first king (1 Sam. 10:1ff). Though Samuel performed the act, it was the Lord who did the anointing. The proof that Saul was anointed by the Lord was that the Spirit of the Lord would come upon him (10:6), and the Spirit did so (10:10).

Being the Lord's anointed meant Saul held a special place in God's favor. However, Saul sinned against the Lord and the Lord thusly rejected him from being king (1 Sam. 15). The Lord has another person in mind to anoint as his favored one: the son of Jesse, David (1 Sam. 16). Samuel anointed David and then the Spirit of the Lord immediately rushed upon David as confirmation of God's favor. The Lord's favor had transferred from Saul to David.

David had great respect for the Lord's anointed, unwilling to harm Saul in the least (1 Sam 24:6, 10; 26:9, 11, 16, 23; 2 Sam. 1:14, 16), despite having already been anointed himself. Observe some of David's writings in the Psalms, what he expresses about the Lord's anointed:

> Great salvation he brings to his king, and shows steadfast love to his anointed, to David and his offspring forever. (Psalm 18:50)

> Now I know that the LORD saves his anointed; he will answer him from his holy heaven with the saving might of his right hand. (Psalm 20:6)

> The LORD is the strength of his people; he is the saving refuge of his anointed. (Psalm 28:8)

> You prepare a table before me in the presence of my enemies; you anoint my head with oil; my cup overflows. (Psalm 23:5)

David celebrated the favor of God that was upon him; his cup of God's blessing overflowed.

The Hebrew word referring to one who is anointed is the source from which the term Messiah is derived. Also, the Greek word that means 'anointed one' is where we get the term Christ. If you can't see where this is going, you haven't been paying attention very well.

Ultimately, it is Jesus who is the Anointed One of God. God's favor is upon Jesus. Observe God's declaration at Jesus' baptism:

> and the Holy Spirit descended on him in bodily form, like a dove; and a voice came from heaven, "You are my beloved Son; with you I am well pleased." (Luke 3:22)

Jesus' baptism was His anointing. Just as was the case with both Saul & David, the Spirit of God immediately descended upon Jesus at the time of His anointing. Both the Spirit and the voice from heaven provided validation that the favor of God was upon Jesus. Jesus is fulfillment of all that pertains to one who is anointed by God, thus His role as Messiah/Christ.

It doesn't stop there. Those to whom Jesus is revealed have also been anointed by God. God's anointing is upon believers!

## Ch. 12: Discovering the Mysterion in the Narratives

> And it is God who establishes us with you in Christ, and has anointed us, and who has also put his seal on us and given us his Spirit in our hearts as a guarantee. (2Co 1:21-22)

Accompanying God's anointing is His Spirit. Those who have been given His Spirit are God's anointed ones. Our cup runneth over. God has anointed us, put His seal upon us, and has given us His Spirit in our hearts as a down deposit for what we are to, one day in the future, receive in totality. God has put His favor upon us!

Certainly, our anointing is not on par with what Jesus was anointed to do (redeem humans from sin), but we are to function as God's anointed ones on earth as we express the true Anointed One through His Spirit who, one day in each of our past, rushed upon us. The anointing of God that we received gives us the spiritual understanding we need to know that the Anointed One abides in us and that we also abide in the Anointed One. John wrote:

> But you have been anointed by the Holy One, and you all have knowledge. ... I write these things to you about those who are trying to deceive you. But the anointing that you received from him abides in you, and you have no need that anyone should teach you. But as his anointing teaches you about everything, and is true, and is no lie--just as it has taught you, abide in him. (1Jo 2:20, 26-27)

We have been anointed to function as Jesus' body on earth. Jesus functions through us, His fellow anointed ones. Jesus is God's ultimate Anointed One, we likewise are God's anointed ones.

Believer, let us live and walk in that anointing! Abide in Him!

### SAUL & DAVID

Saul preceded David as king of Israel. This is emblematic of a theme throughout the Scriptures: the inferior precedes the superior. Saul, the counterfeit king, preceded David, the man after God's own heart.

We see this pattern in the patriarchs. Ishmael preceded Isaac. Ishmael was cast out whereas Isaac received the promise. Esau preceded Jacob, however "the older shall serve the younger" (Gen. 25:23). Esau sold his birthright and Jacob received the blessing.

Likewise, Saul preceded David as king. But the Lord rejected Saul as king, whereas David served as God's *true* king. Even prior to David becoming king "his name was highly esteemed" (1 Sam. 18:30) and Saul was exceedingly jealous (1 Sam 18:8ff).

> And David had success in all his undertakings, for the LORD was with him. And when Saul saw that he had great success, he stood in fearful awe of him. But all Israel and Judah loved David, for he went out and came in before them. (1 Samuel 18:14-16)

That the inferior precedes the superior is reflective of the overarching narrative of redemptive history: Adam preceded Jesus. Adam is the representative head for all of humanity. Adam was made in the image of God. Luke refers to Adam as "the son of God" (Luke 3:38). But Adam proved himself to be a counterfeit. Jesus is the true son of God. Jesus is the true image of God (2 Cor 4:4) and serves as Head of the new humanity (Eph. 1:22 with 2:15).

All of humanity is born into Adam. Adam is our natural head by physical birth. One must be reborn to be in Jesus. Jesus is our supernatural Head by spiritual birth.

The same dynamic applies to the people of God. Physical Israel preceded spiritual Israel. Physical Israel did not receive what was promised (Heb. 11:39). In fact, only a remnant of physical Israel will be saved (Rom. 9:27). In contrast, all of spiritual Israel, those who are in Jesus, will receive the promise ("they shall all know me"; Heb. 8:11).

The inferior Old Covenant preceded the superior New Covenant (2 Cor. 3).

> But as it is, Christ has obtained a ministry that is as much more excellent than the old as the covenant he mediates is better, since it is enacted on better promises. For if that first covenant had been faultless, there would have been no occasion to look for a second. ... In speaking of a new covenant, he makes the first one obsolete. And what is becoming obsolete and growing old is ready to vanish away. (Heb 8:6-7, 13)

## Ch. 12: Discovering the Mysterion in the Narratives

This all emanates from the relationship in contrast of Adam and Jesus, "the last Adam" (1 Cor. 15:45).

Like Adam, Saul was rejected by the Lord and no longer shared in His fellowship. As was said of David (1 Sam. 18:14), Jesus had success in all His undertakings, for the Lord was with Him.

| The inferior precedes the superior | |
|---|---|
| Adam | Jesus |
| First Creation | New Creation |
| Natural Body | Spiritual Body |
| Physical Israel | Spiritual Israel |
| Old Covenant | New Covenant |
| Ishmael | Isaac |
| Esau | Jacob |
| Saul | David |

**DAVID & SOLOMON**

David lived a rather tumultuous life. Even his reign as king was marked with suffering. He endured much conflict and was a man of war.

David's reign was followed by the reign of his son, Solomon. Solomon's reign was a glorious one! Solomon was a man of wealth and wisdom. He reigned during a time of peace. The kingdom of Israel was never as expansive as it was during the reign of Solomon.

The contrast between David and Solomon reflects "the sufferings of Christ and the subsequent glories" (1 Pet. 1:11). David's life resembles the hardships and suffering experienced by the earthly Jesus. The subsequent glorious reign of Solomon resembles the resurrected and victorious Christ.

Among the hardships David experienced:
- Alone as a youth while tending the sheep
- Spears thrown at him from Saul
- Forced to part ways from his best friend
- Felt responsible for the death of many priests (1 Sam. 22:22)
- Sought after by Saul
- Mourned over the deaths of Saul & Jonathan
- Suffered the guilt of his offenses involving Bathsheba
- Suffered the loss of his infant child
- Fled from his rebellious son Absalom
- Cursed by Shimei (2 Sam. 16)
- Mourned Absalom's death (2 Sam. 33)
- Suffered the guilt of his desire to number the people (2 Sam. 24:10)

That's a lot of hardship for one lifetime. It's also the kind of life that can shape one's heart to be a man after God's own heart. David's life of self-denial, in general, and persecution reflected the self-denial and persecution lived by Jesus on earth.

Contrast with the lifestyle and kingdom of Solomon:

> And God said to him, "Because you have asked this, and have not asked for yourself long life or riches or the life of your enemies, but have asked for yourself understanding to discern what is right, behold, I now do according to your word. Behold, I give you a wise and discerning mind, so that none like you has been before you and none like you shall arise after you. (1 Kings 3:11-12)

Solomon was given wisdom that can be compared with no other man. Jesus truly was the wisest person who ever lived. Solomon foreshadowed Jesus because Jesus' personification of wisdom can be compared with no other man.

> I give you also what you have not asked, both riches and honor, so that no other king shall compare with you, all your days. And if you will walk in my ways, keeping my statutes and my commandments, as your father David walked, then I will lengthen your days." (1 Kings 3:13-14)

Because He kept God's statutes and commandments, the kingdom Jesus reigns over has riches and honor and length of days to which every other earthy kingdom is incommensurate.

> Judah and Israel were as many as the sand by the sea. They ate and drank and were happy. Solomon ruled over all the kingdoms from the Euphrates to the land of the Philistines and to the border of Egypt. They brought tribute and served Solomon all the days of his life. (1 Kings 4:20-21)

The people were at peace, numerous, and happy, representing the general state of being for those who abide in Jesus' kingdom. The land Solomon possessed was more expansive than the kingdom of Israel was at any other point in its history. Jesus' kingdom is *most* expansive!

## Ch. 12: Discovering the Mysterion in the Narratives

> And God gave Solomon wisdom and understanding beyond measure, and breadth of mind like the sand on the seashore, so that Solomon's wisdom surpassed the wisdom of all the people of the east and all the wisdom of Egypt. ... And people of all nations came to hear the wisdom of Solomon, and from all the kings of the earth, who had heard of his wisdom. (1 Kings 4:29-30, 34)

Jesus' wisdom surpasses all others. People of all nations come to Jesus and hear His wisdom.

> Now it was in the heart of David my father to build a house for the name of the LORD, the God of Israel. But the LORD said to David my father, 'Whereas it was in your heart to build a house for my name, you did well that it was in your heart. Nevertheless, you shall not build the house, but your son who shall be born to you shall build the house for my name.' Now the LORD has fulfilled his promise that he made. For I have risen in the place of David my father, and sit on the throne of Israel, as the LORD promised, and I have built the house for the name of the LORD, the God of Israel. (1 Kings 8:17-20)

It was in the heart of the earthly Jesus to build a house for the Lord. It was the resurrected and ascended Jesus who did so and continues to do so.

> Thus King Solomon excelled all the kings of the earth in riches and in wisdom. (1 Kings 10:23)

...So does Jesus!

Observe the writings of David and Solomon. David wrote many psalms; several of them dealing with suffering, difficult circumstances, confusion, pain. etc. Solomon wrote books of wisdom with confidence (Proverbs) and beauty (Song of Solomon). Even's Solomon's writing that was filled with questions (Ecclesiastes) was at a higher plane of thought, not a result of hardship. As expressed in Ecclesiastes, Solomon stood above his kingdom, looking out upon the land of his dominion, and wondered what was the point of it all apart from knowing God.

David projects pictures of the crucified Christ; Solomon projects pictures of the glorified Christ.

The trio of Saul, David, and Solomon resemble very closely to the trio of Cain, Abel, and Seth. Cain preceded Abel; Saul preceded David. Cain was rejected by the Lord; Saul was rejected by the Lord. Abel was accepted by the Lord; David was accepted by the Lord. Cain persecuted Abel by murdering him; Saul persecuted David and wholly intended to murder him. Abel signified the crucified Christ; David signified the crucified Christ. Seth replaced Abel; Solomon replaced David. From Seth's lineage came Enosh, when people began to call upon the name of the Lord; from Solomon's lineage came God's Anointed One upon whose name people do call (which was also David's lineage, of course).

Both trios ultimately are symbolic of Adam (fallen humanity) and the crucified and glorified Christ.

| **Counterfeit** | Cain | Saul | Adam |
| **Suffering servant** | Abel | David | Crucified Christ |
| **Replacement** | Seth | Solomon | Resurrected Christ |

## SOLOMON'S TEMPLE

Soon after finishing the building of Solomon's temple and all the furnishings (1 Kings 7:51), the Lord made His presence known (1 Kings 8:1-11). The Lord made His presence known in the temple in such a way that the priests had to evacuate. By the cloud that filled the temple, the Lord was saying: 'I am here.'

> Then Solomon said, "The LORD has said that he would dwell in thick darkness. I have indeed built you an exalted house, a place for you to dwell in forever." (1Ki 8:12-13)

The dwelling place of God: the temple. More specifically, the Most Holy Place where the priests could enter just once a year. And at that, only the high priest. And that, with conditions. The Most Holy Place, and by extension, the entire temple structure, represented the dwelling place of God on earth.

At that time, where would you go to meet God? You'd go to the temple. That's where God took up residence.

We know that God is infinite. He is not constrained by space nor time. It's not like God can be confined within the walls of a building. Solomon acknowledged this during his prayer of dedication:

## Ch. 12: Discovering the Mysterion in the Narratives

> "But will God indeed dwell on the earth? Behold, heaven and the highest heaven cannot contain you; how much less this house that I have built! Yet have regard to the prayer of your servant and to his plea, O LORD my God, listening to the cry and to the prayer that your servant prays before you this day, that your eyes may be open night and day toward this house, the place of which you have said, 'My name shall be there,' that you may listen to the prayer that your servant offers toward this place. And listen to the plea of your servant and of your people Israel, when they pray toward this place. And listen in heaven your dwelling place, and when you hear, forgive. (1Ki 8:27-30)

Solomon's prayer is quite extensive. It begins in verse 23 and extends all the way through verse 53. In his prayer, Solomon 10 times referred to God as abiding in heaven.

We know that God dwells in heaven and is not limited by space, but, symbolically, God's dwelling place on earth was the temple structure. Worshippers would go to the temple to meet God. The temple represented the dwelling place of God for the remainder of the Old Covenant era.

However, that temple is no longer standing. It was torn down. In fact, another temple was built in its place, and then that one was torn down. So, then, where is God's dwelling place on earth today? Where and how does God now dwell on earth?

If the symbolic dwelling place of God in the Old Covenant was the temple, where is the symbolic dwelling place of God in the New Covenant? Of course, the dwelling place of God in the New Covenant is not in a place, but in a people:

> So then you are no longer strangers and aliens, but you are fellow citizens with the saints and members of the household of God, built on the foundation of the apostles and prophets, Christ Jesus himself being the cornerstone, in whom the whole structure, being joined together, grows into a holy temple in the Lord. In him you also are being built together into a dwelling place for God by the Spirit. (Eph 2:19-22)

Believers are the New Covenant temple of God, with Christ as the cornerstone. Christ, in fact, is the true temple of God. There has never been any truer dwelling place of God on earth than Jesus Himself.

Jesus is Emmanuel, meaning 'God with us.' "For in Him the fullness of God dwells bodily" (Col. 2:9). God has never dwelt on earth in any more real way than in the very Person of Jesus.

Jesus is the true dwelling place of God on earth. Jesus is the true temple. "Destroy this temple," Jesus said, "and I will raise it up in three days" (John 2:19).

But as we've already addressed, the New Covenant temple isn't only Jesus. All those who are in Jesus are also being built into the Lord's spiritual temple, "a dwelling place for God." How are we the dwelling place of God? "By the Spirit." Those who partake in union with Jesus become a portion of the dwelling place of God on earth. Being the dwelling place of God on earth provides the impetus for us to live Christ-like. This New Covenant temple is also referred as a city (the New Jerusalem) and as the bride of Jesus.

> And I saw the holy city, new Jerusalem, coming down out of heaven from God, prepared as a bride adorned for her husband. And I heard a loud voice from the throne saying, "Behold, the dwelling place of God is with man. He will dwell with them, and they will be his people, and God himself will be with them as their God… (Rev 21:2-3)

This is not merely a hopeful anticipation for the future. This is a reality now! God dwells in His people *now*, making them His temple.

The Old Covenant temple served as a foreshadowing of Jesus, it pointed forward to Jesus. The New Covenant temple is a reflection of Jesus, intended to resemble Jesus' likeness.

The Old Covenant temple served as a prefiguration of Christ; the New Covenant temple serves as a post-figuration of Christ. To the New Covenant temple, Jesus proclaims "My Name shall be there" (cf 1 Kings 8:29).

> What agreement has the temple of God with idols? For we are the temple of the living God; as God said, "I will make my dwelling among them and walk among them, and I will be their God, and they shall be my people. (2Co 6:16)

## Ch. 12: Discovering the Mysterion in the Narratives

Solomon's temple served as a foreshadowing of Jesus, but also a picture of all those who have been immersed into Jesus. We have become Jesus' dwelling place on earth. "Abide in me, and I in you" (John 15:4). We have been brought into union with Jesus and made stones of the same temple, the dwelling place of God on earth.

Jesus has made His dwelling among us; He will be our God, and we shall be His people.

Praise Jesus!

### ELIJAH'S ASCENSION

Elijah was a prominent prophet of God. The Lord determined "to take Elijah up to heaven" (2 Kings 2:1).

Prior to be taken up, Elijah was sent by the Lord to Bethel. His assistant Elisha journeyed with him. Then Elijah was sent to Jericho. Then the Jordan. After having approached the Jordan, Elijah rolled up his cloak, struck the water with it, and the river parted so that they crossed on dry ground.

Before Elijah was taken up Elisha made one request: "Please let there be a double portion of your spirit on me" (2:9). When Elijah was taken up, Elisha "saw it" and then "he saw him no more" (2:12). After Elijah was taken up, Elisha took up Elijah's cloak, struck the water with it and the river parted again so that Elisha could cross back, again on dry ground.

It was said of Elisha that "the spirit of Elijah rests on Elisha" (2:15). Then Elisha performed a healing of the water in Jericho. During Elisha's subsequent journey some local boys came out of the city and mocked him. The Lord vindicated Elisha by bringing out of the woods a pair of mama bears that mauled the boys. The bears served as God's retributive agents.

The journey Elijah took at the Lord's leading is reminiscent of the initial steps of Israel's conquest of the Promised Land, except in reverse order. The Lord led Joshua and Israel to the Jordan, where the Lord restrained the waters "until all the nation finished passing over the Jordan" on dry ground (Joshua 3:17). Following crossing the Jordan, Israel's journey continued to Jericho, the first city that was conquered. After Jericho fell, Israel advanced to Ai, which was a neighbor town of Bethel.

In summary, Israel went to the Jordan, crossed on dry ground, advanced to Jericho, and then to Ai (next to Bethel). Elijah, in reverse order, went to Bethel, then to Jericho, then to the Jordan where he crossed on dry ground. After Elijah was taken up, Elisha repeated the process: he crossed the Jordan on dry ground, came by Jericho (cf 2:15 & 2:19), and advanced toward Bethel (2:22). Transpiring here is symbolism of a new conquest.

Imagining Elisha standing there watching Elijah being taken up brings to mind the apostles standing there watching Jesus being taken up (Acts 1). Not many days later, the Spirit came upon the apostles at Pentecost (Acts 2). The apostles were granted the power of the Spirit to perform "many wonders and signs" (Acts 2:43).

After Elijah was taken up, Elisha took up Elijah's cloak. Elijah's cloak represented his identity as a prophet of God upon whom the Spirit worked mightily. By taking up Elijah's cloak, Elisha continued Elijah's ministry. At Pentecost, the apostles "took up" Jesus' cloak, so to speak, via the Spirit and they continued Jesus' ministry.

Elisha immediately duplicated Elijah's parting of the Jordan, and went on to perform the healing of water. The apostles duplicated Jesus' wonders and signs (Acts 5:12), including Peter's healing of a lame man (Acts 3). Just as it was evident that "the spirit of Elijah rests on Elisha" (2:15), so too was it evident that the spirit of Jesus rested upon the apostles (Acts 4:13). Perhaps it could also be said of the apostles that they received "a double portion" of the Spirit (cf 2 Kings 2:9).

As the local boys derided Elisha and suffered the consequence of persecuting him, in similar fashion the apostles suffered persecution from the local Jews. Jerusalem suffered the consequence of persecuting Jesus by being mauled by God's retributive agents, the Roman armies, in AD 70. (Persecuting the apostles, and any of Jesus' followers for that matter, was the same as persecuting Jesus [Acts 9:4]). The bears tore 42 lads and the 1st Century Romans sieged Jerusalem for 42 months.

Elisha's continuation of Elijah's ministry parallels the apostles' continuation of Jesus' ministry, which was also the beginning of a new conquest. At Pentecost, Jesus began the new conquest of bringing members of His chosen nation into His promised land. As Elijah and Elisha appeared to undo and then redo the beginning stages of the first, physical conquest, Jesus' new and spiritual conquest is of those upon whom He passes His mantle. Even Elijah's summoning of Elisha is reminiscent of Jesus' calling of His disciples (1 Kings 19:19).

Sisters and brothers, what a blessing and privilege it is to be objects of Jesus' conquest. Jesus triumphed victoriously so that He may win us and we win Him!

## Ch. 12: Discovering the Mysterion in the Narratives

We wear Jesus' cloak, by the Spirit, so that His ministry on earth may be continued through us. May we be ever ready to function in a manner that manifests Jesus.

Praise Jesus!

**RESTORATION FROM CAPTIVITY**

The accounts of Ezra and Nehemiah provide the narrative pertaining to the restoration of Jerusalem. The overarching theme of the restoration is to supply a second exodus; just as the children of Israel were brought out of bondage from Egypt, so also is a remnant of Judah released from captivity to Babylon. The rebuilding of Jerusalem serves as the focal point of this second exodus: God's restoration of His people. Each exodus is prophetic of salvation in Jesus.

The promises of restoration appear primarily in the writings of the prophets. Even though the city of Jerusalem was rebuilt, the promises pertaining to restoration were not fully realized at that time. The restoration of Jerusalem provided a physical picture of the spiritual restoration that was to take place in Christ.

In the 1st Century, the Jews were still awaiting this restoration, more than five centuries after the city was rebuilt. Luke informs us that Simeon was "waiting for the consolation of Israel" (Luke 2:25). The promises made to Israel regarding their restoration had yet to be fully realized. Jesus acknowledged that the coming of John the baptizer was the beginning of the restoration of all things (Mark 9:12). Peter commented that Jesus is the fulfillment of the restoration spoken of by the prophets of old (Acts 3:21).

There is much to be said about the fulfillment of restoration to Israel uttered by the prophets, more than what can be addressed in a later chapter specifically focused on the writings of the prophets.[8] The narratives pertaining to the rebuilding of the city provide a physical picture of the spiritual realities that would later be fulfilled in Christ.

---

[8] Patrick Rauh provides an in-depth and detailed analysis of the rebuilding of Jerusalem finding its ultimate fulfillment in Christ and the New Covenant realities in his yet unpublished book tentatively titled *The Picture of Scripture*.

# Chapter 13:
# Discovering the Mysterion in the Poetic Writings

Jesus and His gospel message are forecasted in the poetic writings as well. This is particularly true of the Psalms. For that reason, we'll briefly examine the other poetic books prior to delving more deeply into the Psalms.

### JOB
The events that happened to Job in the first two chapters of the book are tragic. Job was a very wealthy and God-fearing man (Job 1:1).

> There were born to him seven sons and three daughters. He possessed 7,000 sheep, 3,000 camels, 500 yoke of oxen, and 500 female donkeys, and very many servants, so that this man was the greatest of all the people of the east. (Job 1:2-3)

Yet he lost all of it (Job 1:13-19). Seven sons, three daughters, all dead. All his livestock, either captured or dead. His servants, all dead. The only survivors were a single messenger from each incident that lived to bring Job the horrific news; and they all showed up to Job one right after the other.

Job lost everything, from his perspective, in a single moment. Yet Job worshipped God (1:20), gave praise to God (1:21), and did not sin nor charge God with wrong (1:22).

Though it appeared it couldn't get any worse for Job, it got worse. He then suffered from sores so severe that he became unrecognizable. Despite receiving wicked counsel from his wife, Job refrained from sinning with his lips (2:9-10).

Job's friends visited him. When they saw him they were devastated, overcome with grief, and speechless.

Though there is much to learn and discuss from the many chapters in between, it ended well for Job. He ended up with twice as much as he had before:

> And he had 14,000 sheep, 6,000 camels, 1,000 yoke of oxen, and 1,000 female donkeys. He had also seven sons and three daughters. (Job 42:12-13)

As much as Job was a blessed man prior to his extraordinary trials, his latter days were even more blessed! Looking at the big picture overview of Job's life from the beginning of the book to the end of the book, how would we diagram it?

Does the diagram to the right look familiar? It's the same pattern that we saw in the account of Joseph's life. Ultimately, the diagram reflects the death, burial, and Resurrection of Jesus. If we zoom way out to a bird's eye view of the accounts of Job's life, we see a picture of the gospel of Jesus Christ.

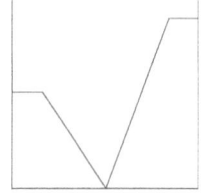

Job's experiences could be summarized as such:

- "blameless and upright, one who feared God and turned away from evil" (1:1b)
- "his suffering was very great" (2:13b)
- "The LORD blessed the latter days of Job more than his beginning" (Job 42:12)

Jesus was blameless and upright, one who feared God and turned away from evil. Jesus' suffering was very great. The Lord blessed the latter days of Jesus more than the former days of His earthly ministry.

What Job experienced was a continued pattern that foreshadowed God's Anointed One. The first and last chapters show us an overview of Job's life and how it reflects the experiences suffered by the Christ. Again, there is much else going on throughout the 40 chapters in between, but the big picture storyline of Job's experiences was Christologically predictive.

Job proclaimed, "Naked came I from my mother's womb, and naked I shall return. The Lord gave, and the Lord has taken away" (1:21). Likewise, Jesus entered the world naked and also left it naked and shamed on the Cross. The Lord "gave" Jesus (i.e., incarnation), then the Lord "took away" Jesus (i.e., Crucifixion). In all the suffering Jesus experienced, he did not sin with His lips (1:22, 2:10).

Fortunately, suffering was not the end of the story for either Job or Jesus. The Lord accepted Jesus' prayer (cf. 42:9). "The Lord restored the fortunes of [Jesus], when he had prayed for his friends" (42:10, cf. John 15:13). As the Lord gave Job twice as much as he had before, so also did the Lord bless Jesus' latter days more than His former days.

*Ch. 13: Discovering the Mysterion in the Poetic Writings*

Job's family was replenished with seven sons and three daughters (42:13). Job saw his family grow, seeing four generations of sons (42:16). Job died having lived a long, full life (42:17).

After being restored, Jesus saw God's family expand with the inclusion of many brothers and sisters (cf. Heb. 2:11-17), the adoption of sons and daughters (Gal. 4:5, Eph. 1:5). God's family has continued to grow for generations upon generations. Jesus' family is still expanding, 2000 years' worth of generations later! And Jesus' life is most certainly "full of days" (42:17). Praise Jesus!

**PROVERBS**

The wisdom of the proverbs is for understanding and instruction. Jesus is the personification of wisdom. Take all the proverbs, wrap them up into a single person, and I present to you Jesus of Nazareth, the Anointed One of God.

The proverbs provide us principles to help guide our living. But more so, they show us the wisdom of the One who can and did truly live accordingly. The proverbs show us Jesus. They also show us the foolishness of those who despise Jesus, His persecutors, the seed of the serpent (Gen. 3:15).

Observe the summary statement (i.e., mission) of the proverbs:

> To know wisdom and instruction, to understand words of insight, to receive instruction in wise dealing, in righteousness, justice, and equity; to give prudence to the simple, knowledge and discretion to the youth-- Let the wise hear and increase in learning, and the one who understands obtain guidance, to understand a proverb and a saying, the words of the wise and their riddles. (Pro 1:2-6)

Jesus is the personification of wisdom and instruction. Jesus is insight. From Jesus exudes righteousness, justice, and equity. Jesus = prudence, knowledge, and discretion.

Consider how we may express a mission statement to explore Jesus intimately. Perhaps it may look something like this:

> To know Jesus, to understand words of Jesus, to receive Jesus in wise dealing, in Jesus' righteousness, justice, and equity; to give Jesus to the simple, Jesus to the youth-- Let the wise hear and increase in Jesus, and

the one who understands obtain Jesus, to understand a proverb and a saying, the words of Jesus and His riddles.

Jesus' riddles consist of his teaching style with the use of parables. In fact, where the word "proverb" is located in verse six, the Septuagint (the Greek translation of the Old Testament) uses *parabolē*, the same Greek word used in the New Testament that is translated parable. Thus, Jesus' parables were a form of proverb.

Observe the call of wisdom in Proverbs chapter 8. Despite wisdom being described as a feminine entity anthropomorphically, wisdom's call is quite reminiscent of something that would be rightly ascribed to Christ. Read Proverbs 8:4-31 as though they were words spoken by Jesus Himself.

We won't spend much more time in the Proverbs. Before we move on, however, consider the teaching of righteousness in the Proverbs. Are we going to suggest that we will obtain such levels of righteousness in our living? Perhaps we should receive the following proverbs as those that describe Jesus, and trust that our only hope for righteousness is in Him, not in any of our efforts and labors. Otherwise, we are relying on a man-centered, works-based righteousness instead of building our hope for righteousness on nothing less than Jesus. Consider Jesus as the principal subject of these passages (sometimes contrasted with His adversaries):

> But the path of the righteous [Jesus] is like the light of dawn, which shines brighter and brighter until full day. (Pro 4:18)
>
> All the words of my [Jesus'] mouth are righteous; there is nothing twisted or crooked in them. ... Riches and honor are with me [Jesus], enduring wealth and righteousness. ... I walk [Jesus walks] in the way of righteousness, in the paths of justice, (Pro 8:8, 18, 20)
>
> Blessings are on the head of the righteous [Jesus] ... The memory of the righteous [Jesus] is a blessing ... The mouth of the righteous [Jesus] is a fountain of life ... The wage of the righteous [Jesus] leads to life ... The tongue of the righteous [Jesus] is choice silver ... The lips of the righteous [Jesus] feed many ... The mouth of the righteous [Jesus] brings

*Ch. 13: Discovering the Mysterion in the Poetic Writings*

> forth wisdom ... The lips of the righteous [Jesus] know what is acceptable (Pro 10:6-7, 11, 16, 20-21, 31-32)
>
> The righteousness of the blameless [Jesus] keeps his way straight, but the wicked falls by his own wickedness. ... The fruit of the righteous [Jesus] is a tree of life, and whoever captures souls is wise. (Pro 11:5, 30)

And so forth.

May we eat of Jesus' fruit, the fruit of the tree of life; for He has captured our souls! And He is so very wise.

Praise Jesus!

**ECCLESIASTES & SONG OF SOLOMON**

Ecclesiastes is another book of wisdom, except from a cynical slant. Ultimately, it could be said that such cynicism would be the result of an approach to life that is apart from Jesus. All they have is to eat, drink, and pass on the fruit of their toil to another. It is all vanity, hollow, void of meaning, without Jesus. To live apart of the life of Christ is not truly living.

The following portion of the book presents a mindset of sadness that could be used to describe the suffering of Jesus:

> A good name is better than precious ointment, and the day of death than the day of birth. It is better to go to the house of mourning than to go to the house of feasting, for this is the end of all mankind, and the living will lay it to heart. Sorrow is better than laughter, for by sadness of face the heart is made glad. The heart of the wise is in the house of mourning, but the heart of fools is in the house of mirth. It is better for a man to hear the rebuke of the wise than to hear the song of fools. For as the crackling of thorns under a pot, so is the laughter of the fools; this also is vanity. Surely oppression drives the wise into madness, and a bribe corrupts the heart. Better is the end of a thing than its beginning, and the patient in spirit is better than the proud in spirit. (Ecclesiastes 7:1-8)

There is no better name than the good name of Jesus; it is "better than precious ointment." The day of Jesus' death is better than the day of His birth. Jesus was willing to suffer, leading to the house of mourning, more than He desired to celebrate with those feasting. Those who look upon the Crucified Christ with sadness of face have their heart made glad in knowing that their atonement has been made secure. Jesus suffered rebuke of the all-wise God. The bribe received from the Jewish leaders revealed their corrupt hearts, and their oppression of Jesus drove Him, the Wise One, into the maddening culmination of death. The end of the betrayal was the Resurrection, therefore "better is the end of a thing than its beginning." Praise the Lord that it ended better than it began!

The Song of Solomon has a very different feel. It celebrates love, adoration, and purpose; purpose fulfilled in one's beloved. Presented in a form like that of a stage production, a man and a woman rejoice in their mutual love.

It should not come as a surprise that we should view the man as Christ. The story projects the love affair between Jesus and His bride. It provides graphic descriptions intended to resemble our love and adoration for Christ, and His love for us.

May we adore Christ with this kind of passion:

> Let him kiss me with the kisses of his mouth! For your love is better than wine; your anointing oils are fragrant; your name is oil poured out; therefore virgins love you. Draw me after you; let us run. The king has brought me into his chambers. (Song of Songs 1:2-4a)

The onlookers celebrate the bride:

> We will exult and rejoice in you; we will extol your love more than wine; rightly do they love you. (Song of Songs 1:4b)

Revel in Jesus' love for us!

> If you do not know, O most beautiful among women, follow in the tracks of the flock, and pasture your young goats beside the shepherds' tents. I compare you, my love, to a mare among Pharaoh's chariots. Your cheeks are lovely with ornaments, your neck with strings of jewels. (Song of Songs 1:8-10)

*Ch. 13: Discovering the Mysterion in the Poetic Writings*

I've never before been compared to a mare among Pharaoh's chariots; but okay, I'm pretty sure that's a good thing.

The celebration of mutual love throughout the Song of Solomon reflects the greatest love story in the history of creation: Jesus and His bride. Praise Jesus that He has so willingly, joyfully, and lovingly betrothed us to Himself!

**THE PSALMS**

What better place to begin in the Psalms than Psalm 1? The first psalm provides a stark contrast between the righteous and the wicked. Who is it that is righteous? It is Jesus. Who is the wicked? All those who are at enmity with Him.

Jesus is the blessed man who did not walk according to the counsel of the wicked, partake in the ways of sinners, nor sit in the seat of scoffers (1:1). Jesus delighted in the instruction of God His Father (1:2; cf. John 12:49). Jesus "is like a tree planted by streams of water" (1:3). Jesus yields His fruit in season; His leaf does not wither. In all that Jesus does, He prospers.

"The wicked are not so" (1:4), they will not stand in the judgment (1:5a). Who will be able to stand in the judgment? Only those who are in Christ Jesus!

Sinners will not be able to abide in the congregation of the righteous (1:5b). Who will abide in the congregation of the righteous? Only those who abide in the Righteous One. "The Lord knows the way of the righteous (i.e., Jesus), but the way of the wicked will perish" (1:6).

Instead of viewing the Psalms from merely a man-centered perspective, as only the expressions of a human author, let us view the Psalms with a Jesus-centered lens. In this way, we can see how Jesus fulfilled the psalms.

Certainly, we are not to disregard the historical context or the setting of the psalm. The backdrop that caused the human author to express what he did will give us greater insight into understanding why it was written. We can't ever remove the context of the human author. Let us utilize the context of the human author's experiences and background to help us further develop our understanding of how Jesus fulfilled the psalms.

For example, David, on many occasions, was fleeing for his life. The third psalm was written in the particular context of David fleeing from his son, Absalom. David had good reason to fear for his life. David knew that when he laid down his head to sleep, it was possible that the enemy could find him in his sleep and kill him. Therefore, anytime David awoke from his sleep he acknowledged that the Lord had sustained him through the night to live another day:

> I lay down and slept; I woke again, for the LORD sustained me. (Psalm 3:5)

We can understand what David is expressing because we know what he was experiencing when he wrote the psalm. Now let us put on our Jesus-Centered Bible Vision goggles, and re-read Psalm 3:5 from the perspective of Jesus: "I lay down (died) and slept (buried); I woke again (raised)."

How did Jesus "wake again"? By the Lord's resurrecting power! The Lord "sustained" Jesus by raising Him from the dead unto life! Because He knew that He would be sustained by God, Jesus "was not afraid of many thousands of people who have set themselves against [Him] all around" (3:6).

As David was crying out to God in His suffering, in a sense Jesus similarly cried out unto God for His life to be sustained. Jesus called out for God to "arise" and to "save" Him (3:7).

Without question, Jesus was not "saved" in the same sense that we describe our salvation as having been saved from our sins. Jesus was saved in the sense that God was not going to allow His Holy One to see decay by remaining in the grave. Jesus was "saved" from the decay of remaining dead and from the guilt and consequence of sin that He bore, sin that leads to death (Rom. 5:12). So, yes, in His suffering and death Jesus can cry out to God, "Arise, O Lord! Save me, O my God!" (3:7).

Observe also the suffering, burial, and resurrection of Jesus prefigured throughout many of the psalms; in particular, this mere excerpt from Psalm 71:

> You who have made me see many troubles and calamities will revive me again; from the depths of the earth you will bring me up again. You will increase my greatness and comfort me again. (Psalm 71:20-21)

## PSALM 22

Several psalms foreshadow the sufferings of the crucified Messiah. One of the more prominent is Psalm 22. Let's examine Psalm 22 from the perspective of Jesus. Instead of viewing it from David's perspective, let's apply the first-person

## Ch. 13: Discovering the Mysterion in the Poetic Writings

pronouns to Jesus. Thus, we'll view the words of this psalm as though they are what Jesus expressed to God the Father in the midst of His suffering and anguish.

> ¹ My God, my God, why have you forsaken me?
> Why are you so far from saving me, from the words of my groaning?
> ² O my God, I cry by day, but you do not answer,
> and by night, but I find no rest.

Of course, the first line is famously quoted by Jesus while on the cross (Matt. 27:46). This should establish our perspective for the duration of the psalm. These words represent Jesus' expression to the Father:

> ³ Yet you are holy,
> enthroned on the praises of Israel.
> ⁴ In you our fathers trusted;
> they trusted, and you delivered them.
> ⁵ To you they cried and were rescued;
> in you they trusted and were not put to shame.
> ⁶ But I am a worm and not a man,
> scorned by mankind and despised by the people.

Jesus was "a worm and not a man" in that He was treated poorly, like the scum of the earth, and was unrecognizable as a man (cf Isaiah 52:14). Being scorned and despised closely resembles the suffering servant of Isaiah 53 (particularly Isaiah 53:3-4). See also Matthew 27:27-30.

> ⁷ All who see me mock me;
> they make mouths at me; they wag their heads;
> ⁸ "He trusts in the LORD; let him deliver him;
> let him rescue him, for he delights in him!"

"And those who passed by derided him, wagging their heads" (Matt. 27:39). Jesus was mocked by those who said "He trusts in God; let God deliver him now, if he desires him. For he said, 'I am the Son of God.'" (Matt. 27:43).

> ⁹ Yet you are he who took me from the womb;
>> you made me trust you at my mother's breasts.
> ¹⁰ On you was I cast from my birth,
>> and from my mother's womb you have been my God.
> ¹¹ Be not far from me,
>> for trouble is near,
>> and there is none to help.

Jesus was God's Chosen One from conception. God did desire to deliver Jesus because Jesus was indeed the Son of God and He trusted in His Father.

> ¹² Many bulls encompass me;
>> strong bulls of Bashan surround me;
> ¹³ they open wide their mouths at me,
>> like a ravening and roaring lion.
> ¹⁴ I am poured out like water,
>> and all my bones are out of joint;
>> my heart is like wax;
>> it is melted within my breast;
> ¹⁵ my strength is dried up like a potsherd,
>> and my tongue sticks to my jaws;
>> you lay me in the dust of death.

Jesus describes the excruciating anguish He suffered by the hands of those who came at him like "many strong bulls."

> ¹⁶ For dogs encompass me;
>> a company of evildoers encircles me;
>> they have pierced my hands and feet—

The piercing of His hands and feet is an obvious reference to the Crucifixion.

> ¹⁷ I can count all my bones— (see John 19:36)
>> they stare and gloat over me;

## Ch. 13: Discovering the Mysterion in the Poetic Writings

> ¹⁸ they divide my garments among them,
>   and for my clothing they cast lots. (see John 19:24)
>
> ¹⁹ But you, O LORD, do not be far off!
>   O you my help, come quickly to my aid!
> ²⁰ Deliver my soul from the sword,
>   my precious life from the power of the dog!
> ²¹ Save me from the mouth of the lion!
>   You have rescued me from the horns of the wild oxen!

Of course, God did not save Jesus from experiencing the Crucifixion, but Jesus was delivered from His place in the grave when He rose on the third day.

> ²² I will tell of your name to my brothers;
>   in the midst of the congregation I will praise you:

This verse is quoted in Hebrews 2:12 to provide evidence that Jesus calls us brothers. The writer to the Hebrews acknowledged that Psalm 22 is from the perspective of Jesus. He wrote "he is not ashamed to call them brothers, saying," and then he quoted Psalm 22:22. Therefore, Jesus will tell of God's name to His brothers (see John 17:6, 12).

> ²³ You who fear the LORD, praise him!
>   All you offspring of Jacob, glorify him,
>   and stand in awe of him, all you offspring of Israel!
> ²⁴ For he has not despised or abhorred
>   the affliction of the afflicted,
>   and he has not hidden his face from him,
>   but has heard, when he cried to him.

Glorify God! Stand in awe! Because God will answer Jesus' cry by raising Him from the dead! God did not despise the affliction of the afflicted (Jesus). God did not hide His face from Jesus, God "heard when [Jesus] cried to Him."

The psalm continues, but for the sake of brevity I have not included the rest of it. The final portion of the psalm emits a disposition of celebration and worship, feasting and satisfaction. This is the celebratory response to the Resurrection and Jesus' glorification as King. We could wrap it up with a modified version of verse 28: "For kingship belongs to Jesus, and He rules over the nations."

**PSALM 30**

See also Psalm 30. Note that the first three verses clearly pertain to the Resurrection. Also "His anger is but for a moment" (when Jesus was on the Cross) … "but joy comes in the morning" (on the day of the Resurrection). What profit is there for Jesus to be dead and remain dead? The Resurrection tells of God's faithfulness (cf. verse 9).

Observe the psalm through the lens of Jesus as He expresses to God His plea for deliverance from the grave and His subsequent celebration. Behold the *mysterion*:

> ¹ I will extol you, O LORD, for you have drawn me up
>   and have not let my foes rejoice over me.
> ² O LORD my God, I cried to you for help,
>   and you have healed me.
> ³ O LORD, you have brought up my soul from Sheol;
>   you restored me to life from among those who go down to the pit.
>
> ⁴ Sing praises to the LORD, O you his saints,
>   and give thanks to his holy name.
> ⁵ For his anger is but for a moment,
>   and his favor is for a lifetime.
> Weeping may tarry for the night,
>   but joy comes with the morning.
>
> ⁶ As for me, I said in my prosperity,
>   "I shall never be moved."
> ⁷ By your favor, O LORD,
>   you made my mountain stand strong;
> you hid your face;
>   I was dismayed.

## Ch. 13: Discovering the Mysterion in the Poetic Writings

> ⁸ To you, O LORD, I cry,
>     and to the Lord I plead for mercy:
> ⁹ "What profit is there in my death,
>     if I go down to the pit?
> Will the dust praise you?
>     Will it tell of your faithfulness?
> ¹⁰ Hear, O LORD, and be merciful to me!
>     O LORD, be my helper!"
>
> ¹¹ You have turned for me my mourning into dancing;
>     you have loosed my sackcloth
>     and clothed me with gladness,
> ¹² that my glory may sing your praise and not be silent.
>     O LORD my God, I will give thanks to you forever!

Praise you, God, for raising Jesus from the dead! We will give thanks to You forever!

### PSALM 69

There are many other psalms we could look at and see a foreshadowing of the Crucifixion. But we'll look at just one more in its entirety: Psalm 69.

> ¹ Save me, O God!
>     For the waters have come up to my neck.
> ² I sink in deep mire,
>     where there is no foothold;
> I have come into deep waters,
>     and the flood sweeps over me.
> ³ I am weary with my crying out;
>     my throat is parched.
> My eyes grow dim
>     with waiting for my God.

Verses 1-4 provide a vivid description of the agony Jesus suffered.

> ⁴ More in number than the hairs of my head
>     are those who hate me without cause;
> mighty are those who would destroy me,
>     those who attack me with lies.
> What I did not steal
>     must I now restore?
> ⁵ O God, you know my folly;
>     the wrongs I have done are not hidden from you.

Jesus was hated "without cause" (see John 15:25); He had done no wrong, yet they attacked Him with lies. Jesus did have to restore what He did not steal in that He righted the wrong that we committed; man sinned against God, Jesus must now be the One to restore it. David acknowledged that God knows his folly; Jesus, of course, did not commit any folly or wrong, but He took upon Himself our wrongs and He was thus not hidden from God's retributive judgment.

> ⁶ Let not those who hope in you be put to shame through me,
>     O Lord GOD of hosts;
> let not those who seek you be brought to dishonor through me,
>     O God of Israel.
> ⁷ For it is for your sake that I have borne reproach,
> that dishonor has covered my face.
> ⁸ I have become a stranger to my brothers,
>     an alien to my mother's sons.

It is for God's sake that Jesus bore the reproach that He did; our dishonor of sin covered Jesus. At the point of the Crucifixion, Jesus' earthly half-brothers did not believe in Him; none were present, thus Jesus was alienated from his mother's sons. Also, the brotherhood of Jesus' disciples made Jesus a stranger to them, save for John.

> ⁹ For zeal for your house has consumed me,
>     and the reproaches of those who reproach you have fallen on me.

## Ch. 13: Discovering the Mysterion in the Poetic Writings

John records that when Jesus drove out the money-changers in the temple the disciples "remembered that it was written, 'Zeal for your house will consume me'" (John 2:17). Also, Paul instructs the saints in Rome to please each other for the good of one another, to build them up (Rom. 15:2). The impetus for doing so was that "Christ did not please himself" (15:3) and Paul backs it up by quoting the second half of Psalm 69:9. Thus, the reproaches of those who reproach God fell on Jesus. Also interesting to note is that Paul's next statement (Rom. 15:4) informs his readers that what was written in former days (i.e., Psalm 69:9, specifically) was written for "<u>our</u> instruction" ("our" meaning New Covenant believers in Jesus).

> [10] When I wept and humbled my soul with fasting,
>     it became my reproach.
> [11] When I made sackcloth my clothing,
>     I became a byword to them.
> [12] I am the talk of those who sit in the gate,
>     and the drunkards make songs about me.

Jesus was made a complete mockery. But Jesus' faithfulness to God led to His deliverance from the grave…

> [13] But as for me, my prayer is to you, O LORD.
>     At an acceptable time, O God,
>     in the abundance of your steadfast love answer me in your saving faithfulness.
> [14] Deliver me
>     from sinking in the mire;
>   let me be delivered from my enemies
>     and from the deep waters.
> [15] Let not the flood sweep over me,
>     or the deep swallow me up,
>     or the pit close its mouth over me.

The deep did not swallow up Jesus, the pit did not close its mouth over Him, for God raised Jesus from the dead! This was the answer to Jesus' prayer...

> ¹⁶ Answer me, O LORD, for your steadfast love is good;
>    according to your abundant mercy, turn to me.
> ¹⁷ Hide not your face from your servant,
>    for I am in distress; make haste to answer me.
> ¹⁸ Draw near to my soul, redeem me;
>    ransom me because of my enemies!
>
> ¹⁹ You know my reproach,
>    and my shame and my dishonor;
>    my foes are all known to you.
> ²⁰ Reproaches have broken my heart,
>    so that I am in despair.
> I looked for pity, but there was none,
>    and for comforters, but I found none.
> ²¹ They gave me poison for food,
>    and for my thirst they gave me sour wine to drink.

Matthew wrote "they offered him wine to drink, mixed with gall, but when he tasted it, he would not drink it. ... And one of them at once ran and took a sponge, filled it with sour wine, and put it on a reed and gave it to him to drink." (Matt. 27:34, 48)

> ²² Let their own table before them become a snare;
>    and when they are at peace, let it become a trap.
> ²³ Let their eyes be darkened, so that they cannot see,
>    and make their loins tremble continually.

Paul quoted these verses in reference to the "hardened" portion of Israel (see Rom. 11:7-11). In reference to their "fall", Paul is clearly addressing the Crucifixion because his next statement is that because of their trespass "salvation has come to the Gentiles." This portion of the psalm (verses 22-28) predictively pertains to the hardened portion of Israel who crucified Jesus.

*Ch. 13: Discovering the Mysterion in the Poetic Writings*

> ²⁴ Pour out your indignation upon them,
>     and let your burning anger overtake them.
> ²⁵ May their camp be a desolation;
>     let no one dwell in their tents.
> ²⁶ For they persecute him whom you have struck down,
>     and they recount the pain of those you have wounded.
> ²⁷ Add to them punishment upon punishment;
>     may they have no acquittal from you.
> ²⁸ Let them be blotted out of the book of the living;
>     let them not be enrolled among the righteous.

God's indignation was poured out on the hardened portion of Israel. He brought judgment on Old Covenant Jerusalem in AD 70 because of their continued evils which culminated in the killing of Jesus. They filled up the measure of their fathers (Matt. 23:32). Verse 25 is quoted in Acts 1:20 in reference to Judas for his role in the Crucifixion.

> ²⁹ But I am afflicted and in pain;
>     let your salvation, O God, set me on high!

Jesus cries unto God for salvation, as if to say "Raise Me, Father! Raise Me!" God did indeed raise Jesus and set Him on high! And Jesus' response was to praise God and give thanks...

> ³⁰ I will praise the name of God with a song;
>     I will magnify him with thanksgiving.
> ³¹ This will please the LORD more than an ox
>     or a bull with horns and hoofs.

There is only one sacrifice in the history of the world that has truly been most pleasing to God. It is Jesus. More than an ox, more than a bull with horns and hoofs, it is Jesus who "offered for all time a single sacrifice for sins" (Heb. 9:12). The sacrifice of Jesus is that which "will please the Lord more than an ox." When men and women who seek God look upon the sacrifice of Jesus, "they will be glad"...

> ³² When the humble see it they will be glad;
> you who seek God, let your hearts revive.
> ³³ For the LORD hears the needy
> and does not despise his own people who are prisoners.

God heard the plea from Jesus who was in need, and God rescued Him. Not only Jesus, but also all those who are in Jesus God has rescued!

> ³⁴ Let heaven and earth praise him,
> the seas and everything that moves in them.
> ³⁵ For God will save Zion
> and build up the cities of Judah,
> and people shall dwell there and possess it;
> ³⁶ the offspring of his servants shall inherit it,
> and those who love his name shall dwell in it.

God will save Zion, His Heavenly Jerusalem! Those who are in Christ Jesus have been raised with Him (Rom. 6:5; Col. 3:1). We shall dwell in the resurrected Jesus and inherit His blessings along with Him! Those who love His name will dwell in the Resurrected Christ!

## PSALM 89

In the previous examples, we can see the psalms being an expression of Jesus to the Father. In Psalm 89, we can see the expression of God the Father to Jesus. Psalm 89 begins with a declaration of God's faithfulness to David (verses 1-4). David, who foreshadowed Jesus' role as king, represents Jesus. Where David's name is used, Jesus' name can be inserted as the truest recipient of God's promises (cf 2 Cor. 1:20).

> ³ You have said, "I have made a covenant with my chosen one;
> I have sworn to David my servant:

## Ch. 13: Discovering the Mysterion in the Poetic Writings

> ⁴ 'I will establish your offspring forever,
>     and build your throne for all generations.'"

God's "chosen one" (v.3) is ultimately Jesus. "David my servant" is a foreshadowing of Jesus, God's greatest servant. Jesus is the offspring who will be established forever (v.4) along with those who are reborn in Him. It was never David's throne that was built to endure all generations; Jesus reigns as the eternal Davidic king.

Observe these words that appear to be written of David, but are actually more true of Jesus:

> ¹⁹ Of old you spoke in a vision to your godly one, and said:
> "I have granted help to one who is mighty;
> I have exalted one chosen from the people.

Of whom is it most true to be a "godly one" and God's chosen one? It is Jesus. Of whom is it most true to be God's servant and the one who has been anointed by God? It is Jesus...

> ²⁰ I have found David, my servant;
>     with my holy oil I have anointed him,
> ²¹ so that my hand shall be established with him;
>     my arm also shall strengthen him.

The accolades continue through verse 25. Then it says:

> ²⁶ He shall cry to me, 'You are my Father,
>     my God, and the Rock of my salvation.'
> ²⁷ And I will make him the firstborn,
>     the highest of the kings of the earth.

The declaration "You are my Father" is more true coming from Jesus than anyone. Jesus is the "firstborn" of the new creation (Col. 1:15-18) and the "highest of the kings of the earth (Rev. 1:5)."

> ³⁰ If his children forsake my law
>     and do not walk according to my rules,
> ³¹ if they violate my statutes
>     and do not keep my commandments,
> ³² then I will punish their transgression with the rod
>     and their iniquity with stripes,

Because of transgressions of men, Jesus was punished with the rod. He received stripes because of our iniquity. But the Father's love for Jesus never waned:

> ³³ but I will not remove from him my steadfast love
>     or be false to my faithfulness.
> ³⁴ I will not violate my covenant
>     or alter the word that went forth from my lips.
> ³⁵ Once for all I have sworn by my holiness;
>     I will not lie to David.
> ³⁶ His offspring shall endure forever,
>     his throne as long as the sun before me.

Despite the Father's love for Jesus never waning, Jesus, God's Anointed One, suffered God's wrath:

> ³⁸ But now you have cast off and rejected;
>     you are full of wrath against your anointed.

The description of the suffering of God's "anointed" continues through verse 45. Then the perspective changes to that as coming from Jesus, calling out to God in His suffering:

> ⁴⁶ How long, O LORD? Will you hide yourself forever?
>     How long will your wrath burn like fire?
> [...]
> ⁴⁸ What man can live and never see death?
>     Who can deliver his soul from the power of Sheol?

## Ch. 13: Discovering the Mysterion in the Poetic Writings

[…]
⁵⁰ Remember, O Lord, how your servants are mocked,
   and how I bear in my heart the insults of all the many nations,
⁵¹ with which your enemies mock, O LORD,
   with which they mock the footsteps of your anointed.

**PSALM 109**

When David (or another psalmist) is expressing his wishes for God to execute justice to his enemies, those are commonly known as imprecatory psalms. Psalm 109 is one such imprecatory psalm. Instead of simply reading the psalm as written about the enemies of David, let's view the psalm as written about those who persecuted and betrayed the true David, the true King of Israel, the Messiah, Jesus of Nazareth.

Observe this modified version of a portion of the psalm, simply by inserting Jesus as the subject of the scorn:

² For wicked and deceitful mouths are opened against Jesus,
   speaking against Him with lying tongues.
³ They encircle Jesus with words of hate,
   and attack Him without cause.
⁴ In return for Jesus' love they accuse Him,
   but Jesus gave Himself to prayer.
⁵ So they reward Jesus evil for good,
   and hatred for His love.

Verse 8 is quoted in Acts 1:20 regarding Judas. Thus, Peter regards Psalm 109 as pertaining to the persecutors, specifically the betrayer, of Jesus. The New Testament does not inform us whether Judas had any children or a wife. If Judas did have children, they were soon to be fatherless; if he did have a wife, she quickly became a widow.

⁸ May his days be few;
   may another take his office!
⁹ May his children be fatherless
   and his wife a widow!

*The Mystery of the Gospel*

Or, if Judas had no children…

> ¹³ May his posterity be cut off;
> may his name be blotted out in the second generation!

Read from the perspective of Jesus, expressing His infirmity to the Father…

> ²¹ But you, O GOD my Lord,
> deal on my behalf for your name's sake;
> because your steadfast love is good, deliver me!
> […]
> ²⁵ I am an object of scorn to my accusers;
> when they see me, they wag their heads.
> ²⁶ Help me, O LORD my God!
> Save me according to your steadfast love!
> ²⁷ Let them know that this is your hand;
> you, O LORD, have done it!

Many took part in condemning Jesus' soul to death. But God saved Him from that condition of death, and Jesus gives great thanks to God, and will praise God in the midst of the congregation of the redeemed:

> ³⁰ With my mouth I will give great thanks to the LORD;
> I will praise him in the midst of the throng.
> ³¹ For he stands at the right hand of the needy one,
> to save him from those who condemn his soul to death.

## PSALM 118

Observe a Christ-centered modification of pronouns for this portion of Psalm 118:

> ¹³ Jesus was pushed hard, so that He was falling,
> but the LORD helped Him.
> ¹⁴ The LORD is Jesus' strength and His song;
> he has become Jesus' salvation.
> ¹⁵ Glad songs of salvation

## Ch. 13: Discovering the Mysterion in the Poetic Writings

are in the tents of the righteous (i.e., Jesus):
"The right hand of the LORD does valiantly,
¹⁶ the right hand of the LORD exalts,
the right hand of the LORD does valiantly!"
¹⁷ Jesus shall not die, but He shall live,
and recount the deeds of the LORD.
¹⁸ The LORD has disciplined Jesus severely (on the Cross),
but he has not given Jesus over to death.

God the Father did not give Jesus over to death as a final destination. God gave Jesus over from death *unto life*, by opening to Him the gates of righteousness...

¹⁹ Open to Jesus the gates of righteousness,
that Jesus may enter through them
and give thanks to the LORD.
²⁰ This is the gate of the LORD;
the righteous (i.e., Jesus) shall enter through it.
²¹ I thank you that you have answered me
and have become my salvation.
²² The stone that the builders rejected
has become the cornerstone.
²³ This is the LORD's doing;
it is marvelous in our eyes.
²⁴ This is the day that the LORD has made;
let us rejoice and be glad in it.
²⁵ Save us, we pray, O LORD!
O LORD, we pray, give us success!
²⁶ Blessed is he who comes in the name of the LORD!

Verse 22 is quoted in reference to Jesus in the Gospels (Matt. 21:42; Mark 12:10-11; Luke 20:17), Acts 4:11, 1 Peter 2:7, and alluded to in Ephesians 2:20. Indisputably, verse 22 pertains to Jesus. It should not be much of a surprise or difficulty for us to believe that the surrounding verses in the same context pertain to Jesus as well.

Jesus is the stone that was rejected. Because He rose from the dead, He became the cornerstone of the new and spiritual temple, the household of God (Eph. 2:19-22). "This is the Lord's doing" (i.e., the Crucifixion & Resurrection); "it is marvelous in our eyes" (v.23). "This (the Crucifixion & Resurrection) is the day that the Lord has made; let us rejoice and be glad in it (v.24).

In the American Church, we have the propensity to think of "this is the day that the Lord has made" and apply it to each and every day. We may even sing "Today is the day that the Lord has made" knowing that the Lord has made each and every day and our appropriate response is that we shall rejoice and be glad in each and every day. It is true that the Lord has made each and every day and we should rejoice and be glad in each and every day, but that's not what the verse is meaning. The verse is looking forward to a future "day" in which the Messiah would suffer death and then be raised from the dead. The day that the rejected stone became the cornerstone is the day that the Lord has made, let us rejoice and be glad in **that** day!

Jesus quotes a portion of verse 26 in Matthew 23. After verbally lambasting the scribes and Pharisees, Jesus basically issued them the commission to "fill up the measure of their fathers" that by killing God's son they would put upon themselves the guilt of their forefathers who killed God's prophets (Matt. 23:29-35). Then (in Matt. 23:37-39), Jesus laments over rebellious Jerusalem, tells them that their temple ("house") will be left to them desolate as He departs, and then He tells them that they will not see Him again until they say "Blessed is he who comes in the name of the Lord" (Ps. 118:26). The Jewish leadership in Jerusalem did not see Jesus again until it was time for them to reject the stone that will become the cornerstone, the night of the betrayal and illegal trial.

Jesus' quotation from Psalm 118 brought forward the context of the entire passage. When speaking or writing in the New Testament era, they would reference a phrase or portion of a passage to draw upon the overall context, not limited to the specific portion quoted. By quoting Psalm 118:26 He is drawing upon the greater context which pertains to the rejection of the stone that became the cornerstone. Jesus tells them in Matthew 23:39 that they won't see Him again until it was time for them to fulfill what the 118th psalm was predicting.

That was the day that the Lord had made; let us rejoice and be glad in *that* day. It was the Lord's doing, *and it is marvelous in our eyes*!

*Ch. 13: Discovering the Mysterion in the Poetic Writings*

**PSALM 119**

The 119th psalm is 178 verses jam-packed full of appreciation and adoration for the law of God. At the time of the writing of the psalms, the law was God's highest expression to mankind. Ultimately, God's highest expression to mankind is in a Person, His Son. Jesus is God's message to mankind. God's message to mankind became flesh and dwelt among us (cf. John 1:14).

During the time of the psalmist, meditating on the law kept one's focus on God.[9] Nowadays, it is meditating on Jesus that keeps one's focus on God, and more potency in doing so. Where the psalmist declares his adoration for God's rules, statutes, precepts, commandments, etc., we can express the same adoration for God through His Son, Jesus, whose righteousness personifies the perfect application of God's rules, statutes, precepts, commandments, etc.

Jesus is the culmination of God's progressive revelation. Let us celebrate Jesus, the One who perfectly expressed living out God's rules, statutes, precepts, commandments, etc. Therefore, when we read of God's rules, statutes, precepts, commandments, etc., in Psalm 119, we have the benefit of seeing Jesus as the reality. Observe this modified stanza of Psalm 119 with Jesus inserted for each reference to God's rules, statutes, precepts, commandments, etc.:

> 97 Oh how I love Jesus!
>   He is my meditation all the day.
> 98 Jesus makes me wiser than my enemies,
>   for He is ever with me.
> 99 I have more understanding than all my teachers,
>   for Jesus is my meditation.
> 100 I understand more than the aged,
>   for I cling[10] to Jesus.
> 101 I hold back my feet from every evil way,
>   in order to cling to Jesus.

---

[9] See also Joshua (Joshua 1:8) and Moses (Deut. 6:6-9).
[10] There are two Hebrew words translated "keep" in the ESV. Both have to do with guarding, protecting, keeping safe, as if protecting with a hedge of thorns. They involve the sense of proximity, keeping near, keeping close. In the cases of a modified translation being to "keep Jesus" (verses 101 & 134 in these passages), I have taken the liberty to modify "keep Jesus" to "cling to Jesus," keeping with the essence of the Hebrew words denoting proximity.

> ¹⁰² I do not turn aside from Jesus,
>    for you have taught me.
> ¹⁰³ How sweet is Jesus to my taste,
>    sweeter than honey to my mouth!
> ¹⁰⁴ Through Jesus I get understanding;
>    therefore I hate every false way.

It was challenging to try to limit to a single stanza our appreciation for Jesus as the fulfillment of God's rules, statutes, precepts, commandments, etc. How about just one more stanza?

> ¹²⁹ Jesus is wonderful;
>    therefore my soul clings to Him.
> ¹³⁰ The unfolding of Jesus gives light;
>    it imparts understanding to the simple.
> ¹³¹ I open my mouth and pant,
>    because I long for Jesus.
> ¹³² Turn to me and be gracious to me,
>    as is your way with those who love Jesus.
> ¹³³ Keep steady my steps according to Jesus,
>    and let no iniquity get dominion over me.
> ¹³⁴ Redeem me from man's oppression,
>    that I may cling to Jesus.
> ¹³⁵ Make your face shine upon your servant,
>    and teach me Jesus.
> ¹³⁶ My eyes shed streams of tears,
>    because people do not cling to Jesus.

Suddenly, Psalm 119 can become a beautiful devotional prayer to diligently seek the great depths of our immersion into Jesus. I will refrain from continuing through the entire psalm; therefore, observe just a few modified verses scattered throughout Psalm 119:

> I will meditate on Jesus and fix my eyes on Jesus. ... Jesus is my delight; He is my counselor. ... My soul melts away for sorrow; strengthen me

## Ch. 13: Discovering the Mysterion in the Poetic Writings

according to Jesus! ... Lead me in the path of Jesus, for I delight in Him. ... Turn my eyes from looking at worthless things; and give me life in Jesus. ... Behold, I long for Jesus; in your righteousness give me life! ... Jesus is better to me than thousands of gold and silver pieces. ... If Jesus had not been my delight, I would have perished in my affliction. ... Jesus is my heritage forever, for He is the joy of my heart. ... Consider how I love Jesus! Give me life according to your steadfast love. ... My lips will pour forth praise, for you teach me Jesus. ... I long for your salvation, O LORD, and Jesus is my delight. (Psalm 119:15, 24, 28, 35, 37, 40, 72, 92, 111, 159, 171, 174)

**PSALM 24**
Let us close this chapter with a Jesus-centered adaptation of Psalm 24:

> ¹ The earth is Jesus' and the fullness thereof, (see 1 Cor. 10:26 & Eph. 1:10)
>    the world and those who dwell therein,
> ² for Jesus has founded it upon the seas
>    and established it upon the rivers. (see Col. 1:16-17)
>
> ³ Who shall ascend the hill of the LORD? (Jesus will)
>    And who shall stand in his holy place? (Jesus will)
> ⁴ He who has clean hands and a pure heart,
>    who does not lift up his soul to what is false
>    and does not swear deceitfully.

Who else among us can claim clean hands and a pure heart? Only Jesus can rightfully make that claim. And we can rightfully make that claim only by being in Him. Only Jesus has not lifted up His soul to what is false. Only Jesus has not sworn deceitfully. Praise Jesus! He it is who shall ascend the hill of the Lord! He it is who shall stand in God's holy place! And by virtue of having been immersed into Him, so will we!

> ⁵ Jesus will receive blessing from the LORD
>    and righteousness from the God of his salvation.

⁶ Such is the generation of those who seek him,
   who seek the face of Jesus.

⁷ Lift up your heads, O gates!
   And be lifted up, O ancient doors,
   that the King of glory may come in.
⁸ Who is this King of glory?
   Jesus, strong and mighty,
   Jesus, mighty in battle!
⁹ Lift up your heads, O gates!
   And lift them up, O ancient doors,
   that the King of glory may come in.
¹⁰ Who is this King of glory?
   Jesus,
   he is the King of glory!

# Chapter 14:
# Discovering the Mysterion in the Prophets

The hidden truth in the prophets is that Jesus is restoring to God a people for Himself in a much different way than was originally perceived. It had appeared God's plan was to make Himself known through a singular ethnic nation. The *mysterion* revealed in the New Testament is that God's plan expressed in the prophets was to make Himself known through Jesus and the spiritual nation that has been immersed into Him, a people for his own possession (cf. Exodus 19:5 & Titus 2:14).

To unveil the fullness of the *mysterion* throughout the prophets would require a series of volumes. This is particularly true of Isaiah alone. The writings of Isaiah are loaded with innumerable Christological implications. We will highlight a few passages of Isaiah, as well as excerpts from the writings of several other prophets.

**ISAIAH 1 & 2**
Right out of the chute, Isaiah's message from the Lord to Judah is one of rebellion and disregard for the Lord (Is. 1:2-3). As the chapter proceeds, religious Jerusalem is severely reprimanded for going through the motions ritualistically, all the while estranged from the Lord. A command for repentance is then issued (1:16-17), followed by this proclamation:

> "Come now, let us reason together, says the LORD: though your sins are like scarlet, they shall be as white as snow; though they are red like crimson, they shall become like wool. (Isa 1:18)

The only way throughout history for the scarlet blood-guiltiness of sin to be made pure as the whiteness of wool and snow is through the atoning sacrificial work of Jesus. Nothing but the blood of Jesus can take away a sinner's sin. Isaiah 1:18 provides a promise of Jesus. The promise was made initially to those who were members of the Old Covenant, but it wasn't until the Crucifixion of Jesus that the promise was realized.

After further scolding through the duration of chapter 1, the Lord again shows His graciousness by providing hope that will arrive in the "latter days":

> It shall come to pass in the latter days that the mountain of the house of the LORD shall be established as the highest of the mountains, and shall be lifted up above the hills; and all the nations shall flow to it, and many peoples shall come, and say: "Come, let us go up to the mountain of the LORD, to the house of the God of Jacob, that he may teach us his ways and that we may walk in his paths." For out of Zion shall go forth the law, and the word of the LORD from Jerusalem. (Isaiah 2:2-3)

The "latter days" Isaiah spoke of occurred more than 700 years after his writings, when Jesus walked the earth in the 1st Century AD. Jesus established the kingdom of God to new heights (i.e., "the highest of all mountains"). Gentiles came into God's kingdom through Jesus (i.e., "all the nations shall flow to it"). It was there and then when Jesus taught us of God's ways "that we may walk in his paths." From Jesus came forth the law/teaching of God, He being the very "word of the Lord" and His gospel message began in Jerusalem.

How is it we may walk in the light of the Lord? By abiding in fellowship with God (1 John 1:5-7) through Jesus who is the light (John 8:12). "O house of Jacob, come, let us walk in the light of the LORD" (Isaiah 2:5). Those who walk in the light of the Lord by abiding in Jesus are the true "house of Jacob."

## ISAIAH 6

Isaiah chapter 6 is famous for the vision given to Isaiah of the throne of God. It's easy to read this chapter and perceive that it is God the Father who is sitting on the throne, as I did for many years. The hidden truth of Isaiah 6 is that it is Jesus who is sitting on the throne.

John informs us that the Jews' disbelief in Jesus is fulfillment of what Isaiah wrote (John 12:37-41). John first quoted from Isaiah 53, and then quotes from Isaiah 6. Next, John remarks that Isaiah saw Jesus!

> Isaiah said these things because he saw his (Jesus') glory and spoke of him. (John 12:41)

The glorious scene of the throne of God in Isaiah chapter 6 displays the glory of Jesus. Isaiah's eyes saw Jesus "the King, the Lord of hosts" (Isaiah 6:5).

## Ch. 14: Discovering the Mysterion in the Prophets

### ISAIAH 11 & 12

In Isaiah chapters 7 through 10 there are multiple passages that are quoted in the New Testament. Each one pertains to Jesus.

In chapter 11, the *mysterion* is overwhelmingly recognized as pertaining to Jesus. He is "the stump of Jesse"; it is Jesus who is the branch that shall bear fruit (11:1).

> And the Spirit of the LORD shall rest upon him, the Spirit of wisdom and understanding, the Spirit of counsel and might, the Spirit of knowledge and the fear of the LORD. (Isaiah 11:2)

The Spirit of the Lord fell upon Jesus at His baptism...while on earth...at His first coming! It is common perception in the modern American Church that the events described in Isaiah 11 pertain to a yet future period of time. However, Jesus' anointing by the Spirit is a past event. The wolf and the lamb dwelling together (11:5ff) is figurative language describing the present New Covenant era when God's Anointed One brings restoration to God's people.

The context of this passage pertains to the restoration of the remnant of Israel (10:20ff). This restoration happens because of God's Anointed One whose "delight shall be in the fear of the Lord" (11:3), and "in that day" (i.e., period of time future to Isaiah) Jesus will "stand as a banner for the peoples" in reference to Gentile inclusion (11:10-16). When does Gentile inclusion occur? It already did occur, in the 1st Century AD as a result of the atoning work of Jesus.

Dearly beloved Christian, you are a member of the restored remnant of Israel. You are among the nations who "inquire" of Jesus, "and his resting place shall be glorious" (11:10). We are presently partakers of the resting place provided by Jesus who has restored us unto God by His grace. Praise Jesus!

How shall we respond to such good news?!?

> You will say in that day: "I will give thanks to you, O LORD, for though you were angry with me, your anger turned away, that you might comfort me. "Behold, God is my salvation; I will trust, and will not be afraid; for the LORD GOD is my strength and my song, and he has become my salvation." With joy you will draw water from the wells of salvation. And you will say in that day: "Give thanks to the LORD, call upon his name, make known his deeds among the peoples, proclaim that his name is

> exalted. "Sing praises to the LORD, for he has done gloriously; let this be made known in all the earth. Shout, and sing for joy, O inhabitant of Zion, for great in your midst is the Holy One of Israel." (Isaiah 12:1-6)

When were wells of salvation first offered for the joyful drawing of water?

> Jesus answered her, "If you knew the gift of God, and who it is that is saying to you, 'Give me a drink,' you would have asked him, and he would have given you living water." (John 4:10)

May we give thanks to Jesus, call upon His name, make known among the peoples His deeds, and proclaim that Jesus is exalted! Jesus has done gloriously; let it be made known in all the earth!

Shout for joy! The Holy One of Israel dwells in your midst by indwelling you with the Spirit of Christ! Praise Jesus!

## ISAIAH 40

Skipping ahead to chapter 40, we dive in to the vastness of beauty that is the last 27 chapters of Isaiah. This portion of Isaiah's book begins with a message of comfort to God's people:

> Comfort, comfort my people, says your God. Speak tenderly to Jerusalem, and cry to her that her warfare is ended, that her iniquity is pardoned, that she has received from the LORD's hand double for all her sins. (Isa 40:1-2)

God's people are to receive comfort from warfare having come to an end (in contrast to the warfare spoken of up through chapter 39 that Old Covenant Jerusalem was to experience). God's people are to receive comfort that their iniquity is pardoned (which only happens through Jesus). God's people are to receive comfort by knowing that not only is their iniquity pardoned but they have received double the blessing from the Lord.

The storyline that results from this message of comfort commences the same way that Jesus' ministry did, with a voice crying in the wilderness to prepare the way of the Lord (Is. 40:3; Mark 1:1-3). The voice continues by crying out that the earth and the people of the earth are temporal, "but the word of our God will

## Ch. 14: Discovering the Mysterion in the Prophets

stand forever" (40:8). What is it that is "the word of our God"? Peter informs us that Isaiah was referring to the gospel (1 Pet. 1:24-25), the same "good news" which Isaiah mentions in the very next verse (40:9).

Jesus came with strength and power (40:10). Jesus tends His flock like a shepherd (40:11). He gathers us, His lambs, in His arms. He will carry us in His bosom and gently lead us.

There is none like Jesus (40:12-27). Jesus is the everlasting God, Creator of the earth (40:28). Jesus does not faint nor grow weary, and He gives power to the faint and strength to the weary (40:29).

Even when the young and vigorous are weary and exhausted (40:30), those whose strength is renewed by Jesus will experience His resurrecting life in a manner as though they will soar through the air like eagles, run without ever being exhausted, walk and never get tired (40:31). Jesus is fulfillment of Isaiah's promises! Praise Jesus!

### CYRUS

As the promises of God that are fulfilled in Jesus continue throughout each chapter, near the end of chapter 44 we come across the mention of Cyrus. That Cyrus is mentioned by name about 200 years before he performs the Lord's purpose is astonishing. More so, Cyrus is described in terms that truly only describe Jesus. "Thus says the Lord, your Redeemer..."[11]:

> who says of Cyrus, 'He is my shepherd, and he shall fulfill all my purpose'; saying of Jerusalem, 'She shall be built,' and of the temple, 'Your foundation shall be laid.'" Thus says the LORD to his anointed, to Cyrus, whose right hand I have grasped, to subdue nations before him and to loose the belts of kings, to open doors before him that gates may not be closed: (Isa 44:28-45:1)

Jesus is God's shepherd. Jesus shall fulfill all God's purpose. Jesus shall build Jerusalem (the New Jerusalem) and lay the foundation for God's temple (the new covenant temple).

The Lord refers to Cyrus as "his anointed" (45:1). The Hebrew word translated "anointed" is the same from which we derive the term Messiah (which

---
[11] Isaiah 44:24a

means "anointed one"). We know that it is Jesus who is truly God's Anointed One. Cyrus provides a picture of Jesus.

Cyrus would subdue the nations before him and show his authority over other kings, via the expansion of his Persian Empire. He would also open the doors to allow for exiles to be set free to return to Jerusalem (see Ezra 1:1-4).

Jesus has been given all authority over heaven and earth. Jesus is the King of kings. Jesus has set the captives free.

The mention of Cyrus has historical fulfillment 200 years after the writing. The *mysterion* of the mention of Cyrus finds its fulfillment another 500+ years later in the Person of Jesus. The hidden truth of the Old Testament is that it points forward to Jesus. The Lord repeatedly uses historical circumstances as a representation of spiritual truths that are realized in the 1st Century.

**ISAIAH 52**

As we continue to pass by several wonderful passages in Isaiah's writings in order to avoid redundancy and excessive length, we'll make a pit stop at chapter 52.

> How beautiful upon the mountains are the feet of him who brings good news, who publishes peace, who brings good news of happiness, who publishes salvation, who says to Zion, "Your God reigns." (Isa 52:7)

The good news to be proclaimed in Isaiah 52:7 is obviously in reference to the gospel of Jesus Christ because Paul informs us such (Romans 10:15). Even though the promise pertains to "the return of the Lord to Zion" (52:8) and the redemption of Jerusalem (52:9), do not be confused. It is neither Jesus' Second Coming nor Old Covenant Jerusalem that is in view. It is the gospel message that is in view. It is the Jesus' First Coming, the proclamation of the gospel, and the redemption of the heavenly Jerusalem that is the ultimate fulfillment of this passage.

The command to "Depart, depart, go out from there; touch no unclean thing" (52:11) is a call to purity, to holiness, to be separate from what is unclean. Paul quotes this passage in the context of New Covenant realities. The temple of the living God (the people, not a building) is to separate herself as pure in the form of lifestyle from that of the world which is unclean (2 Cor. 6:17).

The promise is given that "the Lord will go before you, and the God of Israel will be your rear guard" (52:12). This is militaristic language. The imagery is

## Ch. 14: Discovering the Mysterion in the Prophets

provided that when God's people go to battle, the Lord will be both leading on the front lines while protecting their backs in the rear. This battle is in the Lord's hands and His active duty will assure victory. In other words: 'God's got this.'

How is it that the Lord will lead and protect His people? He answers by proceeding to describe the Crucifixion (52:13-53:12). Isaiah chapter 53 is the most graphic and obvious description of the Crucifixion of Jesus, more than any other Old Testament passage. That's how the Lord chose to fight for His people, on the battlefield of the Cross.

The battle is in the Lord's hands and it will be His Servant (52:13) who will see to it that there will be victory. The victory is won by Jesus' sacrificial atonement! If you have had your sins atoned by the blood of Jesus, you are a member of the Israel for whom the Lord went to battle! And, praise Jesus, the battle is won!

The detailed prophetic account of the Crucifixion in chapter 53 is immediately followed up by the rejoicing of 54:1. The barren one has many children. Paul quoted this passage in Galatians chapter 4 to contrast the Old Covenant and the New Covenant, earthly Jerusalem whose children are born into bondage and the heavenly Jerusalem whose children are born into promise, Hagar and Sarah (the barren one). The barren one produces children of promise.

Rejoice, for Jesus' death, burial, and resurrection provides the precursor for the miracle birth of our spiritual regeneration! The promises of blessing (such as from 54:2-56:8) belong spiritually to you (see Eph. 1:3)!

### ISAIAH 59

Throughout the Prophets, it's common to consistently find two intermingled topics: judgment and blessing. The text flows from one into the other and back again. Among the innumerable applicable texts, we see it in Isaiah 59:18-20:

> According to their deeds, so will he repay, wrath to his adversaries, repayment to his enemies; to the coastlands he will render repayment. So they shall fear the name of the LORD from the west, and his glory from the rising of the sun; for he will come like a rushing stream, which the wind of the LORD drives. "And a Redeemer will come to Zion, to those in Jacob who turn from transgression," declares the LORD.

A pronouncement of judgment (vs.18-19) immediately flows into a promise of blessing (v.20). This happens regularly in the writings of the Prophets. As the prophets pronounce doom upon unbelieving Israel, the message is joined with promises of blessing that God would send a deliverer who will preserve a remnant of Israel.

It's not a coincidence that the concepts of judgment and blessing are intertwined. They both pertain to Jesus. Also, they both pertain to realities of the 1st Century AD.

The judgment Jerusalem suffered from the Babylonians in the 6th Century BC, the judgment spoken of by Isaiah (and other prophets), was neither complete nor final. It was not complete because God preserved Judah alive despite being carried off into captivity. It was not final because God allowed a remnant to return from captivity to rebuild Jerusalem. God's judgment upon Israel was made complete and final in AD 70 when Jerusalem was destroyed by the Romans.

The prophets' promises of blessing are fulfilled by Jesus in the 1st Century through His gospel message. The prophets' pronouncement of judgment upon Israel was also ultimately fulfilled by Jesus in the 1st Century through His retributive judgment on Old Covenant Jerusalem. The destruction of Jerusalem in AD 70 was the complete and final work of what previously occurred in 586 BC.[12] Both the gospel message and the AD 70 destruction of Jerusalem were 1st Century realities that resulted from the work of Jesus, incorporating both judgment and blessing.

The prophets spoke judgment upon Israel. Unbelieving Israel got what it had coming. They disobeyed God, "as they were destined to do" (1 Pet. 2:8). What appears on the surface to be judgment upon unbelieving Israel fulfilled in the Babylonian destruction of Jerusalem contains a hidden truth that is fulfilled in the 1st Century by Jerusalem's rejection of Jesus as the Christ and their subsequent destruction in AD 70, which was both complete and final.

The Lord also promised a redeemer for Israel. The hidden truth is that the Lord's promises to a physical nation were fulfilled in Jesus to a spiritual nation. As physical Israel would receive the retribution for her rejection of God, a

---

[12] I find it to be no coincidence that the destruction of the temple in 586 BC and the destruction of the temple in AD 70 occurred on the same date of the Hebrew calendar. The 586 BC destruction provided an initial fulfillment to the prophets' pronouncement of judgment; the AD 70 destruction was both the complete and final judgment of God upon unbelieving Old Covenant Israel.

## Ch. 14: Discovering the Mysterion in the Prophets

spiritual nation was formed via the gospel message. God fulfilled His promises in a way much bigger than they appeared to be, to a single ethnic nation. God's spiritual nation is comprised of members from *all* nations and ethnicities!

We saw previously in Isaiah's chapter 52 the command to "Depart, depart, go out from there; touch no unclean thing" (52:11). Since Paul saw this verse as applying to New Covenant believers, we can rightly deduce that this call is for spiritual Israel to come out of and be separate from physical Israel. That's exactly what happened in the 1st Century of the early church. Jerusalem believers in Christ separated themselves from Old Covenant Jerusalem by fleeing prior to the Roman destruction, just as they had been warned to do by Jesus in His Olivet Discourse.

Returning to the above passage of Isaiah 59, let's back up a few verses to increase our frame of context. When the Lord saw that truth and justice were lacking, it displeased Him (59:15). "He saw that there was no man, and wondered that there was no one to intercede; then his own arm brought him salvation," God would be the One to provide salvation by His own strength (i.e., via Jesus), "and his righteousness upheld him" (59:16); God's righteousness upheld Jesus, the One bringing salvation. Jesus "put on righteousness as a breastplate, and a helmet of salvation on his head" (59:17a). In addition to bringing salvation, Jesus also will make wail on account of Him all the tribes of the land, even those who pierced Him (Rev. 1:7). Thus, Jesus "put on garments of vengeance for clothing, and wrapped himself in zeal as a cloak" (59:17b).

Then comes verses 18-20 quoted above, 18-19 continuing the theme of judgment whereas verse 20 reintroduces the theme of redemption. The theme of redemption continues in verse 21:

> "And as for me, this is my covenant with them," says the LORD: "My Spirit that is upon you, and my words that I have put in your mouth, shall not depart out of your mouth, or out of the mouth of your offspring, or out of the mouth of your children's offspring," says the LORD, "from this time forth and forevermore." (Isa 59:21)

God's covenant with "those in Jacob who turn from transgression" (v.20; "Jacob" being a synonym for Israel) is to put His Spirit upon them. It is abundantly clear in the New Testament that it is we, members of Christ, upon whom God has put His Spirit. The covenant the Lord is addressing is the New Covenant in Christ, an everlasting covenant "from this time forth and forevermore" (Is. 59:21; cf. Heb. 9:15).

The same theme continues into the next chapter:

> Arise, shine, for your light has come, and the glory of the LORD has risen upon you. (Isa 60:1)

Jesus is our light. Jesus is the glory of the Lord. Jesus has risen upon us!

"Nations shall come to your light" (60:3). When God brings forth redemption like a shining light, which is Jesus, the light will come upon the nations. The "nations" is reference to the true Israel of God, which is comprised of regenerate members of all ethnic nations.

This context continues through chapter 60 and into chapter 61. The beginning of chapter 61 is indisputably referring to Jesus. He says so according to Luke 4:16-21. Isaiah 61 then flows into chapter 62.

## ISAIAH 62

For the sake of Zion and Jerusalem (62:1), the Lord will act. This is in reference to the New Jerusalem, the heavenly city of Zion. When it is revealed that the Lord will bring His righteousness and glory through Jesus, those who are His are given a new name (62:2). And then:

> You shall be a crown of beauty in the hand of the LORD, and a royal diadem in the hand of your God. You shall no more be termed Forsaken, and your land shall no more be termed Desolate, but you shall be called My Delight Is in Her, and your land Married; for the LORD delights in you, and your land shall be married. For as a young man marries a young woman, so shall your sons marry you, and as the bridegroom rejoices over the bride, so shall your God rejoice over you. (Isa 62:3-5)

She who had been called Forsaken (Jerusalem) shall be called "My Delight Is in Her" (New Jerusalem). The land of Jerusalem had been called Desolate but shall be renamed Married.

New Covenant believers collectively have Jesus as a Groom. Jesus has New Covenant believers as His collective Bride. The physical, ethnic Israel of God is

## Ch. 14: Discovering the Mysterion in the Prophets

deemed by God to be named Forsaken and her land Desolate. The spiritual Israel of God, newly created in Christ (Gal. 6:15-16), is His delight.

Though there is plenty more of the *mysterion* present throughout the book of Isaiah, we'll top it off with the concluding verses of chapter 62. If you are indeed in Christ Jesus, this is about you:

> Behold, the LORD has proclaimed to the end of the earth: Say to the daughter of Zion, "Behold, your salvation comes; behold, his reward is with him, and his recompense before him." And they shall be called The Holy People, The Redeemed of the LORD; and you shall be called Sought Out, A City Not Forsaken. (Isa 62:11-12)

Beloved of God, the New Testament informs us that we are His Holy People, the Redeemed of the Lord. We are called "Sought Out, A City Not Forsaken" for we have been sought out. We are the city that has not been forsaken! Praise Jesus!

### JEREMIAH 18

As Isaiah prophesied a mixture of judgment and blessing, so does Jeremiah. However, Jeremiah's message was often more about judgment. The same is true of Ezekiel. In fact, the theme of judgment dominates most of the writings of the prophets. Even so, there's always mixed-in the presence of blessing as the Lord discloses His plan to preserve a remnant for Himself.

We see this duality of judgment and blessing presented to Jeremiah in a very practical way. The Lord informed Jeremiah to go down to the potter's house. While there, the Lord will have a message to share with him.

Jeremiah went to the potter's house and watched him work (Jer. 18:1-4). The potter was making something on his wheel and the clay fell apart in his hands. It was ruined. The potter had to start over. He reworked the same lump of clay and started making something new.

This is a picture of what the Lord did with Israel, involving both judgment and blessing. The Lord began with one lump of clay (Old Covenant Israel), it crumbled (disobeyed the Lord), and the Lord did something new (made a spiritual people in His Son).

Observe the message that the Lord gave Jeremiah after he watched the potter rework his clay:

> Then the word of the LORD came to me: "O house of Israel, can I not do with you as this potter has done? declares the LORD. Behold, like the clay in the potter's hand, so are you in my hand, O house of Israel. If at any time I declare concerning a nation or a kingdom, that I will pluck up and break down and destroy it, and if that nation, concerning which I have spoken, turns from its evil, I will relent of the disaster that I intended to do to it. And if at any time I declare concerning a nation or a kingdom that I will build and plant it, and if it does evil in my sight, not listening to my voice, then I will relent of the good that I had intended to do to it. Now, therefore, say to the men of Judah and the inhabitants of Jerusalem: 'Thus says the LORD, Behold, I am shaping disaster against you and devising a plan against you. Return, every one from his evil way, and amend your ways and your deeds.' (Jer 18:5-11)

The Lord was devising "disaster" against Judah/Jerusalem. They were the clay that fell apart in the potter's hands. They did not turn away from their evil. Their response:

> "But they say, 'That is in vain! We will follow our own plans, and will every one act according to the stubbornness of his evil heart.' (Jer. 18:12)

The Lord will respond to them with calamity (18:13-17). Their next action was to plot to kill Jeremiah (18:18), causing the prophet to cry out to the Lord (18:19-23). The Lord gave Jeremiah another message to give to Jerusalem as the account flows into chapter 19. Here are a few snippets:

> You shall say, 'Hear the word of the LORD, O kings of Judah and inhabitants of Jerusalem. Thus says the LORD of hosts, the God of Israel: Behold, I am bringing such disaster upon this place that the ears of everyone who hears of it will tingle. ... And in this place I will make void the plans of Judah and Jerusalem, and will cause their people to fall by the sword before their enemies, and by the hand of those who seek their life. I will give their dead bodies for food to the birds of the air and to the beasts of the earth. ... "Then you shall break the flask in the sight

> of the men who go with you, ... "Thus says the LORD of hosts, the God of Israel, behold, I am bringing upon this city and upon all its towns all the disaster that I have pronounced against it, because they have stiffened their neck, refusing to hear my words." (Jeremiah 19:3, 7, 10, 15)

This is all bad news for Jerusalem. This is the clay that broke apart in the potter's hands. The good news is that the Lord planned all along to rework the clay into another vessel. The good news is the gospel. The hidden truth is that God's promises are fulfilled in Jesus and all those who are in Christ are members of the *new* Jerusalem. Judgment came upon Old Covenant Jerusalem, the promise of blessing comes upon God's New Jerusalem, the reworked clay.

## JEREMIAH 30 & 31

We see the promise of blessing in chapters 30 & 31 (and elsewhere in Jeremiah's writing).

> For behold, days are coming, declares the LORD, when I will restore the fortunes of my people, Israel and Judah, says the LORD, and I will bring them back to the land that I gave to their fathers, and they shall take possession of it." (Jeremiah 30:3)

Does it appear that the Lord is speaking out of both sides of His mouth? Here He promises to restore the fortunes of Israel; in chapter 19 He promised disaster upon Israel. Which is it? Will the Lord make up His mind?

Is the Lord psychotic or deranged? Forgetful? Does He suffer from multiple personalities? Of course, none of these are true.

Well, then, which is it for Israel? Judgment or blessing?

It is both. Judgment upon the rebellious, earthly nation; spiritual blessings in the heavenly places for the spiritual nation that is in union with Jesus, who is the restoration of Israel. We have to understand God's reworking of the clay.

The promises of blessing in Jeremiah 30 are fulfilled in Christ. God will raise up "David their king" to lead God's people out of bondage (30:8-9). Jesus, of course, is fulfillment of "David their king" who would come in Jeremiah's future. Also, Jesus is the One who leads God's people out of bondage from sin.

As the Lord continues, He includes the covenant formula of "you shall be my people, and I will be your God" (30:22). We'll see the Lord use this covenant formula again and again.

The Lord's promises of blessing continue into chapter 31. We already looked at 31:15 and saw that Matthew regards that obscure verse to have 1st Century fulfillment. Later in the chapter:

> "Behold, the days are coming, declares the LORD, when I will sow the house of Israel and the house of Judah with the seed of man and the seed of beast. And it shall come to pass that as I have watched over them to pluck up and break down, to overthrow, destroy, and bring harm, so I will watch over them to build and to plant, declares the LORD. (Jeremiah 31:27-28)

The Lord divulges to Israel His plan to pluck her up, break her down, overthrow her, destroy her, and bring her harm. The Lord also promises to build and to plant. Here we see both the clay that crumbled and the clay that was reworked into another vessel. This duality of tearing down and building up is also the Lord's thesis statement for the overall message that Jeremiah spoke (Jer. 1:10).

It's only a couple verses later where we find the famous promise of a new covenant which the writer to the Hebrews acknowledged is fulfilled in Christ and all those who are in Him (31:31-34; Heb. 8:8-12). Then there's a promise that Israel will be the Lord's people forever:

> "If this fixed order departs from before me, declares the LORD, then shall the offspring of Israel cease from being a nation before me forever." (Jer 31:36)

However, it is not the ethnic nation that will be before the Lord forever, it is the spiritual nation. The hidden truth of the "offspring of Israel" is revealed in the New Testament to be those who are in Christ, the descendants of Abraham (Gal. 3:29; i.e., the spiritual "offspring of Israel"). More specifically, the offspring of Israel *is* Christ (Gal. 3:16)!

We'll look at just one more passage from Jeremiah:

## Ch. 14: Discovering the Mysterion in the Prophets

> "Behold, the days are coming, declares the LORD, when I will fulfill the promise I made to the house of Israel and the house of Judah. In those days and at that time I will cause a righteous Branch to spring up for David, and he shall execute justice and righteousness in the land. In those days Judah will be saved, and Jerusalem will dwell securely. And this is the name by which it will be called: 'The LORD is our righteousness.' (Jer 33:14-16)

God says He will fulfill the promise he made to Israel. How? He will raise up Jesus, the "righteous Branch." Jesus "shall execute justice and righteousness." "In those days", Jesus will save Judah (a true Jew is one inwardly [Rom. 2:28-29]). Jerusalem (the New Jerusalem) will dwell securely. We, who are saved by Jesus, will be called "The Lord is our righteousness" (cf. Rom. 5:17, 2 Cor. 5:21).

We, dearly beloved, have been granted the righteousness of the Lord through the work of His Son. Praise Jesus! He is our righteousness!

### EZEKIEL 11

The context of Ezekiel's writings is very much the same as Jeremiah's. They both pertain to the destruction of Jerusalem and subsequent captivity of Judah in Babylon. The Lord had Ezekiel perform some very bizarre experiences. Poor Ezekiel.

Amidst the primary theme of doom, judgment, and devastation, the Lord declared through Ezekiel some spectacularly beautiful promises that would later be fulfilled in Jesus, His gospel message, and realities of the New Covenant. We find one in chapter 11:

> And the word of the LORD came to me: "Son of man, your brothers, even your brothers, your kinsmen, the whole house of Israel, all of them, are those of whom the inhabitants of Jerusalem have said, 'Go far from the LORD; to us this land is given for a possession.' Therefore say, 'Thus says the Lord GOD: Though I removed them far off among the nations, and though I scattered them among the countries, yet I have been a sanctuary to them for a while in the countries where they have gone.' Therefore say, 'Thus says the Lord GOD: I will gather you from the peoples and assemble you out of the countries where you have been scattered, and I will give you the land of Israel.' And when they come

there, they will remove from it all its detestable things and all its abominations. And ***I will give them one heart, and a new spirit I will put within them. I will remove the heart of stone from their flesh and give them a heart of flesh***, that they may walk in my statutes and keep my rules and obey them. And they shall be my people, and I will be their God. (Ezekiel 11:14-20)

The new spirit and the new heart are realities of the New Covenant. Recall that in a preceding chapter we established that the promise of land to Abraham is fulfilled spiritually in salvation rest in Jesus. Per Henry Hon, Jesus is "the good land."[13]

Jesus walked in God's statutes. Jesus kept God's rules and obeyed them. Jesus alone is the only One who has ever performed righteously before God. By having been immersed into Christ, believers also are deemed to have successfully walked in God's statutes and kept God's rules and obeyed them. In Christ, believers have become the very righteousness of God (see 2 Cor. 5:21).

Also note the final phrase of the quotation is a reiteration of God's covenant formula: "they shall be my people, and I will be their God."

## EZEKIEL 15

The physical, earthly Jerusalem received a message of condemnation in 14:12-23 (among many, many other passages). That message sets the tone for chapter 15:

> And the word of the LORD came to me: "Son of man, how does the wood of the vine surpass any wood, the vine branch that is among the trees of the forest? Is wood taken from it to make anything? Do people take a peg from it to hang any vessel on it? Behold, it is given to the fire for fuel. When the fire has consumed both ends of it, and the middle of it is charred, is it useful for anything? Behold, when it was whole, it was used for nothing. How much less, when the fire has consumed it and it is charred, can it ever be used for anything! Therefore thus says the Lord GOD: Like the wood of the vine among the trees of the forest, which I have given to the fire for fuel, so have I given up the inhabitants of Jerusalem. And I will set my face against them. Though they escape from

---

[13] Hon, Henry; *ONE: Unfolding God's eternal purpose from House to House*, pages 61-66.

## Ch. 14: Discovering the Mysterion in the Prophets

> the fire, the fire shall yet consume them, and you will know that I am the LORD, when I set my face against them. And I will make the land desolate because they have acted faithlessly, declares the Lord GOD." (Ezekiel 15:1-8)

Jerusalem, when it was whole, was good for nothing! How much less when Jerusalem is charred will it be good for anything? Jerusalem acted faithlessly and will be consumed by fire. The Lord has set His face against them! The land of the worthless vine will be made desolate.

Jerusalem was initially made desolate in 586 BC That desolation, again, was neither complete nor final. Some were left in Jerusalem. Jerusalem was later rebuilt. The desolation of Jerusalem was not complete until AD 70 when it suffered the wrath of the Lamb for having rejected the Cornerstone.

In Ezekiel's future, there will be a true vine that was yet to come (see John 15:1-6). The true and faithful vine will not lead God's people into a land of desolation. Jesus is the true vine! Praise Jesus!

### EZEKIEL 16

Just as chapter 14 leads into chapter 15, so too does chapter 15 lead into chapter 16. Chapter 16 provides the explanation for the judgment pronounced in chapter 15. In chapter 16, Jerusalem is graphically described as an abhorrent whore (16:1-58). The description is brutal and extensive. Jerusalem is promised judgment (16:38) as those who commit adultery and shed blood are judged (which is by death). Yet, at the end of the ruthless onslaught the Lord promised blessing (16:59-63).

Does the Lord suffer from amnesia? Is He confused? How can He lambast Jerusalem so intensely and then follow it up with reassuring them that He will remember His covenant that He made many years prior?

The covenant the Lord promised to Abraham, Isaac, and Jacob was fulfilled in Jesus (see Luke 1:68-79). The life, death, burial, resurrection, ascension, and multiplication of Jesus secured salvation and redemption for God's Israel (spiritual Israel, i.e. the restored Israel, the reworked clay of Jeremiah 18).

When God says "I will atone for you for all that you have done" (Ezek. 16:63), how does God accomplish this? The only way any humans have ever been or can ever be atoned for their sins is through the blood of Jesus. His atoning work on the cross is the only way in which man can be saved (cf. Acts 4:12). We can only rely entirely on Jesus! Praise Jesus!

Therefore, the physical ethnic nation of Israel received the judgment from God as a harlot. It is the Bride of the new covenant community of believers in Christ who receive the promises of restoration and atonement.

## EZEKIEL 34-37

Chapters 34 through 37 of Ezekiel's book contain multiple beautiful pictures of Jesus, His redemptive work, and the realities of partaking in the divine life of Jesus that we can experience today.

In response to the wicked shepherds of Israel (Ezek. 34:1-10), God announced that He will shepherd His people Himself (Ezek. 34:11-31). How will God shepherd His people? Of course, through the Good Shepherd, Jesus (John 10:11, 14). God will set up over His flock His servant David (Ezek. 34:23-24). Jesus is the true David!

Jesus will feed us with good pasture (34:14). With Jesus as our shepherd, we shall lie down in good grazing land. Jesus will seek the lost, Jesus will bring back the strayed, Jesus will bind up the injured, Jesus will strengthen the weak (34:16).

When will God's shepherd bring together His flock? "On a day of clouds and thick darkness" (34:12; cf. Matt. 27:45: "Now from the sixth hour there was darkness over all the land until the ninth hour.").

The human sheep of God's pasture are those who abide in God's Anointed, Jesus. This flock is the true "house of Israel" (34:30).

The passage concludes with a pastoral illustration to the repeated covenant formula: "you are my sheep…and I am your God" (34:31).

The Lord again made promises to the "house of Israel" in Ezekiel 36:22-38. The most well-known portion of that passage is verses 25-28:

> I will sprinkle clean water on you, and you shall be clean from all your uncleannesses, and from all your idols I will cleanse you. And I will give you a new heart, and a new spirit I will put within you. And I will remove the heart of stone from your flesh and give you a heart of flesh. And I will put my Spirit within you, and cause you to walk in my statutes and be careful to obey my rules. You shall dwell in the land that I gave to your fathers, and you shall be my people, and I will be your God. (Ezekiel 36:25-28)

## Ch. 14: Discovering the Mysterion in the Prophets

Only by the blood of Jesus can we be sprinkled clean from all our uncleanness (Heb. 10:22). He gave us "a new heart" (Rom. 6:17) and "a new spirit" (Rom. 7:6). He put His Spirit within us (Rom. 8:11) and caused us to be obedient to Him (1 John 5:2). We dwell in the "land" of salvation rest that God has given us (Heb. 3:7-4:11). These are truths that are revealed to us, dear believers! This portion of the passage also closes with God's covenant formula: "you shall be my people, and I will be your God."

In chapter 37 is the famous vision of the valley of dry bones (37:1-10). This is a representation of resurrection. Christ was the firstfruits of the resurrection, all those who are in Christ are raised with Him (Col. 3:1) and appear as an exceedingly great army (Ezek. 37:10). This vision also depicts the act of regeneration that occurs in the hearts of those who are made alive in Christ!

> Then he said to me, "Son of man, these bones are the whole house of Israel. Behold, they say, 'Our bones are dried up, and our hope is lost; we are indeed cut off.' Therefore prophesy, and say to them, Thus says the Lord GOD: Behold, I will open your graves and raise you from your graves, O my people. And I will bring you into the land of Israel. And you shall know that I am the LORD, when I open your graves, and raise you from your graves, O my people. And I will put my Spirit within you, and you shall live, and I will place you in your own land. Then you shall know that I am the LORD; I have spoken, and I will do it, declares the LORD." (Ezekiel 37:11-14)

Jesus is the true Israel. We are "the whole house of Israel" (37:11). When God opened the grave of our spiritual deadness and raised us to new life, we knew that He is the Lord. He put His Spirit within us and gave us life!

As the promises continue through the chapter, in verse 23 we again find God's covenant formula and in verse 24 we again find reference to the One who fulfills God's promises: God's servant David who will be our king and shepherd. The surrounding promises that are given physical descriptions have a hidden truth. The hidden truth is that the promises that are described in a physical manner are realized in a spiritual manner in Christ.

*The Mystery of the Gospel*

God's covenant formula pertains to a "covenant of peace" and "an everlasting covenant" (37:26). God's covenant to us is eternal and provides the necessary reconciliation (i.e. peace) to make us right before God. Moreover, in the same verse God said He would set us in our land (land of salvation rest), multiply us (as Christ multiplies Himself), and set His sanctuary in our midst forever (via Christ dwelling within those in whom He is multiplying Himself).

The chapter closes thusly:

> My dwelling place shall be with them, and I will be their God, and they shall be my people. Then the nations will know that I am the LORD who sanctifies Israel, when my sanctuary is in their midst forevermore." (Ezekiel 37:27-28)

We again see the covenant formula. Also, observe the New Testament realities: we are God's dwelling place (spiritual temple); the Lord sanctifies Israel (those who are in Christ have been cleansed, sanctified); we are His sanctuary on earth (by His indwelling us) and He will do so forevermore.

This passage is also quite reminiscent of Jesus' prayer in John 17, particularly verse 23. Speaking of us, His believers: "I in them and you in me, that they may become perfectly one, so that the world may know that you sent me and loved them even as you loved me." Jesus prayed that His dwelling place would be with us, that He would be our God because God is in Him. And He prayed that by having God in us we shall be His people so that the nations would know that He is the Lord who sanctifies us into perfect oneness.

God's sanctuary/dwelling/holy place is in us and in our midst forevermore! Dear believer, God abides in us! Praise the Lord!

### EZEKIEL 40-48

In the closing chapters of the book, Ezekiel is shown a vision of a magnificent temple. He provides several very specific details in his description of this temple.

We know that the purpose of the temple is to represent the dwelling place of God on earth. During the Old Covenant era, the Old Covenant temple served to represent God's dwelling place. That is, until Ezekiel watched the glory of the Lord depart the physical structure (Ezek. 10:18).

## Ch. 14: Discovering the Mysterion in the Prophets

In the New Testament era, the dwelling place of God is not in a physical building, but in a people. The members of the New Covenant are collectively the temple of the living God (2 Cor. 6:16). God dwells in His people.

It's easy for us to read very specific details of the temple Ezekiel sees and speculate that he is describing a very real structure with very particular dimensions. Some suggest that this temple is the description of a yet-to-be-built future temple.

However, we have seen God's progressive revelation develop from dwelling in a physical structure to dwelling in a people by His Spirit. We would then have to go backwards, assuming *regressive* revelation to think that God would again dwell in a physical structure after the original physical structure has already been fulfilled by a spiritual temple. It would be going from picture to fulfillment, back to picture again.

The temple Ezekiel sees involves a priesthood and an altar. Once the perfect sacrifice of Jesus' blood was offered, any other blood sacrifices offered to God are a wicked oblation! When Jesus was offered, the veil was torn in two (Mark 15:38). To think that this temple is to be physically rebuilt to again offer sacrifices is to mend the veil back into one and re-hang it, thus re-separating the presence of God from His people. What a heinous atrocity that would be!

What appears to be physical in nature is fulfilled in a spiritual manner. Jesus is the true temple of God and all who dwell in Him (by Him dwelling in them) are also the temple of God. This temple Ezekiel sees is comprised of physical descriptions that represent the true temple of God, which is spiritual in manner.

John also received a similar vision (Rev. 21), except John saw a city. This city is the New Jerusalem, the bride of God. Who is the bride of God but the spiritual nation who has been immersed into Jesus? John also heard the following pertaining to this city:

> "Behold, the dwelling place of God is with man. He will dwell with them, and they will be his people, and God himself will be with them as their God[14]. (Rev. 21:3)

The temple Ezekiel saw and the city John saw were the same thing: the dwelling place of God! The dwelling place of God on earth is in a people.

---

[14] Note that God again used the covenant formula here to John.

Ezekiel's temple represents the people in whom God dwells just as John's city represents the people in whom God dwells.

Ezekiel saw the glory of the Lord leave the temple in Jerusalem, and he also saw the glory of the Lord enter this new temple:

> As the glory of the LORD entered the temple by the gate facing east, the Spirit lifted me up and brought me into the inner court; and behold, the glory of the LORD filled the temple. While the man was standing beside me, I heard one speaking to me out of the temple, and he said to me, "Son of man, this is the place of my throne and the place of the soles of my feet, where I will dwell in the midst of the people of Israel forever. (Ezekiel 43:4-7a)

Ezekiel saw the glory of the Lord enter this temple and heard it said that this is where God will "dwell in the midst of the people of Israel forever." John saw the city of New Jerusalem which is comprised of all believers, and John also heard it said that this city is where God will make His dwelling place forever. Again, Ezekiel's temple and John's city are the same. Dear believer, they are us! Christ in us!

Ezekiel saw a river coming out of the temple (Ez. 47:1-12). This river gets increasingly deeper. It begins ankle-deep, becomes knee-deep, then waist-deep. Eventually, it is all encompassing, unable to pass through because of the rising waters.

This river also gives life. Every living creature that is nourished by this river has life. The fish in it have life. "Everything will live where the river goes" (47:9). Trees along its banks will be sustained: "Their fruit will be for food, and their leaves for healing" (47:12). It will flow all the way to the sea and even turn the sea into fresh water. The river that comes from out of the sanctuary gives life!

Jesus is that river! Jesus flows from the sanctuary of God and gives life to all who are immersed into Him. Jesus provides nourishment to those whom He encompasses.[15]

Jesus is the giver of life. Jesus is the living water (John 4:13-14) and the bread of life (John 6:48). Jesus is the resurrection and the life (John 11:25) as well as the

---

[15] Acknowledging friend Bill Otis for the insight regarding the river of Ezekiel 47.

## Ch. 14: Discovering the Mysterion in the Prophets

way, the truth, and the life (John 14:6). We, who have tasted of the fruit of Jesus, have eaten from the tree of life!

John recorded a vision of having seen the tree of life. Observe the river that provided nourishment to the tree of life:

> Then the angel showed me the river of the water of life, bright as crystal, flowing from the throne of God and of the Lamb through the middle of the street of the city; also, on either side of the river, the tree of life with its twelve kinds of fruit, yielding its fruit each month. The leaves of the tree were for the healing of the nations. (Revelation 22:1-2)

The imagery brought forward into John's vision is that of the river described in Ezekiel 47. A river that 1) provides life, 2) flowed from the throne of God and of the Lamb (i.e., Jesus), 3) it nourishes trees that will "bear fresh fruit every month" (Ez. 47:12), and 4) its leaves are for healing. The tree of life is shown to receive its nourishment from the river of Ezekiel 47!

Jesus is the source of divine life. The tree of life and Ezekiel's river are each depictions of Jesus, the life that is in Him, and the life that He gives to those who abide in Him. We can partake in the divine life that flows from Jesus! Praise Jesus!

The temple Ezekiel saw was a depiction of, first and foremost, the Person of Jesus. In no more real way has God ever dwelt on earth than in the very Person of Jesus. Jesus is the truest dwelling place of God in His Creation. We who have been joined unto Jesus have become members of the same temple. Believers are now members of the temple of God, the city where God dwells on earth. "And the name of the city from that time on shall be, 'The Lord Is There'" (Ez. 48:35b).

### DANIEL

There are a number of immense topics that could be discussed in great length about the book of Daniel. We'll narrow our focus more specifically to chapters 2 through 7, and to that which pertains to the *mysterion*, the gospel of Christ. Chapters 2 through 7 in the book of Daniel comprise a chiastic literary structure with chapter 1 serving as an introduction and establishing the context. [16]

In Daniel chapter 2, Nebuchadnezzar has a dream and Daniel interprets it. In chapter 3, friends of Daniel are thrown into the fiery furnace yet are unharmed.

---

[16] For further explanation of chiastic structure, please see Appendix: Chiastic Structure.

In chapter 4, Nechadnezzar is severely humbled, and then restored. Chapter 5 chronicles the humbling of Belshazzar when the Medes conquer the Babylonian Empire. In chapter 6, Daniel gets thrown in the lion's den but is preserved by God. Chapter 7 records a dream of Daniel and its interpretation.

Chapters 2 and 7 are each of dreams and their interpretation. Both visions pertain to four kingdoms that precede God's

| Ch. 2: | Nebuchadnezzar's dream |
| Ch. 3: | Shadrach, Meshach, & Abednego |
| Ch. 4: | Nebuchadnezzar's humiliation |
| Ch. 5: | Belshazzar's humiliation |
| Ch. 6: | Daniel & the lion's den |
| Ch. 7: | Daniel's vision of 4 beasts |

kingdom. Jesus is the stone that was cut out by no human hand (2:34) and broke in pieces the image that represented the four earthly kingdoms. Likewise, Jesus is presented in chapter 7 as having been given a kingdom whereas the kingdoms represented by the four beasts will have their dominion taken away.

Chapters 3 and 6 both pertain to faithful followers of God suffering severe persecution. The faithful men appear to be given a death sentence, but, by God's mercies, they remain unharmed. However, Nebuchadnezzar's servants are consumed by the fire and the accusers of Daniel were ravaged by the lions. Both accounts conclude with a decree that goes forth throughout the kingdom, to all peoples, nations, and languages declaring the Lord as God (3:29, 6:25-27).

Chapters 4 and 5 record the humiliation of rulers of Babylon. Nebuchadnezzar is humiliated in chapter 4, Belshazzar in chapter 5.

At this point, it would appear that the humiliations in chapters 4 and 5 provide the apex of the chiasm. However, there is a significant difference between the two humiliation accounts. Belshazzar, in chapter 5, is killed and his kingdom given to another nation. Nebuchadnezzar, in contrast, is restored to his kingdom. Thus, we see the following:

    A - Dream of 4 kingdoms preceding God's kingdom (2:1-49)
        B - Faithful ones preserved by God (3:1-30)
            C - Nebuchadnezzar's humiliation (4:1-33)
                X - Nebuchadnezzar's restoration (4:34-37)
            C' - Belshazzar's humiliation (5:1-31)
        B' - Faithful one preserved by God (6:1-28)
    A' - Dream of 4 kingdoms preceding God's kingdom (7:1-28)

## Ch. 14: Discovering the Mysterion in the Prophets

Why is the center point, the item of greatest emphasis, about Nebuchadnezzar? Well, it's not really about Nebuchadnezzar. It's about what Nebuchadnezzar's experience represents.

How would we diagram Nebuchadnezzar's experiences recorded in chapter 4? (See right. Remember this?)

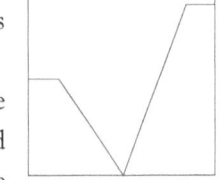

Nebuchadnezzar's experiences in chapter 4 could be summarized as such: he possessed "mighty power" and "glory" (4:30)… "he was driven among men and ate grass like an ox" (4:33)… "I was established in my kingdom, and still more greatness was added to me" (4:36). Even though he began with great glory and had it all restored to him, he still ended better off than he started ("still more greatness was added").

Nebuchadnezzar's humiliation and restoration to increased greatness is part of the pattern established throughout the Old Testament, a pattern that finds its fulfillment in the death, burial, resurrection, and exaltation of Jesus Christ. In fact, Jesus is the true faithful One who suffered severe persecution, was given a death sentence, seemingly went to His doom, but was miraculously restored to increased greatness. Shadrach, Meshach, and Abednego contribute to the pattern as well. They were faithful to God, thrown into seemingly certain death, then restored and "promoted" (3:30). Daniel, also, was faithful to God, thrown into seemingly certain death, then restored and "prospered" (6:28).

We see the *mysterion* at work throughout these chapters. This is also what makes significant the restoration of Nebuchadnezzar. As the center point, the apex, of the chiasm which encompasses chapters 2 through 7, we see the writer's intent to focus the readers on the pattern that is ultimately fulfilled in Jesus. Jesus was humiliated, then restored to increased greatness!

Understanding the chiastic structure also explains why certain events are recorded out of chronological order. Daniel's vision in chapter 7 preceded the events that took place in chapters 5 and 6.

In our culture, we expect our literature to be written chronologically, unless specifically noted otherwise. In their culture, they may be quick to recognize chiastic structure in their literature and would not overlook it as we generally do. If you have ever been puzzled why certain events appear to be out of chronological order, perhaps the author had a purpose other than simply recording a chronological order of events. In this case, the vision in chapter 7 was not randomly misplaced out of order, it was deliberately placed in its proper order as part of a larger chiastic structure. This chaism had purpose: to draw attention to the restoration that occurred as a result of humiliation (i.e., foreshadowing the Crucifixion and Resurrection of Jesus Christ).

May we, along with Nebuchadnezzar, "praise and extol and honor the King of heaven, for all his works are right and his ways just; and those who walk in pride he is able to humble" (4:37). Praise Jesus!

## HOSEA

The life experiences of Hosea documented in the first three chapters of his book depict the redemption story.

At the Lord's command, Hosea married a woman who will commit whoredom. She later left Hosea to pursue her lovers. Hosea finds her on the black market of human trafficking and he purchases her for the equivalent amount that Judas was paid to betray Jesus, symbolizing the price of redemption. Hosea commands her to be faithful to him and he commits to be faithful to her.

It's the classic storyline of boy finds girl, boy loses girl, boy performs heroics to win girl back. That's the same basic premise of the redemption story. Jesus created mankind, Jesus lost fellowship with mankind due to sin, Jesus acted as hero to win mankind back into fellowship with Him. Hosea provided a picture of Jesus by acting as a redeemer.

In prior chapters, we already examined portions of Hosea chapters 1 and 2 in reference to Romans 9 and Joshua 7. Therefore, we won't belabor it now, but we'll briefly look at Hosea 2:23 again. Observe the modified phrasing of the covenant formula that we have seen many times already:

> and I will sow her for myself in the land. And I will have mercy on No Mercy, and I will say to Not My People, 'You are my people'; and he shall say, 'You are my God.'" (Hos 2:23)

In addition to Paul's quotation of this passage in Romans 9, Peter also confirms that this passage, and the covenant formula, is applied to the Gentile-based people of God via Jesus' act as redeemer:

> Once you were not a people, but now you are God's people; once you had not received mercy, but now you have received mercy. (1Pe 2:10)

## Ch. 14: Discovering the Mysterion in the Prophets

Peter applied Hosea's adaptation of the covenant formula to those who are in Christ. Thus, the repeated Old Testament promise of an everlasting covenant that He will be our God and we will be His people are fulfilled in us through Christ.

> Afterward the children of Israel shall return and seek the LORD their God, and David their king, and they shall come in fear to the LORD and to his goodness in the latter days. (Hos 3:5)

We are those who have been purchased by Christ, just as Hosea purchased his wife. We are the children of God who seek the Lord and Jesus our king (the true David). We are those who come in reverence to the Lord and to His goodness. We do this, from Hosea's viewpoint, in the "latter days." These "latter days" are not to be viewed as being exclusively in our future. The entire New Covenant era is the "latter days" from the perspective of the period of time that preceded it. In other words, from the perspective of the BC era, the post-Christ era (i.e., the past ~2000 years and counting) *is* its latter days.

### JONAH

As we work our way through the smaller books of the prophets, we'll find the same recurring themes: repeated warnings of judgment mixed in with occasional promises of a future hope. To avoid further redundancy, also considering that we've already addressed a few of these passages (such as Joel 2:28-32 & Amos 9:11-15), we'll highlight only a few more passages, those that provide an approach that is unique to our journey.

Unique is definitely one way to describe the book of Jonah. Most of the books of the prophets are about a message that the Lord wants to declare. The book of Jonah is more about the experiences of the prophet. The message that the Lord wants to declare through Jonah's voice box is but a minor detail in the grand scope of the narrative. Let's recount Jonah's experiences.

The story begins with Jonah's disobedience: the Lord gave him a message to give to Nineveh; Jonah fled, intending to go as far in the opposite direction as possible. Jonah got on a boat and the Lord brought a nasty, overwhelming storm. The sailors were scared and attributed the severity of the storm to a divine source and assumed that one of them on board was the cause of divine fury. For this reason, they decided to cast lots, and the lot fell on Jonah.

Jonah volunteered to be thrown overboard, possibly because he thought it would get him out of having to go to Nineveh. The sailors initially resisted doing so, but eventually relented and tossed Jonah overboard. The sea ceased from its raging.

We all know what happened next. Jonah was swallowed by a great fish. After three days, Jonah prayed to the Lord, culminating with the proclamation "Salvation belongs to the Lord!" Jonah was subsequently spit out and landed on dry ground.

Jonah then went to Nineveh. He preached a message of repentance, and the Ninevites repented. The king of Nineveh ordered a city-wide fast that included all the animals. His decree concluded with:

> Let everyone turn from his evil way and from the violence that is in his hands. Who knows? God may turn and relent and turn from his fierce anger, so that we may not perish. (Jonah 3:8b-9)

The Lord responded by relenting of the disaster He said He would do to them.[17]

It's commonly understood that Jonah's experience with the great fish foreshadowed the gospel of Christ. After all, Jesus said so Himself:

> But he answered them, "An evil and adulterous generation seeks for a sign, but no sign will be given to it except the sign of the prophet Jonah. For just as Jonah was three days and three nights in the belly of the great fish, so will the Son of Man be three days and three nights in the heart of the earth. The men of Nineveh will rise up at the judgment with this generation and condemn it, for they repented at the preaching of Jonah, and behold, something greater than Jonah is here. (Matthew 12:39-41)

Jonah was the picture. Jesus is "greater than Jonah." The fulfillment is greater than the picture. Jesus is the fulfillment of Jonah's experiences.

---

[17] This relenting was temporary, however, because about a century later Nineveh was overtaken when the Babylonians rose to power and conquered the Assyrians.

## Ch. 14: Discovering the Mysterion in the Prophets

Although Jonah's encounter with the great fish is widely accepted to serve as a foreshadowing of the Crucifixion and Resurrection of Jesus, let's also look a bit closer at the details of the account prior to and following the great fish.

The story began with one disobedient act that brought about the wrath of God. So, too, did Adam's one disobedient act bring about the wrath of God upon mankind.

The casting of lots pinpointed Jonah as the one upon whom the guilt of the wrath of God had fallen. Jesus was the One appointed by God to take upon Himself the burden of God's holy and furious storm. When Jonah was tossed overboard, the wrath of God was appeased and many others (the sailors) were saved from certain doom. Jonah being tossed overboard to presumably certain death appeased the wrath of God just as Jesus' death truly did appease the wrath of God.

Jonah's prayer in the belly of the great fish is reminiscent of the psalms that project the suffering of the Messiah. If you read Jonah 2:2-9 without knowing the context, it would be easy to mistake it for a Davidic psalm.

Jesus, with the voice of thanksgiving, will offer Himself as a sacrifice to God, exactly what Jesus vowed to the Father to pay (cf. 2:9). Jesus also knows that his "salvation" (deliverance from the grave) is sure: "Salvation belongs to the Lord!"

After Jonah was spit out by the fish (symbolizing Jesus' resurrection), he took the message of repentance to Gentiles, and the Gentiles believed (3:5) and repented. This also describes the early church (cf. Acts 15:7b). The belief and repentance of the Gentile Ninevites foreshadows the belief and repentance of Gentiles who respond to the gospel of Jesus Christ.

Jonah 3:10 was said of the Ninevites and could also be said of those who respond to the gospel:

> When God saw what they did, how they turned from their evil way, God relented of the disaster that he had said he would do to them, and he did not do it.

**HAGGAI**

Haggai's ministry occurred after the first wave of Jewish exiles returned from captivity to Jerusalem. They had begun rebuilding the temple but eventually the work on the temple dwindled. The Lord used Haggai to scold the people with a message of "consider your ways" (1:5, 7). The people responded to this charge, determined to get back to building the temple, and the Lord offered the comforting message "I am with you" (1:13).

The obvious application for us in the New Covenant is to be busy building God's house. Of course, God's house is no longer a physical temple structure, it is a spiritual group of people. May we be about the business of building up the New Covenant temple of God, not only by speaking the gospel to the world but also by building up and encouraging those who consist of God's new temple.

> And the LORD stirred up the spirit of Zerubbabel the son of Shealtiel, governor of Judah, and the spirit of Joshua the son of Jehozadak, the high priest, and the spirit of all the remnant of the people. And they came and worked on the house of the LORD of hosts, their God, (Haggai 1:14)

The Lord had already stirred up Haggai's spirit to give the message. Then Zerubbabel and Joshua had their hearts stirred. Here we see prophet, priest, and governor (ruler) all having their hearts stirred to build the temple. Jesus, of course, fulfilled the Old Covenant offices of prophet, priest, and king (ruler), and Jesus' heart is stirred to build God's temple by multiplying Himself in her. The combined offices of Haggai, Zerubbabel, and Joshua project the function of God's Anointed One.

We also see Zerubbabel depicted as a picture of Christ:

> On that day, declares the LORD of hosts, I will take you, O Zerubbabel my servant, the son of Shealtiel, declares the LORD, and make you like a signet ring, for I have chosen you, declares the LORD of hosts." (Hag 2:23)

Zerubbabel is described by the Lord as "my servant" just as He does Jesus (Is. 42:1, 52:13, et al.). Zerubbabel is a "chosen" one of God and is made like the Lord's signet ring.

The signet ring of a king was used to confirm the king's approval. Any envelope sealed with wax that contained the emblem of the king assured the readers that the king was consenting to the message in the letter.

## Ch. 14: Discovering the Mysterion in the Prophets

Ultimately, Jesus is God's signet ring. Jesus is God's stamp of approval. Anything and everything Jesus did served as a validation of what God purposed. Zerubbabel was merely a foreshadowing of Jesus.

Zerubbabel is said to be made like a signet ring "on that day." When is "that day"? We know "that day" is the day God will "shake the heavens and the earth" (2:21). This is connected to the message Haggai gave to Zerubbabel three days earlier (2:1-9):

> For thus says the LORD of hosts: Yet once more, in a little while, I will shake the heavens and the earth and the sea and the dry land. (Hag 2:6)

When does/did/will the "yet once more, in a little while" take place? The writer of Hebrews clued us in when quoting Haggai near the end of chapter 12.

Prior to doing so, the writer to the Hebrews contrasted the old covenant with the new covenant via their respective "mount": "You have not come to [Mount Sinai]...you have come to Mount Zion" (Heb. 12:18-24). The writer then issued a warning: "See that you do not refuse him who is speaking" (12:25a). The cause for the warning has precedent because Israel "refused him who warned them on earth" (which was Moses at Sinai) and "they did not escape." How "much less will we escape if we reject him who warns from heaven"? (which is Jesus who ascended).

"At that time" (the giving of the Old Covenant at Sinai) "his voice shook the earth" (12:26a, cf. Ex. 19:18-19). "But now" (the giving of the New Covenant through Jesus) "he has promised 'Yet once more I will shake not only the earth but the heavens'" (12:26b). The writer then explains the reason for quoting Haggai (with my insertions):

> This phrase, "Yet once more," indicates the removal of things that are shaken--that is, things that have been made *(i.e., Mount Sinai and its covenant)*--in order that the things that cannot be shaken *(Mount Zion and its covenant)* may remain. Therefore let us be grateful for receiving a kingdom *(which is current)* that cannot be shaken, and thus let us offer to God *(because it is current)* acceptable worship, with reverence and awe, (Heb 12:27-28)

The writer to the Hebrews informs us that the Lord's promise to shake the heavens and earth via His prophet Haggai finds its fulfillment in Jesus and His Covenant (i.e., the good news of the kingdom of God). Jesus came and shook up the heavens and the earth!

Let's go back to the message that begins Haggai chapter 2. In this message, the Lord drew to Zerubbabel's attention that the second temple they were rebuilding looked nothing like the glory of Solomon's temple (2:3). Then the Lord encouraged Zerubbabel, Joshua, and all the people to "be strong" and instructed them to "work" (2:4). The Lord again reassured them that "I am with you" and reminded them of the covenant He made with them at Sinai ("according to the covenant that I made with you when you came out of Egypt" [2:5]). Then comes the promise of "Yet once more, in a little while, I will shake the heavens and the earth" (2:6).

The scene at Sinai shook the earth. Jesus will "in a little while" turn the world upside down, shaking both the earth and the heavens. This "little while" lasted until Jesus came, ushered in God's kingdom from heaven, and revealed Himself as fulfillment of the hidden truth contained in the writing of Haggai. Praise Jesus!

## ZECHARIAH 3

Zechariah saw several spectacular visions, particularly in the first six chapters. We'll focus our attention on the vision in chapter 3. This vision pertains to the same Joshua who was the high priest recorded in Haggai. In this vision, we see a picture of the gospel.

Joshua is wearing filthy garments. They are removed and replaced with "pure" clothing. This symbolizes redemption. The filthy garments of sin are removed and the forgiven sinner is made holy and pure.

> Then he showed me Joshua the high priest standing before the angel of the LORD, and Satan standing at his right hand to accuse him. And the LORD said to Satan, "The LORD rebuke you, O Satan! The LORD who has chosen Jerusalem rebuke you! Is not this a brand plucked from the fire?" Now Joshua was standing before the angel, clothed with filthy garments. And the angel said to those who were standing before him, "Remove the filthy garments from him." And to him he said, "Behold, I have taken your iniquity away from you, and I will clothe you with pure vestments." And I said, "Let them put a clean turban on his head." So

## Ch. 14: Discovering the Mysterion in the Prophets

> they put a clean turban on his head and clothed him with garments. And the angel of the LORD was standing by. (Zec 3:1-5)

Not only does this vision portend forgiveness we have in Jesus, it prefigures Jesus Himself. As Satan was standing by Him to accuse Him, Jesus took upon Himself the guilt of sin. He went to the Cross as though He had committed offense. He was raised from the dead as the firstfruits of the new creation, with pure and clean garments.

The following message that the angel of the Lord assured Joshua are words we can easily imagine being spoken directly to Jesus:

> Thus says the LORD of hosts: If you will walk in my ways and keep my charge, then you shall rule my house and have charge of my courts, and I will give you the right of access among those who are standing here. (Zec 3:7)

Jesus did walk in God's ways and kept His charge. As a result, Jesus is worthy to rule God's house and have charge of His courts. Jesus is the One who has been given the right of access into God's kingdom.

> Hear now, O Joshua the high priest, you and your friends who sit before you, for they are men who are a sign: behold, I will bring my servant the Branch. For behold, on the stone that I have set before Joshua, on a single stone with seven eyes, I will engrave its inscription, declares the LORD of hosts, and I will remove the iniquity of this land in a single day. (Zec 3:8-9)

Jesus is the Branch, God's servant, and God's true high priest. Jesus is the stone with omniscience ("seven eyes") upon whom God will engrave His inscription. Jesus removed our iniquity in a single day. That "single day" is, of course, the Crucifixion. What else can we know about "that day"?

> In that day, declares the LORD of hosts, every one of you will invite his neighbor to come under his vine and under his fig tree." (Zechariah 3:10)

Through the atoning work of Jesus, the gospel has gone forth ("invite his neighbor to come"). Because of the day that Jesus removed iniquity, where we come is "under his vine and under his fig tree." We can abide under His shelter, beneath His protection, eating of His fruit, sharing in His life.

Praise Jesus!

As stated at the beginning of this chapter, several volumes would have to be written to exhaust the fullness of the *mysterion* of the good news of the kingdom of God contained in the writings of the prophets. Let the passages addressed in this chapter serve merely as an appetizer for your future exploration of the prophetic writings with the intent of identifying their Christological fulfillment via gospel truth.

Jesus, reveal Yourself to us through the ancient writings!

# Conclusion: What Does This All Mean?

What this all means is that the Old Testament is the story of Jesus. Via patterns, types, shadows, etc., the Scriptures point to Jesus.

What this all means is that attempts to find morals from Old Testament stories may be a severely insufficient understanding of the text. Take, for example, David's slaying of Goliath. It would be easy to try to identify traits of David that we want to emulate: David trusted in the Lord, David was courageous, David was bold to take a stand for God, etc. We might, therefore, want to have the trust, courage, and boldness that David did. But this simply removes Christ from the picture.

We might see David as a hero and our response is to want to play the role of hero like David did. But David's trust, courage, and boldness foreshadowed Christ, the true David. Let us not use the account of David & Goliath to attempt to play the role of hero ourselves by emulating David's character. Instead, may we acknowledge that Jesus is the only one to be exalted, David merely foreshadowed Jesus, and we can emulate Christ because He abides in us and functions through us. It's quite a big difference between moralizing the text and seeing its Christological fulfillment. One view exalts Christ; the other puts ourselves in the spotlight attempting to emulate the role of the hero.

What this all means is that systems of theology and doctrines that are derived from the Old Testament are sketchy at best. They likely miss the point (which is that the truth of Jesus is hidden in predictive shadows) and they provide distractions from seeing a full revelation of Christ. At worst, it can be an affront to Jesus Himself and mislead believers into false teaching.

What this all means is that a literal reading of the text is often *not* the best way to read the Old Testament. Understanding what the text states literally is of great importance, but the literal reading is often not the fullest meaning of the text. There is typically a deeper meaning hidden beneath what is seen on the surface.

What this all means is that theological views that emphasize Israel, especially end-times views involving modern Israel, are misguided. Some Christians are determined to await fulfillment of these promises made to national, ethnic Israel; all the while not realizing that we receive the benefit of these promises by virtue of being in Christ, who already fulfilled these promises. Adhering to the belief that 21st Century Israel plays a role in God's ancient promises misleads believers away from Jesus being central and supreme in all of God's purposes.

What this all means is that modern views that the prophets spoke of the Second Coming of Jesus neglect the fact that the prophets predicted more about the *First* Coming of Jesus and the realities brought about throughout the entirety of the New Covenant era. God spoke through the prophets in a predictive manner to bring attention to the pinnacle of His work in creation: the crucifixion and resurrection of Jesus.

What this all means is that a theological system that built its foundation upon ostensible covenants that the Scriptures don't explicitly mention is a hindrance to truly understanding the fullness and depth of Christ. This particular theology takes God's revelation of Jesus as the focal point of redemptive history and flattens it by putting Him on the same level as the Old Testament covenants, instead of seeing Jesus as the fulfillment of these prior covenants.

What this all means is that contemporary beliefs that are centered on certain aspects of the Old Testament are likely missing the point that Jesus fulfilled it all. Whether it's centering one's Christian life on such things like a modern implementation of the Sabbath, being fruitful and multiplying to produce a quiverfull of children, or elevating the Ten Commandments as God's highest expression to mankind (instead of recognizing Jesus as God's highest expression), the reality is that Jesus fulfilled it all.

What this all means is that Jesus is the focal point of the Scriptures, the focal point of God's purposes in creation, and should be the focal point of our lives. Any man-devised theology or doctrine that steers our attention away from Jesus is worthy of being challenged.

Dear reader, do not put yourself at odds with anyone who believes or teaches any of the above-mentioned items. Believers in Jesus are one in Him. Do not be found alienating yourself from other believers, but rather love one another. This is not a call to set yourself against the person who believes or teaches such things; this is a call to internally challenge the teaching itself.

Consider what you're taught, whether it brings you closer toward a full revelation of Jesus, or is it theology that distracts you from Christ? Consider your approach to the Old Testament: do you see Jesus on display in a predictive

## Conclusion: What Does This All Mean?

manner? Does doing so make you challenge what you thought you knew about the Old Testament?

What this all means is that the true meaning of the Old Testament is hidden within. It was hidden for ages. It was later revealed to be the good news of God's kingdom in the birth, life, suffering, death, resurrection, ascension, glorification, and multiplication of Christ. It will be completed at the restoration of all things in Christ at His return. This is the good news of God's kingdom!

Jesus is the revealing of the mystery of the gospel.

# *Appendix: Chiastic Structure*

A chiasm is a literary device that can be used in poetry and is common in Hebrew literature. It often functions in a format such as A-B-B'-A', where both A and A' are similar or related, and the same with B and B'. The use of chiastic structure generally seeks to emphasize the portion in the center of the chiasm. In the above example, the portion of the chiasm labeled B and B' is the primary emphasis of the writer. Sometimes the center point is emphasized with no counterpart, such as the case with A-B-X-B'-A' or A-B-C-X-C'-B'-A' formats. In these formats, the X represents the writer's primary point of emphasis.

I am certain that there are a multitude of chiastic structures in the Scriptures, most of which I am unaware. One simple example of which I have been made aware is Matthew 6:24:

A - No one can serve two masters
   B - for either he will hate the one
      C - and love the other
      C' - or he will be devoted to the one
   B' - and despise the other.
A' - You cannot serve God and money.

A and A' present a similar thought: you cannot serve two masters. B and B' present a similar thought: hate/despise. C and C' present a similar thought: love/be devoted. The emphasis is found in the center: to love God and be fully devoted to Him.

A much more elaborate chiasm that has been popularly recognized regards the flood account from Genesis 6:10 through 9:19a as proposed by Gordon Wenham.[18] Wenham suggests that there are 31 items in the chiastic structure of the flood story. This chiasm finds its center point in Genesis 8:1: "God remembered Noah."

Wenham observes that this chiasm "begins and ends with a reference to Noah. Then Noah's sons are named and so on…In the closing scene, 'Shem, Ham and

---

[18] Gordon J. Wenham, "The Coherence of the Flood Narrative" *Vetus Testamentum* 28 (1978) 336–348.

Japheth', 'the ark', 'the flood', 'the covenant' and 'food', are mentioned in precisely the reverse order to that found in the opening scene."[19]

Here goes:

    A - Noah (6:10a)
     B - Shem, Ham and Japheth (6:10b)
      C - Ark to be built (6:14-16)
       D - Flood announced (6:17)
        E - Covenant with Noah (6:18-20)
         F - Food in the ark (6:21)
          G - Command to enter ark (7:1-3)
           H - 7 days waiting for flood (7:4-5)
            I - 7 days waiting for flood (7:7-10)
             J - Entry to ark (7:11-15)
              K - Yahweh shuts Noah in (7:16)
               L - 40 days flood (7:17a)
                M - Waters increase (7:17b-18)
                 N - Mountains covered (7:19-20)
                  O - 150 days waters prevail (7:(21)-24j
                   P - GOD REMEMBERED NOAH (8:1)
                  O' - 150 days waters abate (8:3)
                 N' - Mountain tops visible (8:4-5)
                M' - Waters abate (8:5)
               L' - 40 days (end of) (8:6a)
              K' - Noah opens window of ark (8:6b)
             J' - Raven and dove leave ark (8:7-9)
            I' - 7 days waiting for waters to subside (8:10-11)
           H' - 7 days waiting for waters to subside (8:12-13)
          G' - Command to leave ark (8:15-17(22))
         F' - Food outside ark (9:1-4)
        E' - Covenant with all flesh (9:8-10)
       D' - No flood in future (9:11-17)
      C' - Ark (9:18a)
     B' - Shem, Ham and Japheth (9:18b)
    A' - Noah (9:19)

As all of the details of the flood are being expressed, the author revealed the focal point of the entire story is that God "remembered" Noah. The details of the account are important, but amidst all the details the primary point of the

---

[19] Ibid.

author is that God chose to preserve a remnant, delivering Noah (and his family) from destruction. This resembles the redemption story.

Also observe that the number of days likewise point toward the climaxing statement that "God remembered Noah":

    A - 7 days (7:4)
      B - 7 days (7:10)
        C - 40 days (7:17)
          D - 150 days (7:24)
            X - God remembered Noah (8:1)
          D' - 150 days (8:3)
        C' - 40 days (8:6)
      B' - 7 days (8:10)
    A' - 7 days (8:12)

With this understanding of chiastic structure used as a literary devise, we can gain a better appreciation for what Daniel presented.

www.ingramcontent.com/pod-product-compliance
Lightning Source LLC
Chambersburg PA
CBHW031104080526
44587CB00011B/823